FOUR DEAD
IN OHIO

FOUR DEAD IN OHIO

Was There a Conspiracy at Kent State?

NORTH RIDGE BOOKS
Laguna Hills, CA

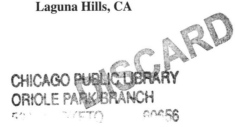

North Ridge Books, P.O. Box 1463, El Toro, CA 92630
NRBooks@aol.com

10 9 8 7 6 5 4 3 2

ISBN: 0-937813-05-2
Library of Congress Catalog Card No.: 94-067230

Library of Congress Cataloging-in-Publication Data

Gordon, William A., 1950-
[Fourth of May]
        Four dead in Ohio: was there a conspiracy at Kent State? /
        William A. Gordon
            p. cm.
        Originally published: The Fourth of May. Buffalo, N.Y.:
        Prometheus Books, © 1990. With new introd.
        Includes bibliographical references and index.
        ISBN 0-937813-05-2
        1. Kent State University—Riot, May 4, 1970. 2. Student
        movements—Ohio—Kent—History—20th Century.   I. Title.
        LD4191.072G67 1995
        378.771'37—dc 20   94-3479
                                                            CIP

Oriole Park Branch
7454 W. Balmoral Ave.
Chicago, IL 60656

For

Cheryl Silverstone
Debra Silverstone
Andrea Gordon
Rebecca Gordon
and
Adam Gordon Fishman

Books by
William A. Gordon

"HOW MANY BOOKS DO YOU SELL IN OHIO?"
FOUR DEAD IN OHIO
THE ULTIMATE HOLLYWOOD TOUR BOOK
SHOT ON THIS SITE

That night they had an outdoor grill at the University Inn, and we were waiting for the meat to be grilled. We were sitting in a corner and a couple came over. A lovely, gray-haired couple. Friendly.

He said, "Excuse me, would you by any chance be the newly elected president?" And I said, "Yes, I am." And I turned to Eva and I said, "Gee, it's nice, isn't it, to be coming back to hometown people."

And without batting an eye this man said to me, "Well, I hope you're going to be tougher than your predecessor. They should have shot four hundred, not four of them."

That is the first word I heard from a member of the Kent community.

> — Dr. Glenn A. Olds, president of Kent State
> (1971-1977), recounting his August 1971
> welcome to Kent State

If it takes a bloodbath, let's get it over with. No more appeasement.

> — California Governor Ronald Reagan, on how
> to handle campus protests, April 7, 1970

CONTENTS

Acknowledgments

There are so many people I have to thank I could probably write another book simply doing that.

Many people opened up their private files to me, swapped information, extended courtesies, or—in a few instances—even provided me with documents suppressed by the courts.

In particular, I would like to thank Professor David Engdahl of the University of Puget Sound School of Law. Professor Engdahl is a constitutional scholar who has written widely about the shootings and the legal issues raised by the use of military troops in civil disorders.

He is also an expert on the evidentiary record, and the most honest lawyer involved in the Kent State case.

The late Reverend John P. Adams, who acted as a liaison between the Kent State victims and various government agencies (and oftentimes as a liaison between the victims and their own attorneys) generously sent me the numerous trial transcripts that are quoted throughout this book.

I would especially like to thank John Dunphy, the reporter who covered the trial for the *Akron Beacon Journal,* and Peter Davies, who wrote an earlier book on the shootings. Although this book is sometimes critical of Davies' reasoning and certain conclusions he reached, I have always been grateful for his help.

Several attorneys spent their valuable time with me, helping me understand the complex legal issues involved as well as their tactics at the trials. I would like to thank Steven Sindell, who represented the victims, and Bernard Stuplinski, Michael Diamant, Jack Schulman, and Edd Wright, who represented the indicted Guardsmen.

Special thanks go to the late Galen Keller, the ACLU paralegal who, in the days before everyone had a computer, summarized, indexed, and cross-referenced the more than 13,000 pages of trial transcripts. With the help of those indexes, I was always able to locate and retrieve information quickly.

Federal prosecutor Robert Murphy courteously returned my phone calls and politely tolerated several very difficult questions I had to ask.

George Houston of the FBI processed my various Freedom of Information requests and facilitated my visit to FBI headquarters in Washington, D.C., in 1980 to study the Bureau's reports.

Judge Donald Young's law clerk, Mike Velotta, allowed me to read many of the pretrial depositions in the federal courthouse in Cleveland before Judge Donald Young ordered them sealed. ·

Those depositions, incidentally, were sealed at the request of the Ohio attorney general's office (which represented the Ohio National Guardsmen and former Ohio Governor James A. Rhodes in the civil litigation) and Kent State University—an institution nominally dedicated to the pursuit of research and scholarship. The depositions were eventually opened to the public, and several of them are cited in this book.

Many other individuals assisted me in various ways. I would like to thank these individuals collectively, and in doing so I apologize to anyone I may have inadvertently left out.

I would like to thank Pat Englehart, Bob Hoiles, Bob Downing, and John F. Greenman of the *Akron Beacon Journal;* Chris Jindra and Stephanie Saul of Cleveland's *Plain Dealer;* William Barrett and Pam Speck of the KSU Alumni Association; Kent State archivists Les Stegh, George Hing, and Nancy Birk, and archival assistants Sylvia Eldridge and Lori Mertel; Dr. Lawrence Dowler, associate librarian of Harvard College; Judith Ann Schiff, chief research archivist of Yale University's Manuscripts and Archives; James J. Hastings, deputy director of the Nixon Presidential Materials Projects, and his staff of archivists, especially Bryon A. Parham; Dennis East and Mary Zimmeth, archivists of the Ohio Historical Society; Doug Moore and Joe Durbin of Kent State News and Information; Benson Wolman, executive director, and Bruce Campbell, legal director of the Ohio ACLU; Greg Rambo, Sanford J. Rosen, and Dean Kahler.

I am also grateful to Bob Carpenter, Rick Sallinger, Dean Keller, Steve Keller, Alan Canfora, Kenneth McIntyre, Virginia Rinehart, Dick Waltz, Scott Bills, Mike Pesarchick, Jerome Stoklas, Jack Radgowski, Phil Long, Rose Ellis, Reece Moorehead, James Siere, Kermit J. Pike, Raymond Galloway, James Polk, Carol Ross, Randy Hibshman, Robert

Morris, Professor Stephen J. Cohen, Dr. Glenn A. Olds, Robert Fildes, Audrey Weprin, Donald Schwartzmiller, Norman Cousins, Marianne Nolan, John Miller, Sue Schisler, Madeline Drexler, Julie Morris, Bill Schmidt, Judy James, Elmer Leeper, Julie Martin, Ronnie and Steve Silverstone, Ron and Margaret Fishman, Ruth and Harry Sabgir, May M. Dowell, John Filo, Howard Ruffner, L. Samuel Copeland, Ronald McNees, Robert Sleeman, Greg Santos, Don Bauer, Richard Burns, Debbie Berger, Donna Zerner, Sandra Bullock, the clerks at the Portage County courthouse, and all the librarians who helped me at Yale, the Ohio Historical Society, the National Archives, the University of Akron, Kent State University, Cleveland State University, the Cleveland Public Library, and the Akron-Summit County Library, particularly the Ayres and McDowell branches.

Before this book was published I asked several individuals to read the manuscript in various draft stages. Dr. Lawrence Dowler, who was head of manuscripts and archives at Yale's Sterling Library, helped me above and beyond the call of duty. I am also indebted to Professor Robert Dyal, Charles Schollenberger, Michael Roberts, Philip Semas, and Paul Keane.

I am sorry to say I cannot thank any professors at Kent State. Although the university pays considerable lip service to preserving the memory of the tragedy, none of the professors I approached would help me when I asked for help. In fact, one professor, after telling me he could not put my manuscript down, went on to complain about the writing. He told me "I like dry, analytical stuff."

At least several individuals at Prometheus Books, the original publisher of this book, were able to recognize that this book is an important contribution to our understanding of what happened at Kent State on May 4, 1970. I would like to thank Doris Doyle, senior editor, for her support and encouragement, and my copy editor, John D. Van Fleet, who caught more than a few grammatical atrocities and improved this book in countless ways.

Finally, I owe more than I can express to my grandmother, the late Hannah Schulman Gordon Mendelson, and to my parents, Mrs. Frances Gordon and the late Professor Dennis Gordon.

William A. Gordon
March 1995

For truth there is no deadline.

> — Heywood Broun,
> *The Nation,* December 30, 1939

Tell the truth and run.

> — Yugoslavian proverb

Preface

The Kent State shootings occurred in broad daylight and in front of several hundred witnesses.

They were subsequently investigated by 300 FBI agents, the U.S. Department of Justice, a team of private attorneys who prosecuted the victims' wrongful death and injury claims, and several teams of enterprising journalists.

Despite this, the same questions that were asked on May 4, 1970— and in the immediate aftermath—are still being asked today.

The questions include:

• Was there a conspiracy among the Ohio National Guardsmen to shoot the students?

• Did an informant for the FBI fire his pistol, prompting the Guard to return fire?

• Did Ohio Governor James Rhodes, who interrupted a political campaign to visit Kent the day before the shootings, follow up on his threats to "get rid" of the demonstrators?

• Or, as journalist Norman Cousins and others have asked: "Had a decision been made at a national level that the student demonstrations across the nation had gone far enough and that an example had to be made?"

This book is the first study that tries to answer these questions—and a few others—since the litigation ended and most of the investigative files were publicly released.

In recent years the FBI has released more than 8,000 pages of its investigative reports. This book draws on those reports, as well as the 47-volume transcript produced from the three-month-long wrongful death and injury trial, the criminal prosecutions of eight Guardsmen, and independent investigations conducted by the Ohio Highway Patrol, the Ohio National Guard, and Kent State.

In addition, I conducted more than 200 interviews over a period of 19 years. These interviews were with a broad cross-section of figures who played key roles in the Kent Affair: the attorneys who argued the cases, White House and Justice Department officials, eyewitnesses, law enforcement officials, friends of the parents of the four students who were killed, and the few Ohio National Guardsmen who were willing to talk for attribution.

I drew several conclusions about the shootings, all of which are spelled out in Chapter Two, "Find the Smoking Guns."

However, before discussing those conclusions—and before providing a background to the events that led up to the shootings on May 4, 1970—there are a few issues I think ought be addressed first.

One is that even though this is the first, and to date, only major examination, and reappraisal of the killings, I realize that neither this book nor any other studies historians may write in the future will end the debate over what happened at Kent State.

That is because cases like Kent State never get completely resolved. One needs only to take a quick look at the more than 600 books about the assassination of President Kennedy—or for that matter, the copious literature on the Julius and Ethel Rosenberg spy case, the guilt or innocence of Sacco and Vanzetti, and virtually any other 20th century historical controversy—to appreciate the fact that no single journalist, scholar or historian has ever really "solved" or "resolved" anything.

As an author who has studied this case more thoroughly than anyone, I believe I have a fairly good idea of what happened.

I feel very comfortable with the conclusions I reached.

However, I certainly would not make any claims that I know the truth—the whole truth or the unadulterated truth. Only the Guardsmen who were on Blanket Hill know what prompted them to open fire under the very suspicious circumstances that occurred.

I probably should also point out that what journalists, scholars and historians do (or at least what the best ones do) in historical controversies like this one is examine the evidence available to them. They cut through the enormous amount of nonsense and propaganda that is inevitably said and written and try to sift fact from fiction.

Even if they are not miracle workers who can singlehandedly solve all the mysteries (even Woodward and Bernstein could not do that), they can at least suggest reasonable answers and, to borrow the language of the academic historians, "demythologize" the events.

This is basically what I did.

I also broke ranks with most conventional history-tellers and told the story of the Kent State killings in a manner that is rather unique.

While this book is primarily an investigative account, on occasion I told the story through the use of carefully selected satirical devices.

For example, I was too polite to call the National Guard officers perjurers. So, to demonstrate that virtually every important point in their testimonies was contradicted by an unusual number of witnesses, I resorted to devices such as a "Myron Pryor Box Score" and a "Major Jones Credibility Chart."

History should record that there was a significant cover-up of what happened at Kent State and then a complete breakdown in the judicial processes.

There were all kinds of crimes committed at Kent State in May of 1970, yet no one—students, Guardsmen, or government officials—were held accountable in any of the courts.

This book examines why that came about. It also focuses on the one issue that dominated public debate: whether or not the National Guardsmen conspired to kill the students at Kent State.

The Historical Significance of May 4

Before examining that question, the shootings need to be placed in historical context.

The question needs to be asked: How historically significant was it? What are historians likely to conclude about May 4?

The university has done a very poor job explaining what May 4 is all about. Amazingly, when it built a memorial on campus,* it released a report stating a memorial was needed not because four people were gunned down, or because Kent State became an American battleground in the middle of an unpopular war.

No, Kent State commissioned the memorial, according to its own committee, because May 4 "sensitized America to regimented lines of communications and authority. May 4 changed forever how future demonstrations—peaceful and otherwise—must be perceived, analyzed, understood, and settled non-violently. Hence, a University Memorial is needed."

---

*The memorial was built not to memorialize the victims, but the "event." The university never had much sympathy for its dead.

I cannot think of a dumber reason to spend $100,000 on a memorial—or even to keep alive the memory of May 4.

So, to help steer Kent State's scholars in the direction of the debate, I would like to say first that besides the fact that the war in Vietnam was brought home, Kent State was a rare incident in American history in which the militia was used against American citizens.

It was not "the first military volley aimed at a civilian crowd in the history of the United States." A book, *The Kent Affair,* co-authored by two Kent State English professors, made that claim, but there are actually some long-forgotten precedents.

Although virtually no one remembers it today, National Guardsmen or militiamen from various states killed civilians during several labor riots in 1877. These killings occurred in Martinsburg, West Virginia; Baltimore; Pittsburgh; and Buffalo.

The fact that the military is used so infrequently against American citizens is, of course, why the tragedy was so shocking. What may not seem uncommon in other parts of the world—killings of civilians by governments or armies in Beijing, South Africa, or in unstable South American countries—is not supposed to happen here.

The shots at Kent State were heard literally around the world, and for many of us who were college students during that divisive era, it seemed like the entire country was on the threshold of being torn apart over the war in Vietnam.

In the aftermath of Kent State and President Richard Nixon's invasion of Cambodia (which triggered the demonstrations), student protests forced more than 200 college campuses to shut down completely, and classes were disrupted at hundreds of other universities.

The uproar, however, proved to be short-lived. Except for some sporadic protests the following year and in 1972, the campuses quieted down. Nixon seemed to pursue his policy of deescalating American involvement in Vietnam at his own pace.

Kent State was not "the single most influential event contributing to the end of Vietnam." That is what some students at Kent State claimed when they asked for the memorial, but there is no evidence that the killings changed the course of history.

Since the early 1980s, there have been a number of scholarly reappraisals of the Vietnam conflict. To my knowledge, not a single historian has argued that the Kent State tragedy had much of an impact on the conduct of American policy in Vietnam; although the killings and the resultant national uproar probably forced Nixon to withdraw U.S. troops from Cambodia before he intended to.

Kent State will probably be remembered more as a message to those who opposed government policy in Vietnam. The killings indicated to them—in quite unmistakable terms—what the consequences would be if they raised their voices too loudly against the war.

In fact, that message had been delivered to college students as early as a year before the shootings. In a little noted speech delivered at General Beadle State College in Madison, South Dakota, on June 3, 1969, President Nixon spoke about the antiwar protests and the civil disturbances that were racking American cities at the time. He compared them to an insurrection, and said: "The Nation has survived other attempts at insurrection. We can survive this one."

To those who used force in their protests, Nixon warned: "We have the power to strike back if need be, and we can prevail."

The government certainly prevailed at Kent State—and its deadly crackdown against protestors was overwhelmingly approved of by the general public.

A poll taken by the Gallup Organization for *Newsweek* in May 1970 indicated that most Americans wholeheartedly supported the National Guard's actions.

In fact, the poll indicated that 58 percent of the public believed the demonstrators themselves were primarily responsible for the student deaths. Only 11 percent of the public faulted the National Guardsmen who pulled the triggers.

Which brings us, I think, to a significance of the Kent State shootings that historians have hitherto overlooked.

On the basis of the public opinion polls taken at the time, and the circumstantial evidence presented in this book, I would argue that these were the most popular murders ever committed in the United States.

PART ONE

ONE

Four Days in May

Thursday, April 30, 1970

President Richard Nixon announced on national television that he was sending American combat troops into Cambodia on a mission to destroy Communist sanctuaries there.

The announcement angered many college students, who felt that Nixon had broken his promise to wind down the war in Vietnam. Many students, in fact, felt that the invasion was a major escalation of the war.

The following day protests were held on college campuses throughout the country, including one at noon on the campus of Kent State.

Friday, May 1, 1970

At Kent, an ad hoc group of less than half a dozen graduate students led an antiwar rally at noon on the campus Commons. This rally, attended by perhaps 500 students, was peaceful and memorable for only one event. That event was the burial of the U. S. Constitution—which was a symbolic gesture. The students charged that Nixon violated the Constitution by not consulting Congress before ordering the invasion.

Late that evening, after 11:00 P.M., there was a disturbance in the business section of downtown Kent. Windows along several blocks were smashed, bonfires were set in the street, and at least two stores were looted.

As far as we know, the disturbance downtown was spontaneous. No evidence later surfaced suggesting that any group or individuals had planned the disturbance in advance as part of an antiwar protest.

The Justice Department's summary of the FBI report states: "We are not sure how the incident on this night started." However, most accounts have noted that the first night of springlike weather and the antics of a motorcycle gang, the Chosen Few, doing motorcycle tricks on the street, helped contribute to events getting out of hand.

Saturday, May 2, 1970

During the day all kinds of wild rumors spread throughout the town of Kent. Some residents of the town actually believed that a revolutionary group, the Weathermen, would be flying their own private airplanes into Kent that night.

Fear seemed to grip the city, and many local officials and townspeople were convinced that dedicated subversives or "outside agitators," who they blamed for the Friday night disturbance, would be back to cause more trouble on Saturday night.

Kent Mayor LeRoy Satrom was convinced that the student group, the Students for a Democratic Society (SDS), was choreographing the events. Kent's chief of police, Roy Thompson, seemed to concur. Thompson later told the *Cleveland Press* he felt "Armageddon was at hand."

As history shows, these officials could not have been more mistaken. The SDS was never linked after the fact to any of the protests on campus (which one would expect had the organization been pulling the strings. Radical groups like to claim responsibility for acts of violence so they can get their names in the press).

After the shootings, the FBI and other law enforcement agencies searched diligently for underground or subversive plots behind the protests at Kent State. If there is anything notable about their investigations, it is their failure to produce any evidence of any organized or left-wing plots.

It must be noted, however, that local merchants had one very legitimate reason to be jumpy. On Saturday afternoon, several local merchants reported receiving anonymous telephone threats. The merchants were told to put antiwar slogans in their windows "unless they wanted to risk having their shops burned or damaged" on Saturday night.

Mayor Satrom spent most of the day meeting with various state and local officials, and about 5:00 P.M. called Ohio Governor James A. Rhodes' office and asked that National Guardsmen be sent to Kent to protect the city that night.

Since no acts of violence had yet occurred, the Guard decided to instead send several detachments of troops, already mobilized for a trucker's strike in northeast Ohio, to the Rubber Bowl in Akron, about ten miles outside Kent, where they were placed on standby alert.

About 7:30 that evening, an antiwar rally was held on the Commons. Again, none of the subsequent investigations were able to determine which groups or individuals were responsible for organizing this event.

We do know that after the rally began, the crowd marched around the campus as leaders beckoned other students, particularly those residing in dormitories, to join the protest. By 8:05 P.M., a crowd estimated at between 500 and 1,000 converged on West Hall, the University's Army ROTC building. Some students started throwing rocks at the building, and within minutes a few individuals stepped out of the crowd and tried to burn the building down.

That should not have been too difficult a task. The building, which originally had been built as a temporary housing unit for Army personnel during War World II, was made of wood. But repeated attempts to ignite the building with matches and railroad flares seemed to fail.

Police did not arrive on the scene to prevent the arson attempts, and about forty minutes later, a fire was finally started after a young man "dipped a cloth into a gasoline tank of a parked motorcycle."

Kent firemen did rush to the scene, but they met resistance from several demonstrators who tried to prevent them from extinguishing the blaze. According to the Report of the President's Commission on Campus Unrest (henceforth known as the Scranton Commission Report, after its chairman, William Scranton): "Members of the mob . . . slashed and stabbed the hose with pocket knives, an ice pick, and a machete. They threw rocks at the firemen, who then withdrew. At this point, the fire seemed to subside."

Kent Fire Chief Fred Miller later told me that the reason he ordered his men to retreat was because they could not do their job without protection from the police.

Why were not the police there to help? The failure of the city and campus police to stop the would-be arsonists and assist the firemen later became the subject of considerable speculation.

The city police department was only a few blocks away, in downtown Kent, and the campus police headquarters was even closer—just a few hundred yards from the building.

Statements made to the FBI by Chester Williams, the university's security director, and Tom Kelley, a KSU police detective, confirm that the campus police stood by and merely observed the scene for more than an hour while the demonstrators tried to burn the building and harassed the firemen.

Even more disturbing were the conclusions of an internal University fact-finding body commissioned by then-Kent State President Robert I. White. The university's own report stated: "The persons involved in the actual incendiarism were few, were separated from the main crowd, and could easily have been apprehended by the police."

Adding to the puzzle is the fact that no more than five to ten minutes after the firemen retreated—supposedly because of the lack of police protection—another law enforcement agency, the Portage County Sheriff's Department, arrived on the scene (in lieu of the city and campus police). Two of the deputies, Ross Jamerson and Walt Moore, told me in separate interviews that even though there were only four or five sheriff's deputies present, those few men managed to disperse the crowd by firing tear gas.

Only after the Portage County deputies chased the crowd from the scene did the Kent State police emerge from their surveillance points and take positions around the building. At that point, the fire seemed to have died on its own.

Meanwhile, the crowd, apparently emboldened by the lack of police response, headed toward downtown Kent. Along the way they did some additional damage, setting fire to an archery shed and destroying a fence and a telephone booth.

At 9:30 P.M. the crowd reached Kent's main intersection and encountered the National Guard, which had just entered the city. After a brief skirmish in which several members of G Troop, 107th Armored Cavalry, the unit which fired into the crowd two days later, were hit by flying rocks, the troops forced the crowd back onto the campus, where the ROTC building was now burning furiously out of control.*

Later, there were a few minor incidents in which some Guard mem-

---

*The fact that the arson attempts only succeeded *after* the demonstrators had been chased from the building—and the city and campus police's refusal to protect the building—are only two of the disturbing peculiarities surrounding the fire. We know now, for

bers chased some of the students around the campus. But by midnight, a sweep of the campus indicated that the students had returned to their apartments or dorms.

The Guard then took positions throughout the city and campus. They were now very much in control.

Sunday, May 3, 1970

Unfortunately, the events at Kent State happened to coincide with the elections in Ohio. One politician who could have tried to defuse the volatile situation instead decided to impress the electorate.

That politician was the incumbent governor of Ohio, James A. Rhodes. With the primary only two days away, Rhodes was trailing his opponent, Robert Taft, Jr., in the race for the Republican senatorial nomination.

On the morning of May 3, a desperate Rhodes abruptly changed his campaign plans and helicoptered into Kent, where he had his picture taken next to the charred ruins of the ROTC building. Then the governor met privately with the highest ranking Guardsman in the state of Ohio, Adjutant General Sylvester Del Corso, and with other high level local, state, and federal officials in a conference room at the Kent fire station.

We still do not know all the details of what was said at that meeting or what decisions were reached about how to handle any further protests in Kent. But afterward, reporters were invited to a press conference, at which Rhodes and the other officials took turns denouncing the violence in Kent in the strongest of terms.

Rhodes, without specifying who he was referring to, claimed that "we are up against the strongest, well-trained militant revolutionary group that has ever assembled in America . . . They're worse than the brownshirts and the Communist element and the night riders and the vigilantes. They are the worst type of people that we harbor in America . . . [They intend] to destroy higher education in Ohio."

After Rhodes ended his speech, a reporter asked General Del Corso

---

example, that the KSU police knew as early as the afternoon before the fire that the building would be attacked, and that KSU Detective Tom Kelley even told an NBC camera crew not to leave Kent that evening so they would not miss the blaze.

For a complete examination of the circumstances surrounding the fire, see Chapter Three, "Who Burned ROTC?"

how long the Guard would remain in Kent. Rhodes, butting in, answered: "*Until we get rid of them*" [emphasis added].

Rhodes added: "Ohio is not only a target. *The only thing is we have done something different. Instead of prolonging a fifteen-day [demonstration] at Columbia and a twelve-day [demonstration] at Harvard and three years at Berkeley, we are going to do something about it and with them*" [emphasis added].

Rhodes did not specify what he had planned, but his threats to crack down were echoed by Ohio Highway Patrol Chief Robert Chiarmonte and by Kent Police Chief Roy Thompson, who also answered questions at the press conference.

Chiarmonte even raised the specter of shooting. Chiarmonte warned: "The next phase we have encountered elsewhere is where they start sniping." If that happened, he promised, "they can expect us to return fire."

Chief Thompson, answering a question a few minutes later, was even more ominous. He said: "I'll be right behind with the National Guard to give our full support—anything that is necessary. Like Ohio says, use any force that is necessary, *even to the point of shooting*. We do not want to get into that, but the law says we can if necessary" [emphasis added].

These threats, of course, raise an interesting question. Were they made spontaneously, or was the subject of shooting students broached—either specifically or in hypothetical terms—during the private meeting that was held before the press conference, or in any other meeting held by government officials that weekend?

There is no evidence directly linking Governor Rhodes or anyone else attending the meeting to the shootings the following day. Still, the fact that not one, but two, different law enforcement officials raised the spectre of shooting, and that shooting occurred the next day, makes one wonder whether there might not be more here than they are admitting.

Sunday afternoon was uneventful. Some of the students fraternized with the troops who assembled to guard the ruins of the ROTC building. One was Allison Krause, who was one of the coeds killed the next day.

According to her boyfriend, Barry Levine, Allison spotted a lilac in the barrel of a Guardsman's rifle. After an officer came over and ordered the soldier to remove the flower, she said: "Flowers are better than bullets."

The phrase was later engraved on her tombstone.

About 8:00 P.M. on Sunday evening, students held another rally on the campus Commons, presumably to vent more anger over the invasion of Cambodia.

This rally started peacefully enough, but the Guard officers were worried that the peace might not last.

At 9:00 P.M. an officer read the Ohio Riot Act and ordered the crowd to disperse.

When the students refused to leave, the Guard cleared the Commons with tear gas. Part of the crowd then moved to the home of Kent State President Robert I. White, "where they were dispersed by tear gas by state police."

Other members of the crowd, having nowhere to go, decided to stage a sit-in at the intersection of Lincoln and Main Streets, by the main gate of the campus. They sang "Give Peace a Chance" and other pacifist songs.

At 10:30 P.M. one of the students borrowed a bullhorn from the police and issued a list of "nonnegotiable demands." The student demanded that:

• The war be stopped (apparently before all the students went home that night);

• The university abolish its ROTC program;

• The National Guard be removed from the campus;

For good measure, the student also demanded that everyone's tuition be reduced, that all future demands of the Black United Students, whatever they might be, be met, and the curfew be lifted in town.

The student with the bullhorn also demanded to speak with Mayor Satrom and Kent State President White, and unfortunately, he led the crowd to believe that Satrom and White were on their way, even though neither had any intention of addressing the crowd.

Thirty minutes later, a National Guardsman announced that the 1:00 A.M. curfew in town had been moved forward to 11:00 P.M., that very moment. According to the Report of the Scranton Commission: "The students, previously nonviolent, became hostile. They felt that they had been double-crossed. They cursed the Guardsmen and police and threw rocks at them."

The Guardsmen responded by attempting to disperse the crowd with tear gas, but this time they also fixed bayonets. They chased the students around campus for about forty minutes, and several students were stabbed by Guard bayonets. The President's Commission also reported that "three Guardsmen received cuts and bruises from thrown stones and a wrench."

Monday, May 4, 1970

Despite the events of the weekend, classes resumed as usual, with the Guardsmen continuing to occupy the campus.

Some students prepared for another rally on the campus Commons at noon. The rally had been announced the previous Friday, and was still scheduled, despite a "special message to the University community"—a flyer signed by Robert Matson, Vice-President for Student Affairs, and Frank Frisina, the student body president, announcing that all assemblies would be prohibited by order of the National Guard.*

At 10:00 A.M., National Guard General Robert Canterbury met with President White and other University officials to discuss the situation as it stood. Although no one was later willing to assume responsibility for the decision, both Canterbury and White left the meeting knowing that the students would be forcibly dispersed.

General Canterbury arrived on the Commons at 11:30 A.M., saw the crowd forming, and ordered Lieutenant Colonel Charles Fassinger to have the Guardsmen break up the rally. Fassinger then hastily assembled soldiers from G Troop of the 107th Armored Cavalry from Ravenna, and from Companies A and C of the 145th Infantry Battalion from Akron and Wooster.

The troops were armed with M-1 rifles, .45 caliber pistols, and shotguns. According to the Scranton Commission, these men, who "had an average of three hours of sleep the night before," and who had been on duty for about a week due to the truckers' strike, were given no more than fifteen minutes' notice that they would be moving against the crowd.

Guard Chaplain John Simons later reported to the FBI that some Guard officers expressed concern to General Canterbury "that not enough Guardsmen were available and that the students were not informed" that the rally could not be held.

Simons told federal investigators that General Canterbury not only dismissed these concerns, but he even joked about the upcoming con-

---

*Actually, no formal state of emergency had been declared, making it unclear whether the Guard had the authority to prevent students from rallying. The flyer was distributed in some buildings on campus, but many students had no idea that rallies would be banned.

frontation, saying that he and Adjutant General Sylvester Del Corso "had a great time chasing these students around the other night, even throwing some rocks back at them."

In his book, *Kent State: What Happened and Why,* James Michener also reports that a faculty member pleaded with General Canterbury not to move against the students, who had, until that time, remained peaceful.

Canterbury reportedly responded: "These students are going to have to find out what law and order is all about."

Shortly before noon, the students were still peaceful, and there was little activity at the rally. The students were mostly milling around.

Nevertheless, at approximately 11:55 A.M., Kent State patrolman Harold Rice, escorted by three Guardsmen, was driven around the Commons in a jeep. Rice announced through a bullhorn that the assembly was unlawful, and ordered the students to disperse.

The announcement incensed the crowd. Students threw rocks at the jeep, shouted "Sieg Heil," and cursed the troops.

For several minutes the Guardsmen fired tear gas into the crowd. Most of it blew away because of a 14 MPH breeze; so the Guard advanced toward the students, firing more tear gas as they marched ahead.

Unfortunately, in the last minute scramble to assemble the troops, no one checked to see if the troops had brought enough tear gas along.

Later, no officer would admit that it had been his responsibility to ensure that the troops were adequately supplied.

Within minutes the students retreated. Rock throwing and steady cursing continued, but the Guard clearly had the situation under control.

The Guardsmen continued to chase most of the crowd off the Commons and up the steep hill between Taylor Hall, which houses the University's journalism and architecture schools, and Johnson Hall, a student dorm.

Then, in a logistical move, at 12:07, the men of C Company, 145th Infantry, parted from the main contingent and moved to a grassy knoll by the northwest corner of Taylor Hall (between Taylor Hall and Prentice Hall, another dorm).

The apparent purpose of this move was to secure the corridor between Taylor and Prentice Hall, preventing the students, who had just

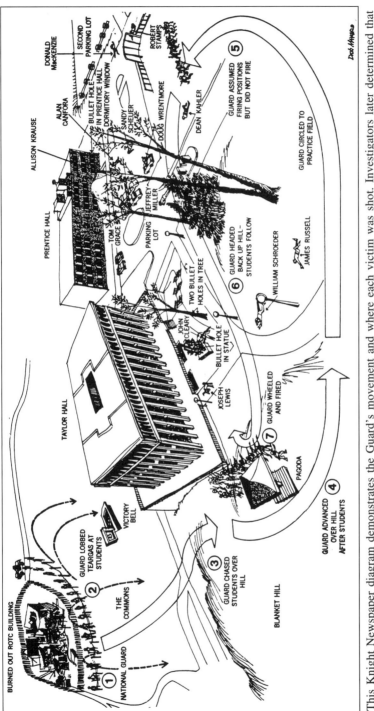

This Knight Newspaper diagram demonstrates the Guard's movement and where each victim was shot. Investigators later determined that William Schroeder was actually in the parking lot near Sandy Scheuer. Alan Canfora and Tom Grace eventually admitted they were on the Taylor Hall hillside, beyond the tree with the bullet holes.

been chased to the opposite side of Taylor Hall, from circling around the building and returning to the Commons.

C Company stayed in that location for the next half hour, and was not involved in the shooting itself.

The main detachment, now numbering 77 men, reached the crest of Blanket Hill by the northeast corner of Taylor, where the now-famous Japanese Pagoda stands.

The Pagoda is an eight-foot-tall concrete architectural landmark, and it was by the Pagoda (or the shelter, as the Justice Department suggestively called it) that the shooting started at 12:24 P.M.

By ten minutes after noon, the Commons had been cleared of students, who were still fleeing from the oncoming Guard.

Instead of stopping at the crest of the hill, however, the troops continued straight ahead. Acting as if they were following a script from the Keystone Cops, the Guardsmen marched right in between the students they had just been chasing, then down a moderately steep hill, and onto a practice football field, where they were forced to halt when they encountered a chain link fence.

The Guardsmen turned 90 degrees to their left, only to discover that the crowd they had been chasing had regrouped behind them.

The troops were now boxed in on two sides. There were students in front of them (mostly in the Prentice Hall parking lot) and students to their right (scattered along the hillside of Taylor Hall).

At this point, if the Guardsmen wanted to return to the Commons, they would have to march back through a crowd of about 1,000 students (both protestors and bystanders) who were now blocking their path.

While it cannot be said that the Guardsmen were in serious trouble (hundreds of reinforcements were nearby; one unit was just a few hundred yards away), the Guardsmen had clearly blundered and relinquished control of the situation, which was now a stand-off.

As might be expected, the move down to the field infuriated some of the Guardsmen. They felt that their officers had placed them in a vulnerable and precarious position.

Sergeant Matthew McManus, for example, later blasted General Canterbury as "a blind fool." And Sergeant Lawrence Shafer told a reporter, with much justification, "the shootings could have been prevented with proper leadership . . . If that general had had his head out of his ass, he never would have put us in that situation."

For the next ten minutes, the Guardsmen remained on the football field while their officers tried to figure out what to do next.

During this time the troops continued to keep the crowd at a distance by firing more tear gas at them. A few protestors darted as close as they dared to throw rocks or tear gas cannisters at them.

As Peter Davies later noted in his studies, military discipline also seemed to deteriorate while the Guardsmen were on the practice field. At least three frustrated Guardsmen threw rocks or tear gas cannisters back at the students. The Scranton Commission reported: "Some among the crowd came to regard the situation as a game—'a tennis match' one called it—and cheered each exchange of tear gas cannisters."

After five or ten minutes, the Guardsmen stopped firing tear gas, and many Guardsmen and students believed (erroneously, as it turned out) that the supply had been exhausted.

Although most students maintained a healthy distance, a few rock throwers got a little bolder, and the Guard appeared ready to resort to additional measures.

Shortly before 12:20 P.M., about ten soldiers from G Troop knelt and assumed a firing formation, aiming their rifles directly at the most vociferous members of the crowd, who were in the parking lot adjacent to Taylor and Prentice Halls.

Photographs show that there were very few students in this area, but one of them, Alan Canfora (who was later wounded), emerged from the crowd, walked to within a close distance of the riflemen, and waved a black flag in front of them.

Canfora's action undoubtedly further provoked the soldiers.

As the troops knelt, an unidentified soldier stood behind them, and according to a number of witnesses, fired one and possibly two shots into the air.

No explanation for this firing has ever surfaced, and no officer has ever admitted firing this shot, which is why it has always been the subject of speculation.

One lawyer later suggested the shot may have been a dry run for the volley which followed. Others thought this might have been an signal to shoot which the soldiers did not respond to.

Although anything is possible, more than likely the shot was an improvised warning that the Guardsmen were prepared to open fire into the crowd if the students did not keep their distance.

By 12:20 P.M., the two senior officers, General Canterbury and Colonel Fassinger, decided that the troops should return to their point of origin, the ROTC building. To do so, the Guardsmen had to march back up Blanket Hill, where hundreds of students were now blocking their path.

These students might have posed a threat to the Guardsmen, but they scattered as soon as the Guardsmen started marching toward them with bayonets fixed.

The Guardsmen continued their slow ascent up Blanket Hill toward the Pagoda. Many students, assuming the confrontation was over, began returning to their afternoon classes.

As Davies and others have noted from studying the photographs of the Guard's ascent, the Guardsmen on the far right flank closest to the students (the men of G Troop) kept a careful watch on the crowds at the bottom of Taylor Hall and in the parking lot adjacent to Taylor and Prentice Halls.

It is not clear how much rock throwing there was at this point. The Guardsmen, of course, later claimed they had been subjected to a life-threatening rock attack. The Justice Department concluded, however, that there was less rock throwing than there had been earlier, when the Guardsmen were stationary targets on the practice football field.

Several witnesses reported that, as the Guardsmen got closer and closer to the Pagoda, some of them hesitated from time to time, half-turning to point their rifles again at the most vociferous students in the parking lot below.

When the Guardsmen reached the crest of Blanket Hill, by the Pagoda, they appeared ready to round the corner of Taylor Hall and to pass completely out of sight of the demonstrators.

At 12:24, when the men of G Troop were just a few feet from the corner of the building, they suddenly stopped, turned about-face, lifted their rifles to their shoulders, and opened fire into the crowd of students below.

The shooting went on for thirteen seconds, and when it was over, four students were dead or dying, and nine others were wounded. One was paralyzed for life.

The Guard advances on the students, firing tear gas. (Previously unpublished photo by L. Samuel Copeland.)

Guardsmen kneel on the practice field and take aim at the students. (Photo by John P. Filo.)

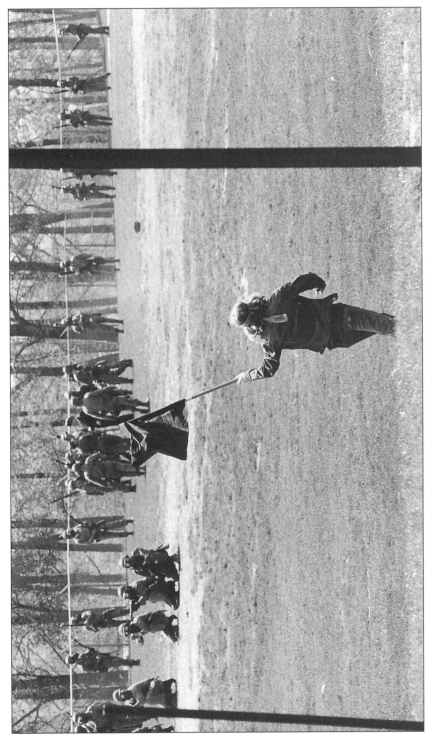

Alan Canfora provokes the Guard by waving a flag. (Photo by Howard E. Ruffner.)

Guardsmen watch students closely as they ascend Blanket Hill. (Photo courtesy KSU Archives.)

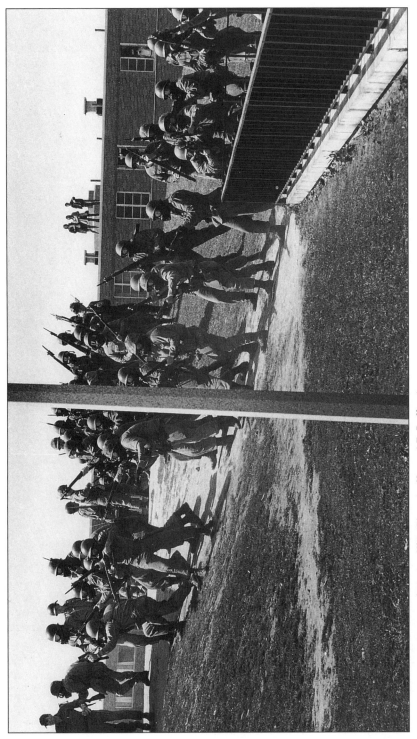

The Guard turns at the crest of Blanket Hill. (Photo by Howard E. Ruffner.)

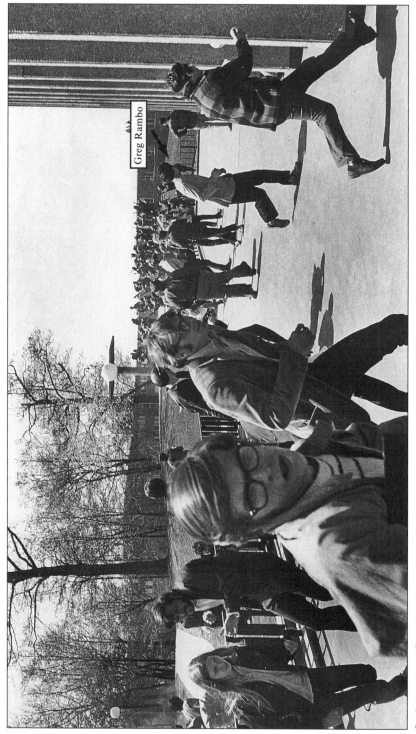

Students scatter. (Photo by *Akron Beacon Journal*.)

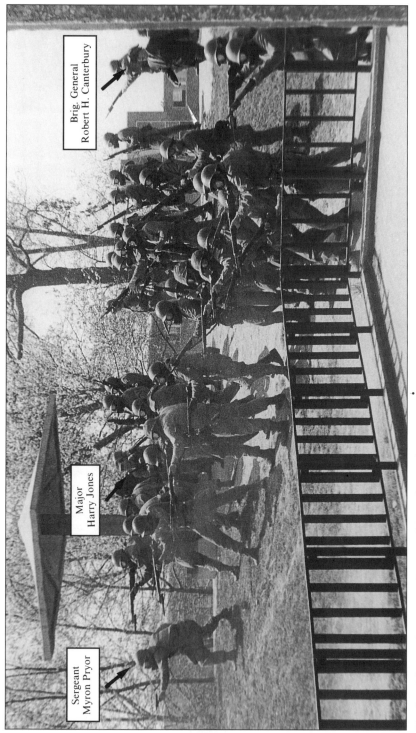

Brig. General
Robert H. Canterbury

Major
Harry Jones

Sergeant
Myron Pryor

The Guard fires on the students. (Photo by John A. Darnell, jr.)

Canterbury attempts to stop the shooting. (Photo by John A. Darnell, jr.)

Jones tries to regain control and calm the Guardsmen. (Photo by John A. Darnell, jr.)

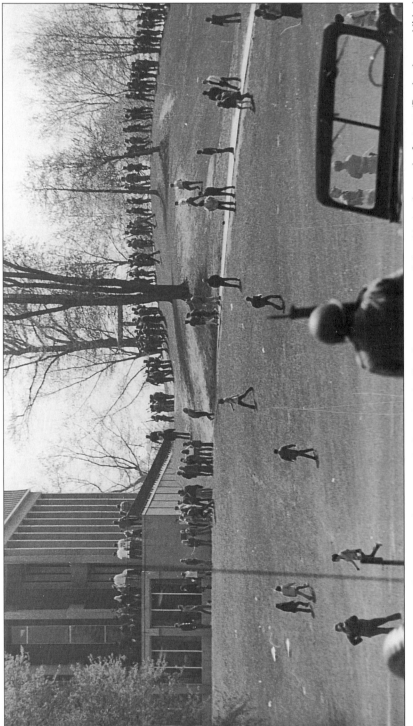

Taken moments after the shooting stopped, this photo clearly shows that the Guard was not surrounded and had a clear path of retreat. (Previously unpublished photo by L. Samuel Copeland.)

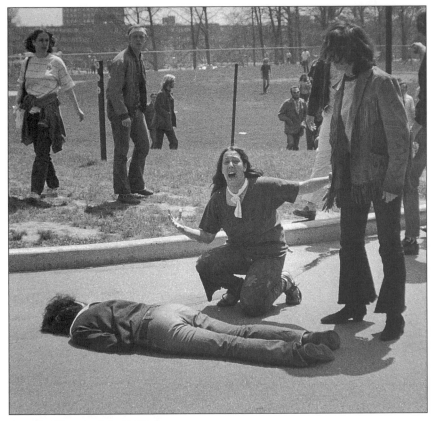

Anguish. (Photo by John P. Filo.)

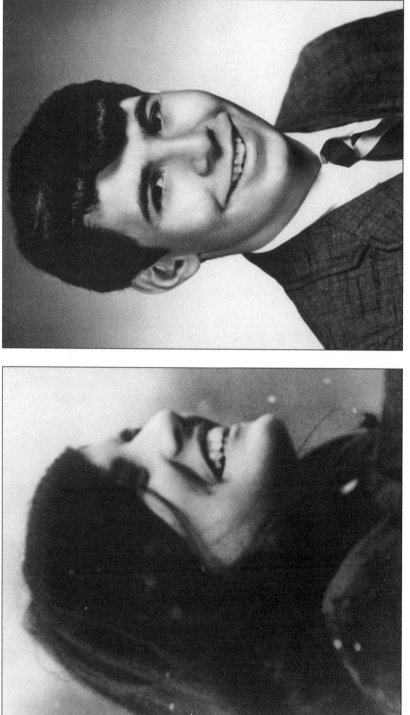

Jeffrey Miller.

Allison Krause.

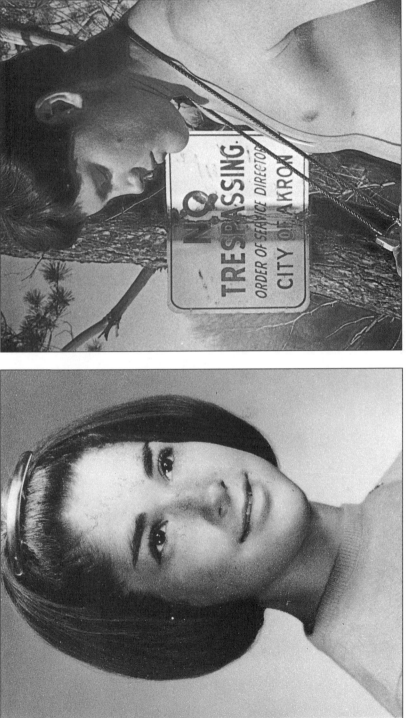

William Schroeder.

Sandra Scheuer.

TWO

The Search for the Smoking Guns

> You will recall, Holmes, that you once observed
> to me: It is of the highest importance in the art of
> detection to be able to recognize, out of a number
> of facts, those which are incidental and those
> which are vital.
>
> – Edmund Aubrey,
> *The Case of the Murdered President*

Immediately after the shootings, the National Guard offered two (and many thought conflicting) explanations as to why they fired on the students.

General Robert Canterbury, who was the senior officer present, issued a prepared statement saying: "A crowd estimated at several hundred closed in and assaulted the Guard force again with rocks and pieces of concrete. A single shot was fired, followed by several other shots, these by Guardsmen."

Canterbury was not willing to say that there was definitely a sniper present, but Adjutant General Sylvester Del Corso, who was not at the scene, was. Speaking from his office in Columbus, Del Corso told reporters: "A sniper opened fire against the guardsmen from a nearby rooftop." His deputy, Assistant Adjutant General Frederick P. Wenger, also issued a similar statement that the troops were simply defending themselves against a sniper.

A few days later, however, Del Corso was forced to retract the Guards' position. Del Corso admitted the Guard was unable to produce any evidence of a sniper at Kent State.

Which was what all the subsequent investigations determined: that the sniper only existed in the imaginations of the spokesmen for the National Guard.

Both the Scranton Commission Report and the Justice Department's summary of the FBI investigation, which was prepared for a possible prosecution of the soldiers, noted there were not any witnesses who saw anyone shoot at the soldiers.

Even the firing troops could not say they saw anyone shoot at them.

Moreover, the troops did not follow sniper maneuvers, which would have required them to take evasive action and pinpoint the location of a sniper in order for selected marksmen to return fire.

And if that were not enough, the troops fired in the wrong direction. Had there been a sniper, he or she would have, by definition, fired from a concealed or elevated position (say, from behind them, or atop Taylor Hall or one of the nearby dormitories).

The troops did not fire in any of the directions. Instead, they fired point blank into the crowd.

In the years that followed, certain officers would occasionally try to resurrect the specter of a sniper, and on those occasions, their comments would get reported uncritically in the media.

For the most part, however, the Guard dropped the sniper story and only continued to maintain they fired out of necessity to protect themselves against a wild and crazy mob.

Canterbury, speaking for the soldiers, claimed from the very beginning—in a press conference the day after the shootings—that "some of the students were within 10 feet of the Guardsmen."

Del Corso said in his statement: "All (77) Guardsmen were hit by rocks and bricks. Guardsmen facing almost certain injury and death were forced to open fire on the attackers."

In effect, the Guard argued that the students behaved like lemmings—or, to use perhaps a better analogy, like kamikazes, unconcerned about the possibility that if they got too close to the soldiers, they might run into the Guardsmen's bayonets or get themselves injured.

Were the students on a suicide mission? Let us examine each and every element of the Guards' claim of self-defense, starting with their claims that the students mercilessly pelted them with rocks, bricks, and chunks of concrete.

In one of their most memorable efforts to argue self-defense, the attorneys for the Guardsmen, during the 1975 wrongful death and injury trials, brought into the courtroom huge sacks of rocks recovered from the 1,300 square foot area of the confrontation.

The rocks were brought into the courtroom in huge potato sacks bearing the label "Bulls-eye."

The idea the attorneys were trying to plant in the minds of the jurors was that all of the rocks recovered from the scene were actually thrown, and that the protestors always hit their mark.

The attorneys for the victims were very much placed on the defensive by this ploy. Although their arguments were not as memorable as the huge sacks, they were able to point out that if an individual walked outside Taylor Hall today, he or she might be able to pick up as many rocks as were picked up by authorities after the shootings; since many of the rocks were indigenous to the grassy hillside and nearby parking lots.

All the sackfuls proved, of course, was how many rocks were found on the ground after the killings. There was no way of determining how many were actually thrown or hit the National Guardsmen.

The dozen or so photographs taken by various photographers in the minutes before the shootings were actually more helpful in showing what the students were doing in terms of rock throwing. Interestingly, the photographs taken just before the shooting started and during the first few seconds of gunfire fail to capture more than a handful of missiles flying through the air.

In fact, virtually all of the photographers testified there never was any barrage of rocks. Many other eyewitnesses said basically the same thing.

At the trial, it seemed as if only the Guardsmen could see the rocks.

The Guard's attorneys were also reduced to arguing that the photographers and the witnesses were all looking the wrong way.

Of course, had there been a real "rock attack," and had the Guardsmen been subjected to serious danger by the students, it would have had to follow that a number of Guardsmen would have been hurt by the demonstrators.

However, when it came time to produce evidence in court of injuries sustained by the soldiers, the Guard's attorneys could only produce two photographs documenting any Guardsmen were injured.

A review of the 1975 civil trial record reveals that the attorneys entered into evidence a photograph of a bruise that James McGee sustained on his right bicep sometime on May 4 (although it was never specified at what point on May 4), and a photograph of Sergeant Lawrence Shafer's badly bruised arm in a sling.

Shafer told the FBI he was hit on the arm about 10 to 15 minutes before the shooting. And although his arm was badly bruised, the injury did not prevent him from picking up his rifle 10 to 15 minutes later and wounding a student giving him the finger. The student was identified by the Justice Department as Joseph Lewis, Jr.

There are, of course, other reasons why the Guards' claim of self-defense was challenged from the beginning.

One question was raised simply by looking at the Guardsmen's physical position just before they started shooting. The troops were marching past Taylor Hall and were about to round the corner of the building and pass out of sight of the demonstrators, who were off to the troops' right flank.

Even if the students had launched a last-minute major assault as the Guard reached the crest of the hill, the Guardsmen could have escaped harm by walking another five or ten feet behind the northwest corner of Taylor Hall. The rocks would have simply bounced off the building.

The Guardsmen were not surrounded, as every official investigation concluded. The Justice Department summary noted that: "Regardless of the location of the students following them, photographs and television film show that only a very few students were located between the Guard and the Commons. They [the Guard] could easily have continued in the direction in which they had been going."

Not only were the Guardsmen not surrounded, but apparently the students never came as close to the soldiers as the troops claimed.

At the 1975 wrongful death and injury trial, "shooters"* like Lawrence Shafer, William Perkins, and James Pierce swore under oath that as many as 100 rock-throwing protestors charged their ranks, with some coming as close as 30 to 50 feet of the soldiers.

There is no question that some of the students followed the Guards-

---

*"Shooters" is the term some of the Guard's lawyers used when referring to the soldiers who fired.

men up the hill. But the photographic evidence shows that most of the students maintained a safe distance from the rifles.

The FBI subsequently measured the distance between the victims and the Guard's position and found that the closest student hit, Joseph Lewis, Jr. was wounded while standing 60 feet away. The next closest victim, John Cleary, was wounded approximately 90 to 100 feet from the Guardsmen. After Cleary, Alan Canfora and Tom Grace were wounded approximately 150 to 175 feet from the Pagoda.

The Justice Department's summary of the FBI report states that none of the fatalities "was in a position to pose even a remote danger to the National Guard at the time of the firing."

The FBI determined that Jeffrey Miller was standing about 250 feet from the soldiers when he was killed, and that fatalities Sandra Scheuer, Allison Krause, and Bill Schroeder all fell at distances ranging from 330 to 375 feet from the Pagoda—more than the distance of a football field.

Had the students been an immediate threat to the soldiers' lives, one would expect that there would have been a number of fatalities and wounded students found very close to the soldiers. Instead, the people who were killed and wounded were found in locations that aroused profound suspicions about the Guards' claim of self-defense and their motives for shooting.

So, if the Guardsmen wildly exaggerated the reported rock attack . . . if the students never got that close to the Guardsmen . . . and if the Guardsmen had a clear path of retreat, what prompted the Guardsmen to stop, do an almost complete about-face, and start shooting the students?

Could the Guardsmen have panicked?

Many people who did not want to believe the worst about the soldiers' motives are convinced they must have.

That, after all, is a reassuring notion.

And it is, in fact, easy to see why a reasonable person might reach this conclusion. While the Guardsmen's stories do not stand up to close scrutiny, no one can dispute the fact that there was some rock throwing, flag waving, verbal abuse, and movement by the students.

James Michener, in his book *Kent State: What Happened and Why,* argued that people have been asking the wrong questions about the Guardsmen. What was important, Michener suggested, was not what a

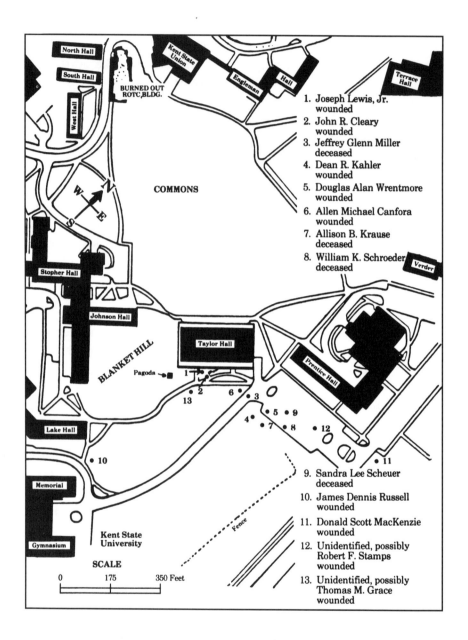

1. Joseph Lewis, Jr.
   wounded
2. John R. Cleary
   wounded
3. Jeffrey Glenn Miller
   deceased
4. Dean R. Kahler
   wounded
5. Douglas Alan Wrentmore
   wounded
6. Allen Michael Canfora
   wounded
7. Allison B. Krause
   deceased
8. William K. Schroeder
   deceased
9. Sandra Lee Scheuer
   deceased
10. James Dennis Russell
    wounded
11. Donald Scott MacKenzie
    wounded
12. Unidentified, possibly
    Robert F. Stamps
    wounded
13. Unidentified, possibly
    Thomas M. Grace
    wounded

This FBI chart shows the incredible distances between most of the victims and the
Guardsmen. (Note: The Bureau incorrectly guessed victim Thomas Grace's position.
Grace was actually a few feet away from Alan Canfora.)

Distances Between the
Guardsmen and the Victims

VICTIM	ESTIMATED FEET FROM FROM THE FIRING LINE	
	(FBI)	(BCI)
Joseph Lewis, Jr.	60	71
John Cleary	111	110
Thomas Grace	?	200
Alan Canfora	225	225
Jeffrey Miller	255-270	265
Dean Kahler	285-300	300
Allison Krause	300	343
Doug Wrentmore	330	329
James Russell	375-390	375
William Schroeder	390	382
Sandra Scheuer	390	390
Robert Stamps	495	495
Donald MacKenzie	735-750	730

The first figure reported is the more conservative estimate which appears in the Justice Department's Summary of the FBI report. The second represents measurements taken by the Ohio Bureau of Criminal Investigation.

Of the 13 students known to have been shot, seven played varying roles in the protest, while the other six were bystanders. The specifics of what each student did on May 4 can be found in the "Notes" section.

rational person would conclude about the extent of the danger long after the event was over, but:

> What would a hot, tired Guardsman think if he caught a glimpse of moving students coming at him on his blind right flank? He could very reasonably think that he was about to be attacked by 'a howling, vicious mob prepared to tear him apart.'

The problem with that explanation is that the notion that the "shooters" panicked does not easily reconcile with several other key pieces of the puzzle.

For example, there is the duration of the shooting. The shooting lasted for a relatively long period of time: 13 seconds.

We know that because a student named Terry Strubbe made a tape recording of the entire confrontation. Federal prosecutor Robert Murphy later characterized that tape as "one of the most shocking pieces of evidence. You sit there, and you hear that gunfire, and you think it's never going to end . . . That's a pretty heavy concentration of fire."

And the shootings went on much longer than one might expect in a panic situation. 67 shots were fired, according to an acoustical analysis of the Strubbe tape conducted by the Cambridge, Massachusetts firm of Bolt, Berenek, and Newman.

As Peter Davies has argued elsewhere, both the duration of the firing and the number of rounds expended are not consistent with any theory that the Guardsmen panicked.

If a few Guardsmen panicked, the volley probably would have lasted only a few seconds, and ended as soon as the students ran for cover.

That is not what happened. Several of the commanding officers had to work frantically to stop their troops from firing. In some cases the senior officers, including General Robert Canterbury and Major Harry Jones, had to physically grab the "shooters."

The Justice Department summary states that some Guardsmen "had to be physically restrained from continuing to fire their weapons."

Davies argued "the totally unnecessary prolongation of the shooting" probably meant the troops "continued shooting to insure hitting those singled out for punishment."

Also, one has to ask: could that many Guardsmen have panicked with the weaponry they had at their disposal? The M-1 rifle which most Guardsmen carried is in itself a relatively bulky and unwieldy weapon.

While it is easy to understand how an accident could happen with a .45 caliber pistol (which the officers had), it does not seem likely that the 28 Guardsmen who admitted firing could have all panicked for thirteen seconds with their nine-pound rifles; which, after all, are as heavy as some bowling balls.

Snapping a rifle to your shoulder, taking aim, and pulling the trigger not just once, but three or four times, as some "shooters" admitted doing, requires some effort (and presumably some thought).

The Question of Motive

Which brings us to the question of motive. People, as a general rule, do not kill for frivolous reasons.

If the shootings were deliberate, the Guardsmen would have needed some reason to want the students dead, possibly (although not necessarily) beyond the fact the Guardsmen were subjected to abuse and wanted to put an end to the demonstration.

It is really quite easy to understand why some of the Guardsmen may have entertained murderous thoughts. The shootings, of course, did not happen in a vacuum. They occurred during a time when the nation was bitterly divided over the war, and when student protestors were alienating and angering millions of middle class Americans, including many in conservative rural Ohio, where most of the Guardsmen came from.

As early as one year before the tragedy, *Time* magazine noted that the country had lost its patience with antiwar protestors.

"If there was one word that summarized the feelings of much of the U.S. toward radicals," *Time* editorialized, "it was 'Enough!'"

The hatred of protestors also manifested itself after the shootings, when there was an extraordinary outpouring of sympathy and support for the National Guardsmen, and a directly proportional outpouring of anger directed at college students.

In his book, James Michener described this phenomena at length, documenting that "a depressing number [of students] had been told by their own parents that it might have been a good thing if they had been shot" had they joined the protests.

Only a few months after the shootings, the prosecutor for the original state grand jury publicly admitted that he agreed with "what he called the 'average' opinion of most people in the Kent-Ravenna area: 'Why didn't the Guard shoot more of them?'"

The president of the United States, Richard Nixon, had little sympathy for the victims, either. Years later, we learned from the White House tapes that he once ordered his aides to find thugs to beat up people who protested against his Vietnam policies. And in his cold-blooded statement released in response to the shootings, Nixon came, as *Newsweek* put it, very close to saying the students got what they deserved.

J. Edgar Hoover, the director of the FBI, definitely felt that way. A memo has surfaced that Hoover sent to five of his top assistants on May 11, 1970. In it, he admitted telling White House aide Egil Krogh "that the students invited (the shootings) and got what they deserved."

Immediately after the shooting, many of the townspeople and Guardsmen who were on the campus reacted in the following manner:

"How do I feel? I feel it's about time somebody let them have it."

The important question, of course, is: If all of these people who either sent the Guardsmen, or investigated them after the fact, or lived in Kent, felt this way about protestors, what were the Guardsmen themselves thinking?

Did the Guardsmen who had these rifles in their hands— and who were thrust into what were admittedly difficult circumstances—feel the same way?

Although that question cannot be answered definitively, we do know, that to a certain extent, or at least in the cases of some of the soldiers, the answer is yes.

"Shooter" James Pierce "didn't feel they [the demonstrators] were people but 'savage animals.'" That is what Pierce wrote in the after-actions report his Guard superiors asked him to fill out.

Two G Troopers, Sergeant Lawrence Shafer (who did fire) and Lieutenant Alexander Stevenson (who denied firing, although not all the attorneys believed him) both admitted that while they had manned command posts the night before the shootings, they had bayoneted men who were sitting in cars.

Shafer admitted under oath that he had bayonetted a disabled Vietnam veteran who had bad-mouthed him because he had been in no mood to take any guff.

Other witnesses, including students and faculty members who approached Guardsmen to gauge the situation on Sunday and Monday, reported to being threatened by very short-tempered Guardsmen.

How short-tempered were they? In his book, *Kent State: What Happened and Why*, James Michener, tried to capture their frame of mind as they ascended Blanket Hill.

Describing their condition, Michener wrote:

> They have been on duty for nearly a week, sleeping at odd times and in odd places. They have eaten irregularly and have been subjected to taunts and ridicule. They are bewildered by the behavior of college students and outraged by the vocabulary of coeds. It is hot. They have been stoned. They have chased a lot of oddly dressed students back and forth and have accomplished nothing except the indignity of having their own tear gas thrown back at them.

Apparently one of the Guardsmen Michener interviewed told him there was "a strong feeling running through the Guard that 'we've taken enough.'"

Michener also introduced what at that time was disturbing new evidence about the Guards' conduct.

This evidence came in the form of an eyewitness account by a student named Peter Winnen, who had returned to Kent State as a student after serving in Vietnam. As Michener quoted Winnen, while the Guardsmen were on the practice field: "I saw them go into a huddle, and it was quite obvious that a decision of some kind had been reached."

Accepting Winnen's observation of a huddle, at one point in his book Michener wrote it seemed likely:

> that on the football field, while the students were being obnoxious and the stones were drifting in, that some of the troops agreed among themselves, 'We've taken about enough of this crap. If they don't stop pretty soon we're going to let them have it.'

In the absence of proof, Michener seemed content to let this question of murder slide. In fact, later in his book, Michener ignored the evidence he had introduced, concluding the shooting "was an accident, deplorable and tragic."

One man was not willing to let the matter slide. That was Peter Davies, a Staten Island insurance agent who had immigrated to England in 1957.

Davies had been appalled by the shootings, and he began collecting documents and photographs and studying the official reports issued by the Justice Department and the President's Commission on Campus Unrest.

By May 1971, Davies was becoming increasingly convinced that the shootings were deliberate. Michener's book reinforced Davies' belief that there had been a murderous conspiracy, and Davies was determined to do something about it.

Two months after Michener's book was published, Davies completed a book-length report in an attempt to get the Justice Department to conduct a full investigation.

Seizing on Winnen's statement that the Guardsmen had huddled on the practice football field, Davies carried the argument further and sketched a scenario of how he thought the Guardsmen decided to shoot the students.

Davies' report stated that, at an undetermined point of time during the confrontation, "a few Guardsmen, perhaps no more than eight to ten" decided to shoot the students to teach them a lesson.

The report suggests that a prearranged signal to fire was agreed upon, and he thought that the signal was the firing of a .45 caliber pistol by First Sergeant Myron Pryor, the senior noncommissioned officer of G Troop. (In the photographs, Pryor can be seen out in front of the men with his left arm stiffly outstretched. The photograph gives the impression that Pryor fired his .45 directly at the students.)

Davies also argued that the reason the shooting happened at the crest of Blanket Hill was because the Guardsmen were on high ground and the crest of the hill provided an excellent view of the students on the Taylor Hall hillside and in the Prentice Hall parking lot below. Davies argued that the Pagoda was a convenient landmark for the Guardsmen to make their stand.

The linchpin of Davies' theory was the manner in which the Guardsmen turned to face the students at the Pagoda. In a letter to this author Davies wrote:

> It is the precision and neatness with which these several Guardsmen started shooting that just does not fit the explanation of panic and fear and confusion . . . How can we possibly accept that 8 Guardsmen, within the same second, all suddenly decided, as individuals, that their lives were in danger and spun around together in a coordinated unit and commenced shooting? . . . All I can say is those men had super mental telepathy up there or they knew beforehand what they were doing.

Re-examining the Conspiracy Question

Of course, quite a bit has happened since Davies made these very serious and highly publicized charges.

Since then, two trials have been held (one criminal and one civil). Neither of these trials centered around the question of conspiracy (the trials focused primarily on the issue of excessive force), but the trials nevertheless provided some new information about whether or not there was a conspiracy.

The FBI has also released its full report, including the eyewitness statements its agents collected from the various witnesses: students, faculty members, Guardsmen, and other law enforcement officials.

Davies also became embroiled in several controversies. The specifics of those controversies (covered in later chapters) are not as important as the fact that he lost some of his strongest supporters, including some sympathetic reporters who gave his theorizing generous coverage.

Despite these developments, since the mid-1970s, no one has taken a fresh look at Davies' conspiracy theories or the more recent wave of theorizing that the conspiracy was much larger: that the Guardsmen were only pawns in a larger game to choreograph a fatal confrontation on a college campus.

What follows here are some of the questions that have not been asked, but should have been, in the attempts to decipher the puzzle of the Kent State killings.

Davies' conspiracy theory rested heavily on his claim that the Guardsmen seemed to act in a concerted fashion when they fired. Did that claim hold up?

Yes. In fact, Davies overlooked some of the strongest passages supporting his theory.

In his conspiracy report, Davies cited the statements of six eyewitnesses who told an internal Kent State fact-finding commission (the KSU Commission on Campus Violence) that they were under the impression the Guardsmen acted in concert.

A careful reading of that report indicates that the commission actually heard sixteen, not six, witnesses, who, in the words of the report's author, stressed "the approximate simultaneity of the movements of the Guardsmen who fired, and the impression created that an order had been given."

In fact, the FBI, which interviewed more eyewitnesses than any other investigative body, found even more witnesses that suggested the Guardsmen acted in concert.

When I reviewed the eyewitness statements collected by the FBI, I looked for certain common denominators, including descriptions of the Guardsmen's turn toward the students. I found that twenty-four witnesses used the words "turned together," "in unison," or similar phraseology in describing the Guardsmen's turn. Dozens of other witnesses—about 90 in all—simply stated the Guardsmen turned, without explicitly stating that a number of Guardsmen acted identically at the same time.

How many Guardsmen turned at once?

That cannot be pinned down, but there is no testimony to contradict the estimate "shooter" James McGee gave during the 1975 civil trial. McGee suggested "maybe ten."

In Davies' scenario the conspiracy was supposedly hatched in the huddle on the practice football field. The Guardsmen were subsequently asked about the huddles at the 1975 civil trial. What do we know about these huddles now?

The Guardsmen made no attempt to conceal the fact that discussions took place among the officers on the practice field. Colonel Charles Fassinger testified he conferred with General Robert Canterbury. So did Major Harry Jones.

Major Jones and Captain Raymond Srp both testified that they conferred with Sergeant Myron Pryor. Pryor, interestingly, denied talking to anyone.

Every officer who was questioned admitted that discussions took place on the field. At the same time, they denied that the possibility of shooting students was ever discussed before it actually happened. These officers characterized the huddles as strategy sessions in which the officers simply discussed what their next moves would be and how to get off the practice field.*

---

*There is some evidence to suggest that some officers may have lied on this point. In his after-actions report to his superior offices, "shooter" James Pierce claimed that Sergeant Pryor gave a contingency order to his men: "If they rush us, shoot them."

Pryor denied this. However, another Guardsman (who fired into the air) told the FBI he heard an identical order, although he was not able to identify the source.

Even if the officers told the truth—that they only held innocent tactical huddles—couldn't some of the enlisted men have held their own conspiratorial huddles at the same time?

There is nothing to rule out that possibility. Curiously, though, while the officers seemed to manage to converse with each other, the enlisted men suspected of being involved in a conspiracy swore that it was too difficult to hold conversations because of all the noise.

Are there any reasons to believe that the troops did not conspire to kill the students at Kent?

Yes. Besides their denials, there is the fact that all of the enlisted men were wearing gas masks that concealed their identities. As Jack Schulman, one of the Guards' attorneys at the criminal proceedings, noted, most of the enlisted men did not know who they were standing next to. If there had been a conspiracy, several Guardsmen of equal rank would have had to enter into a murderous pact on the spur of the moment with strangers.

Murderous conspiracies are usually hatched after some deliberation by people who know and trust each other.*

If it would have been too difficult for the enlisted men to agree on a murderous conspiracy, could they have simply responded to an officer's order to fire?

No officer admits that he gave such an order, but the theory does seem to be the one most consistent with the evidence as we now know it.

How could such an order have been executed?

Given the noise level, it seems unlikely that an order could have been given by the usual method—a verbal command.

Davies was convinced that the first shot was actually a signal that told the other Guardsmen to start firing. That notion was disproved by the

---

*One important reason the Guardsmen were not able to identify their neighbors was because some of the "shooters" (Barry Morris, James Pierce, and James McGee) had removed their sewn-on name tags from their uniforms. As Guardsman Rudy Morris testified, those name tags "are part of our uniform." One can legitimately ask why any Guardsmen would remove his identifying tag—unless, perhaps, he knew or at least had some advance inkling that somebody might get shot and he did not want to be identified in any of the subsequent investigations.

acoustical analysis of the Terry Strubbe tape recording commissioned by the Justice Department. The analysis indicated that there were only fractions of seconds between the first, second, and third shots, indicating that shot number one could not have been the proximate cause of the others.

It turns out that it really does not make much difference who managed to squeeze the first trigger.

Under the circumstances, it seems much more likely that there was a hand signal to fire.

This possibility was never seriously explored because Colonel Fassinger assured the FBI during its initial investigation that the Guard did not employ hand signals.

At the 1975 civil trial, however, Major Jones demonstrated to the jury the different signals soldiers use in combat.

Jones testified: "You tap a man on the helmet (and) point to a specific point or target." The purpose of the tapping, Jones testified, was to get the soldier's attention. However, if the soldier was already looking at the officer: "I suppose you could use the point method . . . You want to point to what you specifically want him to fire at. You have a specific thing you want him to lay fire power on."

Assuming the signal theory is correct, which officer would have given the order to shoot?

No one seriously suspects General Canterbury, Colonel Fassinger or Captain Srp. All of these officers were either marching in front of or off to the right of the G Troopers who fired and were not in a physical position to give a signal to fire.

The question of who else might have issued such an order was examined to some extent at the 1975 civil trial. Most of the questioning was directed toward the two officers who brought up the rear of the line. These were two career soldiers: Major Harry Jones and Sergeant Myron Pryor, the senior noncommissioned officer of G Troop.

Is there any reason to believe that Major Jones gave a signal to shoot?

The victims' attorneys did not actively pursue this theory at the trial, even though one of their own witnesses, a former student named Robert Pickett, volunteered that the shooting started after Major Jones made some type of waving motion with the riot baton he was carrying.

The full FBI report, when it was released, contained several additional statements supporting this notion. The report reveals that there were four other witnesses who noticed Jones motioning with his baton immediately before the troops, as if a command had been issued.

Student witnesses Howard Bluestein and Stewart Feldstein told the FBI they saw an officer drop his baton. Student James Minard said he saw the stick go up and down, and student Arturo Sanjiel said the officer made some kind of a swinging motion.

What did Major Jones have to say about this?

Jones himself lent some credence to the notion that the shooting followed one of his baton movements. When he was deposed for the 1975 civil trial, Jones testified that he was constantly giving his men hand signals, telling them to stay in formation and "Hurry up."

He testified that he heard the first shot ("an explosion," he called it) after he gave one of his signals. However, Jones swore that "Hurry up" and "Stay in formation" were the only types of orders he issued on May 4. He denied giving an order to fire, and insisted "there is no such thing as a baton signal." (Probably because National Guard are not normally issued riot batons. The riot baton Jones was carrying had been borrowed from Captain Ron Snyder, who became infamous for bringing his own private arsenal of weapons and riot control paraphernalia with him to the campus.)

Is it possible that the troops might have misinterpreted Jones' signalling and erroneously thought he was giving an order to fire, when in fact he did not?

Jones insisted at the trial that his "Hurry up" signal "differs greatly" from the combat signal to fire: "I don't see how anybody could misinterpret that."

And, of course, Jones was not talking about one Guardsman. The "Big Screw-Up Theory," if you want to call it that, assumes that a number of Guardsmen—perhaps as many as four or five—could have simultaneously misinterpreted the same signal. While that may be theoretically possible, the chances of that happening, realistically, seem to be rather remote.

Who do we believe then? Major Jones, who says he did not order the firing, or the five students whose statements suggested that Jones' motioning was connected to the firing?

Ultimately, this is an unanswerable question. Had this specific issue ever been presented to a jury, it would have boiled down to what attorneys call a "swearing contest." The jury's verdict would have hinged on whose testimony seemed the most believable.

To assist the reader in evaluating the charges, I have included a chart, appropriately titled "The Major Jones Credibility Chart." It indicates that the major was contradicted by other witnesses on a host of different issues, and his denials that he started the Kent State shootings have to be considered in that context.

It should be mentioned, though, that even if Major Jones was contradicted quite frequently, it does not necessarily follow that he was not telling the truth when he denied giving an order to fire. A jury would have also had to take into account several other factors.

For instance:

• Witnesses agree that Jones tried to stop the shooting once it started. One could infer from his actions that he was not the one who started it.

• Although he never testified at any trial, I found a Guardsman who was willing to testify that the major was "mighty mad" at the troops. This Guardsman was Private Jeffrey Jones (no relation). Jeffrey told me: "I know he was against the shootings. I'm pretty sure he was not the one who gave the order to fire, if there was one."

• Supporting Jeffrey Jones' assertion, another Guardsman who was on the firing line, Richard Love, told his superiors that as soon as the firing ceased, Major Jones demanded to know: "Who gave you men the order to fire?"

That indicates that not only did Jones not give the order to fire, but that he immediately suspected that someone else did.

Could that someone else have been Sergeant Myron Pryor?

Other witnesses suggested that, but the case against Pryor, like the case against Jones, is fraught with an unusual number of denials and contradictions.

We do know this much. We know that Sergeant Pryor, like Major Jones, was bringing up the rear of the troops.

After the troops turned by the Pagoda, Pryor was photographed out in front of his men intently aiming a .45 caliber pistol at the students. Pryor stood out because he was slightly shorter than the rest of the Guardsmen and because he carried a handgun while most of the enlisted men carried M-1 rifles.

As with the case against Jones, a number of witnesses gave statements to the FBI to the effect that the shooting started after a Guardsman fitting Pryor's description did something that called attention to himself.

A number of witnesses had kept their eyes on Pryor. A review of the FBI statements reveals that there are seven witnesses who were under the impression that this Guardsmen was a leader or that he acted before the rest of the men under his command.*

Did these witnesses ever testify in court?

Of the seven, only John Filo, the photographer, ever testified at any of the trials.

I never heard or read a satisfactory answer as to why the other six never appeared, but one member of the victims' trial team speculated that these other witnesses, even though their testimony suggested the troops may have followed Pryor's behavior, probably saw too many rocks or thought the students were closer to the Guardsmen than they actually were—and that would not help their wrongful death and injury claims.

Perhaps the most important reason these witnesses never testified, though, was because the victims' attorneys could never agree among themselves what they wanted to prove, even at the trial.[†]

Then did the victims' attorneys let Pryor off the hook?

Not really. The attorneys produced two other witnesses who told an even more specific and disturbing story about what Pryor did just before the firing.

These witnesses testified that just before the shooting started Sergeant Pryor tapped the Guardsmen he was trailing on the back before they pivoted and about-faced with him.

One of the witnesses was Harry William Montgomery, an ex-Marine who saw combat duty in Vietnam before returning to Kent as a student. Montgomery testified that he had kept his eye on Pryor most of the time because "I carried a .45 for six months in Vietnam . . . and I identified with it." Montgomery testified that Pryor tapped the three or four Guardsmen in front of him "on the back, on the hindside there or whatever." Then "almost simultaneously, the men that were directly in front of him, seemingly he had communications with, turned and began firing."

---

*The statements of these witnesses appear in the Notes section.

[†]Colonel Charles Fassinger's reaction to this was: "Amen. Talk about scattered . . ."

A second witness, Charles Deegan, testified that he saw essentially the same thing.[*]

How did Pryor respond to this allegation?

Pryor denied tapping anyone as a signal to commence firing. He testified that he did not know why he or any of the other Guardsmen turned to face the students, and insisted that he just turned at the same time as the other soldiers without anyone ordering them to do so.

What did the other Guardsmen have to say about this tapping scenario?

Unfortunately, the plaintiffs' attorneys, after calling Montgomery and Deegan as witnesses, never systematically asked the other Guardsmen if these accounts were accurate.

In reviewing the trial testimony, I could find only two other instances in which the plaintiffs' chief counsel, Joseph Kelner, asked any "shooters" if Pryor tapped them as an order to fire.

Kelner posed that question to Lawrence Shafer and James Pierce, and both denied that Pryor tapped them.

And on this point it appears they answered truthfully.

In fact, the FBI's chart indicating where each Guardsmen was standing on the firing line, based on a photograph taken by John Darnell, demonstrates that neither Shafer nor Pierce were even close enough to Pryor for their sergeant to have touched them. Anyone listening to Shafer's and Pierce's testimony might have thought that Kelner was pursuing a blind alley.

Actually, he was just posing the right questions to the wrong Guardsmen!

Then which Guardsmen should have been asked whether Pryor tapped them as a signal to fire?

Whoever was on the far left flank closest to Pryor. But this is the kick. Not one of the Guardsman would admit to being in that location.

---

*Interestingly, the two key witnesses against Pryor, Montgomery and Deegan, were both Vietnam War veterans who had served in the Marines before returning to Kent to resume their studies. So was Peter Winnen, the student eyewitness who said he saw the Guardsmen huddle.

The most damaging evidence against the Guardsmen came from former soldiers who knew what to look for in combat situations.

After the shootings, the FBI showed each Guardsman John Darnell's photograph of them shooting—the one showing Pryor in front of his men, intently raising his pistol at the crowd of students.

The FBI asked each Guardsman to pinpoint or approximate his location on the firing line, and every Guardsmen placed some distance between himself and Pryor.

Whose testimony should we believe then: the witnesses who swear Pryor tapped his men as an order to fire, or Pryor, who denied it?

That question also cannot be answered definitively. Pryor's denials throughout the trial were extensive. To keep track of all his denials, one needs a box score. That box score is provided on the pages that follow.

What then can we conclude with certainty?

One: That not all the right screws were turned in the investigations.

For this, you have to blame the National Guardsmen. If Colonel Fassinger had told the truth when he was asked about whether the Guardsmen employed hand signals, and if the Guardsmen standing next to Pryor would have admitted where they were standing, investigators might have been able to ask the right questions and determine if Pryor gave the order to fire by tapping his soldiers.

Two: There is strong circumstantial evidence that there had to have been an order to fire. The claims by the Guardsmen that the shootings occurred in the absence of an order simply are not believable.

Three: That triggers were not pulled accidentally at Kent State. The shootings appear to have been deliberate—and while the "smoking gun" still eludes us, we can say with some confidence that there appears to have been extensive perjury at the trials.

Even conceding all the mitigating or extenuating circumstances, the Guardsmen literally appear to have gotten away with murder.

Assuming this theory is correct—that there was an order to fire—is there any reason to believe that anyone higher in command—that is, higher than an officer at the scene—ordered the shootings?

This question is asked repeatedly on campus. A surprising number of people are convinced that Richard Nixon himself arranged the shooting.

There is even a published account in *Gallery* Magazine of a secret conversation between Nixon and Governor Rhodes in which Nixon supposedly told Rhodes "to make a goddamn good example of someone at Kent State."

The trouble with that account is that the source cited was an unnamed low-level intelligence operative, who only heard of the alleged conversation secondhand. There is no reason to believe this operative would have been privy to conversations between a governor and a president, or any conspiracies being launched in the highest levels of government.

There is also no evidence that Nixon or anyone else in his administration was involved in the shooting. In fact, Nixon's telephone logs, released by the National Archives, indicated he personally did not have any phone conversations with anyone in Ohio until after the shootings.

The scenario also does not make sense. In the "Nixon-ordered-the-killing" version, Nixon would have had to call Governor Rhodes; Rhodes would have had to say "sure, boss, I'll kill some students for you" (as if he took such orders from Nixon); and then Rhodes would have had to relay the order to one of his generals, who would tell a subordinate officer; and down possibly one more level in the chain of command.

Just because Richard Nixon despised protestors and might have wanted a crackdown against protestors of his Vietnam policy does not mean he did any more than fantasize about it.

A president who could not spy on Democrats in the same city without getting caught probably was not capable of having choreographed a murderous confrontation between hundreds of soldiers and college students on a few days' notice.

The "it-was-a-big conspiracy, the darkest-page-in-American-history" theorists overlook all the bungling on May 4 and the fact that just about every decision the officers made was made at the last minute. That's why the officers, when they moved against the students, never formulated a plan as to how to accomplish the mission; why the officers seemed unfamiliar with the terrain and why just fifteen minutes into the mission, they marched their troops into a fence; and why the troops did not bring enough tear gas along. This is all evidence of lack of planning, and it also explains why command authority broke down so quickly and why the soldiers seemed to start taking matters into their own hands.

Even if the officers or enlisted men discussed the possibility of shooting students before it actually happened, my belief is that the order to fire probably was not issued until the circumstances presented themselves at Blanket Hill.

The best evidence we have now is that a Guardsman with some authority—a sergeant, perhaps—simply passed a threshold of tolerance for the demonstration.

Whether he felt anger, fear or frustration—or more likely, a mixture of these emotions—I suspect he finally thought: "To hell with these kids. It's time to teach these bastards a lesson."

Of course, no one was willing to confess. Which is understandable.

After all, how would you like to go down in history as the man who started the killings at Kent State?

The Major Jones Credibility Chart

QUESTION	WHAT JONES CLAIMED	PROBLEM
Did Jones ever serve in a command capacity?	At the 1975 civil trial Jones portrayed himself as a liaison officer who only relayed orders and did "the bidding of the general."	Captain Srp testified that Jones seemed to be issuing most of the orders. Jones also was quoted in a 1970 Knight Newspaper report as saying: "The troops were under my command."
Did the major, who was carrying a .22 Beretta, fire his pistol?	Jones said he did not.	At least three .22 bullets were discovered afterwards. Jones was the only Guardsman known to have carried a .22 caliber pistol.
A .22 Beretta is not a standard National Guard weapon. Why was Jones even carrying this gun?	Jones testified he forgot his regularly assigned .45 at the Akron Armory and had no time to retrieve it. Therefore he borrowed the .22 from his friend and subordinate officer Captain Ronald Snyder.	Jones could have borrowed a regulation National Guard .45 from any one of the hundreds of Guardsmen subordinate to him. Instead, he borrowed a privately owned weapon that was ultimately untraceable.
Did Major Jones know that by merely possessing this pistol he was violating National Guard regulations?	Jones denied violating any regulations.	He did admit in the course of his official duties he taught officers on matters pertaining to civil disturbances. Also, Colonel Fassinger testified that after the shooting he chewed out Jones for carrying the pistol. Fassinger said, "That's a mild way of putting it."

QUESTION	WHAT JONES CLAIMED	PROBLEM
Who checked Jones' pistol after the shooting to determine if it had been fired?	Captain Snyder.	If Jones fired his gun, would Captain Snyder have turned in his friend and superior officer? And would Snyder have implicated himself for loaning Jones the contraband pistol?
Did Jones ever threaten to shoot a student taunting him before the troops opened fire?	Jones admitted, "I had a conversation with him," but said he was not sure if he threatened to shoot the student: "The thing was, I got his attention and he left."	Captain Srp claimed Jones waved his pistol at a particularly obnoxious student and said, "Come on, I'll fix you." Other students told reporters that an officer said, "Come on, come on," to a student, as if challenging the student to give him an excuse to open fire.
Was Major Jones reluctant to identify himself in photographs taken at the Pagoda?	Jones refused to positively identify himself in the photos. He testified that an officer prominently photographed resembled him, but suggested the person may have been someone else because "I definitely had glasses on" and the person photographed did not.	Other Guardsmen had no problem identifying Jones. He was the only officer wearing a soft baseball-like cap instead of a steal helmet. Jones was also the only officer with a riot stick; and he and General Canterbury were the only officers not wearing gas masks hiding their identity.

The Myron Pryor Box Score

QUESTION	WHAT THE WITNESSES SAID	
Did Pryor serve in a leadership capacity?	Captain Srp said he did. Guardsmen Barry Morris James Pierce, and James McGee attributed various orders to him.	D
		E
Did he fire his pistol while the Guardsmen were on the practice football field?	Barry Morris, who testified he was standing only six feet away from Pryor, said he did.	N I
		E
Did Pryor order the Guardsmen to remove their identifying name tags?	Barry Morris testified that he did.	D
		E
Did he give a contingency order on the field: "If they rush us, shoot them?"	James Pierce wrote this in his after-actions report.	V E
Did Pryor fire on Blanket Hill?	At the civil trial, John Filo, John Darnell, Harry William Montgomery, and Charles Deegan said he did. Students Stewart Pennell, Jr., Rick Levinger, Lewis Joel Goldberg, Dale Alan Morckel, William Penoyer, and Karl Kessler, in their statements to the FBI, referred to a Guardsman with a handgun firing first. Had they been called to testify, witnesses William Gerstenslager and Debra Shryock would have also claimed he fired.	R Y T H I N G
Was Pryor's pistol loaded?	Captain Srp said the pistol was fully loaded, but that no bullets were expended.	
Did Pryor give a signal to shoot by tapping the Guardsmen standing next to him and by pointing to targets?	Harry Montgomery and Charles Deegan claimed he did.	

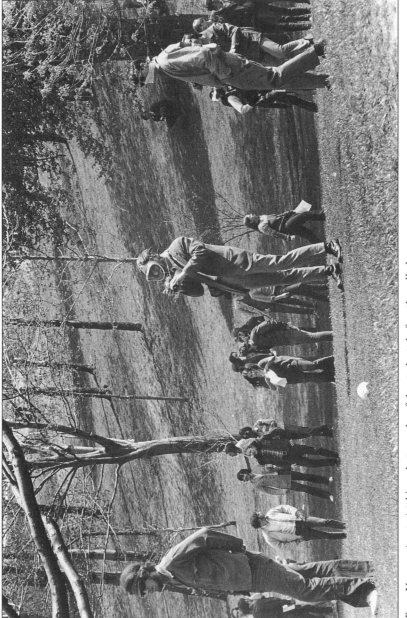

Terry Norman (center) taking photographs of the students before the rally began. (Photo by Kent State University News Service.)

THE STRANGE CASE OF
TERRY NORMAN

To this day, many people in Kent believe that the man who started the Kent State shootings was not a National Guardsman, but a 21-year-old part-time Kent State student named Terrence Brookes Norman.

Norman was the only person on campus (other than a Guardsman or a law enforcement official) known to have been armed with a weapon. He came to the noon rally equipped with a camera, a gas mask, and a .38 caliber pistol, which he concealed under a tan sports coat, and was involved in a highly suspicious incident on Blanket Hill shortly after the smoke cleared and the Guard left the Pagoda.

Some of the details of the incident are still in dispute, but we know this much. He was involved in a scuffle with another student. Norman drew his pistol and pistol-whipped him.

When that happened, several men started chasing Norman across the length of the Commons to the ruins of the ROTC building, where the campus police and the National Guardsmen had set up lines. The gun was then confiscated by the campus police in the presence of several witnesses.

In the days after the shootings, Guard General Sylvester Del Corso, who had claimed the Guard fired in response to sniper bullets, tried to link Norman to the shootings. At one point Del Corso issued a statement claiming that Norman fired four times, "but not at us; he told us he shot at the demonstrators in self-defense."

However, Del Corso backed off that statement, and admitted he had no evidence that Norman was involved in the shootings.

The campus police, which had confiscated the gun, seemed to exonerate Norman when it declared that a sight examination of the pistol revealed that the gun had never been fired.

As it turned out, though, Norman was working on May 4 as an informant for both the campus police and the Akron office of the FBI, taking pictures of demonstrators for possible prosecution. That meant that if Norman had fired his gun, possibly firing the shot which prompted the Guardsmen to turn and fire, both the KSU police and the FBI had real motives for covering up his actions.

For years, rumors about Norman swirled around the campus. Then, in 1973, there was a major development. When the investigation was re-opened, John Martin, the captain in charge of A Company, 145th Infantry, sent Congressional investigators statements from two of his men who saw Norman surrender his weapon. One Guardsman thought he overheard Norman admit firing the gun—and even admit shooting a student.

On the basis of the Guardsman's statements, Indiana Senator Birch Bayh publicly charged that Norman may have been "the fatal catalyst" for the shootings. However, once this highly publicized charge was made, other witnesses surfaced, and they corroborated Norman's version of what happened on Blanket Hill.

In the most significant development, the *Akron Beacon Journal* located the student who admitted jumping Norman. The student, Tom Masterson, told a reporter he took out his frustration over the gunfire on Norman, who he recognized as a police informant. Masterson confirmed that Norman drew the pistol to protect himself, and said he never saw Norman fire the gun, much less shoot a student.

Significantly, none of the Guardsmen who were indicted or sued subsequently tried to pin the shootings on Norman at the trials.

Norman's claims that he had nothing to do with the shootings were also supported by the results of a professional analysis conducted of the tape recording of the gunfire. The study, commissioned by the Justice Department, indicated that all three of the first shots were fired by M-1 rifles, and not by the .38 caliber pistol Norman turned over to police. That meant that Norman could not have been the "fatal catalyst."

Having said this, the historical record should also reflect the fact that there are an unusual number of loose ends to the strange case of Terry Norman—some of which are quite disturbing.

For instance, we know now that the FBI lied not only about the fact Norman was an informant for them, but also about the results of its ballistics tests. The FBI had assured Congressional investigators that Norman's gun had never been fired on May 4. In fact, the lab tests actually showed that the gun sent to the FBI had in fact been fired at some point since its last cleaning. The lab tests were included in the full FBI report, which I examined at FBI headquarters.

The campus police also improperly tried to influence witnesses into changing their stories. One witness who chased Norman across the Commons, Harold Reid, told me he was under the impression Norman had shot a student until he was told by KSU Police Detective Tom Kelley at

KSU police headquarters—while Reid was still writing his statement—that Norman's gun had not been fired.

We also know that while the Guardsmen were on the practice football field, Norman positioned himself between the Guardsmen and the students and threw rocks at the students. This was witnessed by student Tom Masterson, who claims Norman may have thrown as many as a dozen rocks; by Guardsman Dennis Breckenridge; and by Guard Captain John Martin, who, in a report to his superior officers, wrote he asked himself at the time: "What is this idiot doing?"

Since Norman was an informant for the FBI, and since FBI informants have acted as *provocateurs* in other cases, the question was asked: could Norman have been trying to provoke an incident between the students and the Guardsmen?

Also bizarre is the fact that Norman approached the Guardsmen while they were on the practice football field, just minutes before they retreated up Blanket Hill and opened fire. There are even photographs of Norman surrounded by Guardsmen on the practice field.

There are unanswered questions as to how many guns Norman was armed with on May 4. Some witnesses, including members of an NBC camera crew assigned to cover the disturbances, swear they saw Norman showed off a .357 magnum in the NBC crew car the day before the shooting. Norman turned in a different weapon—a .38 caliber pistol—to the campus police and the FBI after the shootings.

There is also the question of why, when the FBI asked the KSU police to turn over the police officers' statements about their interrogation of Norman, 13 police statements mysteriously disappeared from the desk of a police officer and had to be rewritten.

These loose ends are certainly bizarre, but they do not change the most important conclusion about Norman. That is: he did not start the Kent State shootings.

Whether he fired his gun at some other point remains debatable, but on that narrow but very important issue, Norman appears to have been someone who was simply in the wrong place at the wrong time—with his pistol.

In the history of the Kent State shootings, Terry Norman rates several detailed footnotes, and for those who wish to know more about the strange case of Terry Norman, those footnotes can be found in the "Notes" section.

Guardsmen in front of the burning ROTC building, May 2, 1970. (Photo by Wide World Photos.)

THREE

Who Burned ROTC?

If you happened to watch NBC's dramatization of the Kent State shootings, which initially aired on February 8, 1981, you saw the Hollywood version of the ROTC fire.

In it, a couple of radicals who incited the students one day earlier stood on the campus Commons and innocently watched a boisterous crowd try to burn the building down.

The crowd seemed to get nowhere, and there were even some comic moments inserted to show how ill-prepared and incompetent the demonstrators were. At one point two jocks grabbed a barrel and tried to ram the door of the building. They missed, bounced off the side of the building, and fell flat on their faces.

The crowd applauded and the jocks curtsied.

Then the mood suddenly turned serious when out of nowhere appeared six dark, sinister, mysterious-looking figures. They looked like Ku Klux Klansmen, only they were dressed in black clothing.

Each mysterious figure tossed a torch into a window of the building, thereby immediately starting a conflagration. The camera then shifted to the cutesy female radical, who turned to her clean-cut boyfriend and asked: "*Who* are these people?"

Her friend shrugged and whispered "I do not know" with an air of puzzlement.

Of course, this scene was filmed to leave us with the impression that anyone could have started the ROTC fire.

Anyone, that is, except the original demonstrators who tried to burn the building.

The fact that *anyone* could have set the blaze is one of the few accurate details about the NBC version of that night.

The real perpetrators were never apprehended or even identified—and in that vacuum, there have been all sorts of rumors, speculation, and theorizing as to who might have set the fire.

One of the most popular theories (at least at the University) is that government *provocateurs* deliberately set the blaze to give authorities an excuse to call out the militia, who could then suppress the student protests against the war.

The fire, after all, was the one act of violence that resulted in the calling-out of the National Guard.

If there had not been a fire, the Guardsmen would not have come onto the campus and the students might not have been killed on May 4.

It probably should be stressed that there is no evidence to prove that the ROTC fire was deliberately set for this purpose.

Still, if one examines the circumstances surrounding the fire, one cannot help but notice there are quite a few irregularities . . .

ITEM: The Kent State police knew, at least as early as the afternoon before it actually happened, that an attempt would be made to burn the ROTC building. Kent State Police Detective Tom Kelley gave an interview to the *Akron Beacon Journal* (published on August 8, 1973) in which he admitted that he talked with three members of an NBC camera crew (newsman Fred DeBrine, cameraman Jorge Gomez, and soundman Joe Butano) on the afternoon of May 2, 1970, as the crew prepared to leave Kent and return to its home base in Akron.

Kelley admitted telling the crew: "Don't pack your cameras. We are going to have a fire tonight."

Gomez even told me he even knew in advance the exact time the fire would be set. He stated that Kelley told him the fire would be set at 8:00 that evening—which was, give or take a few minutes, about the time that the crowd converged on the building.

ITEM: The Kent State University Police Department was not the only local law enforcement agency that knew in advance that the building was targeted for arson that night. In August 1970, Roy Thompson, then chief of the Kent Police Department, testified before the President's

Commission on Campus that his informants warned him that the ROTC building was one of several in Kent targeted for destruction that night.

The Kent Fire Department also expected the arson and was prepared to respond in advance. Attorneys for the parents of the slain students deposed Fred Miller, the late fire chief of Kent, and reported in one legal brief that Miller "took the unusual step of having his firemen 'stand by' so that most of the firemen, including volunteers, were at the fire station" several hours before the call actually came.

In addition, the firemen monitored the radio transmissions of the city police department, so that when the fire was finally set, the firemen did not have to wait for a call. They went to the building on their own initiative.

ITEM: Even though Detective Kelley admitted that the campus police knew there would be a fire, the KSU police made no attempt to stop the arsonists. At 7:45 that night a call went over the radio telling the KSU police to don their riot gear, yet the police's own logs show that the campus police did not show up at the building until at least 9:15, an hour and a half later.

ITEM: Statements provided by Chester Williams, the University's Director of Safety, and Detective Kelley, confirm that the campus police monitored the demonstrators and even had officers in the crowd.

Williams told the FBI: "We had two squads of University police mobilized and waiting in assembly points." Yet, "when the ROTC building was set on fire," Williams continued, "we [the police] were observing," not trying to stop the crowd from starting the fire.

ITEM: The University's own internal fact-finding commission, the KSU Commission on Campus, had an extremely difficult time understanding why the police established what the commission euphemistically called "a policy of nonintervention."

The commission documented three instances in which a student, a faculty member, and a local clergyman all independently warned the campus police that people on campus were openly talking about the impending fire.

The study also concluded: "The persons involved in the actual incendiarism were few, were separated from the main crowd, and could easily have been apprehended by the police."

ITEM: The same report also confirmed "that it took an extraordinarily long time to ignite the ROTC building." One of the witnesses before the commission was quoted as saying: "That fire went out several times, and they [the arsonists] had to work on it."

The study also noted: "Many other witnesses testify to several unsuccessful attempts to rekindle a real blaze, and most of them express amazed wonder why the police, with all the opportunity they had, did nothing to prevent the arson."

ITEM: The Kent firemen, who responded to the calls that the building had been set on fire, even though the campus and city police would not, may have completely doused the small blaze that was initially set.

An FBI report says the firemen succeeded, but KSU Police Chief Donald Schwartzmiller said there was still a small fire smoldering when the firemen left, because of the lack of police protection.

The KSU Commission on Campus Violence reached the same conclusion as Schwartzmiller, but suggested that the blaze at that time was small enough that it could have been doused with a hand fire extinguisher.

ITEM: The fire did not actually burn out of control until after the crowd had been chased from the building and KSU policemen took positions around the building.

The KSU commission concluded that when the crowd had been chased away from the building, they "had thought themselves thwarted of their intent."

These strange facts raise a host of disturbing questions:

Why did the Kent State police ignore all the warnings about the fire?

When confronted with the revelations, the police tried to pretend the warnings never reached them. Chief Schwartzmiller claimed that Detective Kelley never told him about any of the intelligence reports that Kelley shared with the NBC camera crew.

But weren't there signs tacked to trees on campus asking: "Why is ROTC still standing?" And weren't those signs posted during the rally on Friday, the day before the fire, where they must have been seen by the police and University officials?

Of course. Schwartzmiller even admitted that he saw them, but he told me he did not take them seriously. He said that everybody on campus, including students who did not support the antiwar protests, had been talking about "ROTC going" for months, and he thought it was just another example of the boy crying wolf.

Even so, one would assume that the police would at least have taken some precautions, and done something once the students gathered around the building.

What were the police doing when the students started to assault the building?

Copies of the campus police logs show mysterious gaps between 8:00 P.M. and 9:15 P.M. If one looks at the logs for all other times during the weekend of May 1-4, one sees that the campus police radio was very busy, with transmissions recorded approximately every few minutes. However, during the time of the fire there are hardly any entries. Then, after the fire, the transmissions returned to normal.

What explanations did the police give for not stopping the demonstrators?

Different stories have been told at different times by different officials. Schwartzmiller's immediate supervisor, Chester Williams, who was Director of Safety and Public Services at the University, gave what appeared to be the official version when he said the campus police force was too small to cope with a crowd of that size—especially one that he characterized as being quite vicious.

Williams asked: "Can you take 22 men [the number of men on the campus police force] and disperse 500 to 1,000 in the mood that was evident? . . . It is my feeling that there's not any building worth a life."

That sounded reasonable enough, and I accepted that explanation until I interviewed Ross Jamerson and Walt Moore, two of the Portage County Sheriff's Deputies that actually dispersed the crowd. Both of them told me that only four or five deputies were able to chase away the students with what Moore said was just one tear gas gun.

Moore, who led the deputies, said he "thought [he] was loony as hell afterwards" for committing his men against so many students, but that "we responded to a call for help as any other policeman would. How could you do anything less?"

Is it possible that authorities might have deliberately held the police back and allowed the building to burn? Perhaps, as some students later charged, because the University was thinking of tearing the building down anyway and wanted to collect the insurance?

Anything is possible, but there is at least one other explanation that might account for the police not showing up for so long.

In 1971, there was a report in *Rolling Stone* magazine. The author of the piece, Joe Eszterhas, had heard complaints from several campus police officers that Schwartzmiller had been drinking heavily that night and that, as a result, he could not take command.

Eszterhas confronted Schwartzmiller with this allegation and asked if there was any basis to it. Eszterhas quoted Schwartzmiller as saying: "Hell, no. If you really want to know, I was getting laid, and if you want I'll bring her in as a character reference."

Schwartzmiller, perhaps realizing that his alibi made him look just as derelict in duty, later claimed that Eszterhas had his days of the weekend mixed up, and that he was with his lady friend on Friday night, not on Saturday, while ROTC was burning.

Schwartzmiller also told me that he did not have a drink that entire weekend. However, I discovered some documents in the Kent State archives that support the drinking complaints that Eszterhas had heard. One of the documents I found, a "personal and confidential" memorandum from former Kent State President Robert I. White to Safety Director Chester Williams, dated July 3, 1970, included a long list of complaints that several Kent State police officers lodged against Schwartzmiller in a meeting with Dr. Robert Beer, one of White's top assistants. One complaint read:

> Once again, he [Schwartzmiller] was highly intoxicated when West Hall [the ROTC building] was fired; for example, in driving to the service center to pick up rope to cordon off West Hall, he drove over curbs and walkways three or four times due to his inability to drive.

Another memo in the archives, written by Chet Williams to White, with the intent of defending Schwartzmiller, had the effect of damning him. In responding to the allegations made against Schwartzmiller, Williams stated: "He [Schwartzmiller] had been drinking [the night of the fire] and was sent home by me. He was not drunk but the scent of alcohol was apparent."*

---

*In denying the allegations that he was too drunk to take command, and that as a result, demonstrators succeeded in burning the ROTC building, Schwartzmiller told me

Assuming Schwartzmiller was too drunk to order his men to disperse the crowd, would that completely explain why the demonstrators were almost given a free rein to burn the ROTC building on Saturday night? Or could there be other factors involved here—perhaps something else going on here that might have even driven Schwartzmiller to drink?

Some revisionists have built elaborate theories around the police's failure to act. Some are convinced that the Kent State police deliberately did not try to prevent the arson because they knew there were *agents provocateur* in the crowd and the police wanted them to succeed.

The revisionists often cite instances of *provocateurs* being unmasked during protests on other college campuses, and even at Kent State after the shootings. In 1972, for example, a member of the left-wing Vietnam Veterans Against the War was caught trying to sell his fellow vets illegal weapons, and he supposedly tried to convince them to commit acts of violence. The vets turned him in to the Kent city police, only to discover he was actually an informant for the KSU police.

It is also well known now that during the late 1960s and early 1970s, the FBI had in effect a counterintelligence program, code-named COINTELPRO, that was deliberately designed to discredit and destroy the New Left movement on the campuses.

The theory that Schwartzmiller deliberately held the police back would only make sense if the *provocateurs* were in the employ of the Kent State police. The revisionists have pointed fingers at the FBI and military Intelligence, and suggested that their provocateurs set the blaze.

What they are suggesting is that someone involved in a conspiracy to burn the building, phoned the campus police and told them: "Don't commit your men. We're sending in our secret agents to burn one of your buildings. Please do not arrest them, and let's keep this our secret."

---

that a lieutenant in his department was after his job and that he and five other officers conspired against him. Schwartzmiller called these officers "The Golf Course Six," because they made the charges during a meeting with a University vice president at the University's golf course.

Another internal University memo in the University archives, sent by Vice President Richard E. Dunn to President White, dated July 27, 1970, indicates that the University suppressed the allegations because it wanted to "prevent a sticky, probably public, controversy which could badly hurt the University." The University accomplished this by quietly demoting Schwartzmiller and reassigning him to overseeing security at the University's golf course.

If some of the theories about provocateurs are that silly, why do these suspicions about provocateurs persist?

For three reasons. One: The students who tried initially to start a fire bumbled for 45 minutes, and some of their friends did not think the protestors were capable of burning the building.

Two: The building did not burn until after the demonstrators left the scene, and the police took up positions around the building.

Three: If there were undercover agents involved in the arson attempts—or even if there were just informants in the crowd, throwing rocks at the building or goading others to set the blaze—some other pieces to the Kent State puzzle—pieces that are otherwise inexplicable—would very neatly fall into place.

For example, "dirty tricks" by undercover agents would explain why the state of Ohio, after it subsequently indicted 25 students and faculty members for their part in the disturbances that weekend, dismissed the charges after only a few cases went to trial.

In December 1971, after it disposed of four of the 25 indictments, the state claimed it had insufficient evidence to proceed with the prosecution with the rest.

Looking back, that was one of the more surprising developments in the Kent Affair. It was especially surprising when one considers how unpopular protestors against the Vietnam War were, and how public officials at every level had promised to vigorously prosecute those responsible for acts of violence.

The official explanation: that there was insufficient evidence to convict any students, defies common sense. With all the witnesses who were present that night, and with all the photographs that wound up in the hands of investigators, one would think that the state of Ohio had more than enough evidence to throw more than a few people in jail.

The Justice Department's summary of the FBI report stated very clearly: "The FBI feels that it has identified 13 persons involved in the burning of the ROTC building and the harassment of firemen."

Yet, out of that 13, only one person was later convicted of an offense—and that was for a misdemeanor offense of interfering with the firemen's attempts to stop the blaze.

Are we really supposed to believe this evidence against the 13 just disappeared?

I do not think so. In fact, had the Kent 25 indictments not been dropped, the person who would have gone on trial next would have been a former student named Douglas Cormack. I found a statement Cormack gave to the FBI in which he confessed to hindering the firemen's efforts and threw rocks at the Guardsmen. Prosecutors should have been able to convict Cormack on the basis of his FBI statement alone.

Why Cormack was not brought to trial remains a mystery. Just as it ultimately remains a mystery why the police ignored all the advance warnings about the fire; why they still did not protect the building for more than an hour once it was assaulted; and who set the blaze.*

These are good questions. Now how about some good answers?

The answer may be that somebody does not want us to know what really happened at Kent State.

Are you going to tell us what you think? Did or did not these secret government agencies play any role in the events preceding the Kent State shootings?

I think we should be content to ponder the possibilities.

Besides, if you think all of this is ridiculous . . . wait until you see what happened in the courts during the first decade after the shootings!

---

*The FBI had better information as to who helped start the fire than anyone has previously realized. I found in the FBI files an extraordinary confession by a then 18-year-old high school student, George Walter Harrington, who was visiting his brother in Kent that weekend. Harrington admitted throwing rocks at and breaking a window in the ROTC building, tugging at the firemen's hoses in the attempt to prevent the firemen from extinguishing the fire, and acting as a middleman in the actual igniting of the building. According to his own statement, Harrington took a rag from the man who soaked it in the gasoline tank of a motorcycle and handed it to another man who dipped the rag "in the corner window of the ROTC building," which started the fire. Harrington even confessed to removing "screens from the window and [breaking] out the window with our bare fists" because he and the dipper "felt the fire needed air."

Harrington's extraordinary confession is mentioned prominently in several internal FBI memos about the fire—even in memos sent to William Sullivan, who was then the Bureau's Director of Domestic Intelligence and one of FBI Director J. Edgar Hoover's top lieutenants.

The state of Ohio also knew what Harrington did. His name appears on a suspect list of the Ohio Bureau of Criminal Investigation, which provided information to the state grand jury that indicted protestors.

Why Harrington, whose confession of wrongdoing appears to be the strongest among all the demonstrators, was never indicted before the grand jury—and why his name has never surfaced publicly before—remains a mystery.

PART TWO

The actions of some students were violent and criminal and those of some others were dangerous, reckless, and irresponsible. The indiscriminate firing of rifles into a crowd of students and the deaths that followed were unnecessary, unwarranted, and inexcusable.
- Report of the President's
Commission on Campus Unrest

Number of students who spent time in jail as a result of the two grand jury investigations:
None

Number of National Guardsmen who were successfully prosecuted:
None

The second part of this book deals with the almost nine years that May 4 and the various legal issues it raised dragged on and on both in and out of the courts.

We will start by looking at the response of the criminal justice system and see how well the criminal courts worked.

First, we will look at how Ohio authorities convened a "special" state grand jury that was such a fraud that Richard G. Zimmerman, a columnist for the Cleveland Plain Dealer called it "a cover-up surpassed only by Watergate."

Then we will examine the results of that grand jury's investigation.

We will see:

• Why the grand jury's report was eventually burned in a wastebasket;

• How the Guardsmen escaped prosecution, despite recommendations that they be brought to trial; and

• How the charges brought against the student protestors were also dropped when Ohio officials thought "the time was right." (In other words, after a sufficient amount of time had passed and Ohio officials thought there was no more public interest in May 4.)

Then we will examine the Justice Department and Nixon White House's strange pattern of behavior in blocking the federal grand jury investigation that had been requested after the state's cover-up had been exposed.

The Nixon administration went to extraordinary lengths to block a trial of the Guardsmen and officially closed the case three times over a period of three years.

Eventually the Justice Department was pressured into reopening its investigation and indicting eight soldiers.

We will see what prompted the Justice Department's turnaround and explore why many suspected (as the next president of Kent State, Dr. Glenn A. Olds, put it) the White House had "something hidden in the box."

We will also examine the question that just about everybody who demanded the federal grand jury asked:

Did the Justice Department really have its heart in the prosecution, or did the prosecutors just go through the motions of the trial to forever silence their critics while at the same time keeping a "lid" on what really happened at Kent State?

FOUR

The Early Coverup

May-June 1970

Immediately after the shootings the FBI conducted what their files describe as "a complete preliminary investigation" of the events at Kent State.

FBI Director J. Edgar Hoover assigned over 300 agents to the investigation. The agents studied everything from the backgrounds and credit ratings of the dead students to what certain professors taught in their classrooms.

The agents looked high and low for subversive conspiracies, and also looked in vain for evidence to support the Guardsmen's initial contentions that they only fired after a sniper fired first.

Although it was clear that the FBI's sympathies were with the Guardsmen and not with the students,* the Bureau did at least take sworn statements from all the Guardsmen.

Those statements, with all the other information, were shipped over to the Justice Department's Civil Rights Division for a determination of whether anyone—students or Guardsmen—violated any federal laws in connection with any of the incidents at Kent.

On June 19, 1970, Robert Murphy, the Civil Rights Division attorney

---

*According to a memorandum Hoover dictated to his top lieutenants, made available under the Freedom of Information Act, Hoover told White House aide Egil Krogh he felt "the students invited (the shootings) and got what they deserved."

who was assigned to head the Justice Department's investigation, prepared a memo for his superior, Assistant Attorney General Jerris Leonard, entitled "Kent State: Preliminary Conclusions and Recommendations."

This six-page memo outlined the state of the evidence as it existed, as well as Murphy's recommendations for what the Department of Justice should do to prosecute violations of federal law.

Murphy recommended against prosecuting any of the commanding officers or Ohio Governor Rhodes. Even though Murphy felt "their conduct showed foolhardiness and negligence," he pointed out that stupidity was not a federal crime and there was nothing the federal government could do about it.

As for the Guardsmen who fired, the most applicable law, Murphy argued, was a statute passed during the Reconstruction era that was originally intended to guarantee that freed slaves (or any other ordinary citizens, for that matter) would not be shot or killed by policemen or militiamen without receiving due process of law.

Murphy wrote:

I do believe that our initial findings indicate that some National Guardsmen intended to, and did, summarily punish members of the crowd by shooting at them, thereby killing, injuring, and intimidating them. The difficult part of proving a violation of 18 U.S.C. 242 is proving that the specific intent of the Guardsmen was to deprive the crowd of their constitutional rights. To recap very briefly, the facts which generally indicate the requisite specific intent are as follows:

(1) There was no sniper;

(2) The Guard was not surrounded and could have continued in the direction in which they were going;

(3) Only a few students were within 30 yards of the Guard—none was closer than 20 yards;

(4) Even if the Guard believed they were being charged by the students, other alternatives—specifically bayonets and a limited supply of tear gas— were available;

(5) At least three responsible members of the Guard, including the captain in charge of Troop G, state specifically that the lives of the Guardsmen were not in danger; and

(6) The Guardsmen were undoubtedly angered by the actions of the students and were frustrated in their inability to either contain or disperse them.

 The memo continued:

Proving these six points circumstantially proves intent and intent can rarely be proven in any other way. It is also the law in the Sixth Circuit that in deciding the issue of intent it is reasonable to infer that a person ordinarily intends all the natural and probable consequences of acts knowingly done and knowingly committed. A person who shoots a gun intends to hurt him.

Murphy conceded that only "one case shows specific intent beyond a reasonable doubt: the admission of (Sergeant Lawrence) Shafer that he shot (Joseph) Lewis because Lewis made an obscene gesture at him."

However, Murphy considered the statements that four other Guardsmen (Barry Morris, James Pierce, James McGee, and Ralph Zoller) provided to the FBI as "admissions in varying degrees, of the knowing use of unlawful force."

Murphy recommended that a federal grand jury be convened within six weeks to indict these five Guardsmen plus Sergeant William Herschler, who was alleged by his sergeant, Matthew McManus, to have fired his rifle into the crowd eight times, "and any other [Guardsmen] that the Grand Jury may develop as a defendant."

In conclusion, Murphy wrote:

We have a case against at least six National Guardsmen for violations of U.S.C. 242. If indictments are obtained we would attempt to try them jointly.*

----

*In the same memorandum Murphy noted that the student protestors also deserved to be prosecuted, but argued that as a tactical move, it would be preferable if the prosecuting attorney of Portage County, Ohio, Ronald Kane, who was publicly talking about convening a state grand jury, handled the prosecutions of the students himself.

"My basic reason for desiring a local prosecution," Murphy wrote, "is that I believe that a federal prosecution of the persons responsible for the ROTC burning will seriously jeopardize our chances to conduct extensive and frank interviews regarding the shootings with students and faculty members. The FBI's investigation into what certain professors taught in their classes has already had that effect."

June-July 1970

The case that Murphy wanted to present to a grand jury was not presented until almost four and a half years after he made this recommendation
to prosecute the National Guardsmen.

The reasons for the delay will probably be debated for years to
come. As we will see later in this chapter, some became convinced the
Nixon White House tried to squelch the investigation because the Nixon
administration had "something hidden in the box"—that is, something it
did not want to risk being revealed at a trial.

Others felt the White House and Justice Department's motives in trying to block a prosecution were explicable in more conventional political
terms. As Arthur Krause, the father of one of the slain students, once put
it, the case was just "political dynamite." As Krause once told me: "going
after the National Guard was like attacking motherhood and apple pie."

Whatever the reasons for the delay, we do know what happened after
Murphy recommended bringing charges against the six Guardsmen.

Department records subsequently released under the Freedom of Information Act reveal that on June 22, 1970, Jerris Leonard, the head of
the Civil Rights Division, forwarded Murphy's recommendations along
with a detailed 35-page factual summary of the FBI report, that Murphy
prepared with one of his colleagues, to Attorney General John Mitchell.

From what we can piece together from internal Department memoranda and from the Department's subsequent actions, it appears that the
Department's initial efforts were uniformly directed toward washing its
own hands of the case and toward urging Ronald Kane, the Portage
County Prosecutor, to conduct a county grand jury investigation.

Kane had been publicly talking about convening such an investigation ever since May 4, but had not taken any action for almost three
months. Publicly, Kane said that he could not conduct the investigation
until he obtained adequate funding from the state of Ohio.

Since Kane's office was small, he lacked both the resources and the
manpower to handle a prosecution of any magnitude.

An internal Justice Department shows that, shortly after Leonard and
Attorney General John Mitchell reviewed Murphy's recommendation, the
two senior Department officials met and decided that instead of accepting
Murphy's recommendation to convene a federal grand jury, they would
instead "assist Mr. Kane initially in the development of what we believe
were clear violations of state statutes on the part of the Guardsmen."

This memo, written by Leonard and sent to the heads of the Department's Internal Security and Criminal divisions on July 7, indicates that whatever Leonard and Mitchell privately felt about possible federal violations by the soldiers, they at least agreed the Guardsmen should be prosecuted by Ohio officials.

According to this memo, on June 25, 1970, Leonard personally traveled to Ravenna, Ohio, to meet with Kane and to "pledge our support and assess his interest and capabilities."

Leonard's plan was that if Kane agreed to present the case to a county grand jury, the Department would assist him, presumably by loaning him attorneys. The Justice Department would then defer any plans for a federal grand jury.

After returning to Washington, Leonard also sent Kane a letter advising him that Department attorneys would prepare a memorandum "setting forth a factual account of the shooting on May 4, 1970, a list of possible witnesses, and an analysis of Ohio law."

At Leonard's request Robert Murphy then prepared a 14-page memorandum for Kane entitled "Potential National Guard Defendants in the Kent State Shootings." The memo identified the same six soldiers Murphy felt were liable to prosecution under federal law and identified six Ohio statutes, ranging from malicious shooting to assault, any one of which might be used to prosecute the six Guardsmen.

The memo ended by saying:

> Taking all the known facts into consideration, the shooting of the students was neither "necessary nor proper."
>
> In conclusion, each of the six identified Guardsmen should be prosecuted under Ohio law.*

Late July-Early August 1970

Until this point, all of these memoranda and recommendations had circulated privately within government circles. That changed on June 23,

---

*The wording of this memorandum is particularly important because Ohio has a statute that renders guiltless "police officers . . . (and) members of the organized militia" who kill or wound rioters—provided that the force they use is "necessary and proper." The Justice Department advised Kane that the Ohio statute would not pose a barrier to the prosecution of the Guardsmen.

1970, when the *Akron Beacon Journal* published a banner headline story revealing for the first time that six Guardsmen were in danger of being prosecuted. The article paraphrased the contents of the Justice Department's 14-page memorandum to Kane, which had been made available to a *Beacon Journal* reporter.

Ironically, this leak set into motion a chain of events that removed both Kane and the Justice Department from the prosecution picture.

The result of this was that the Guardsmen were spared from prosecution.

The news leak had quite a few repercussions. Not only did disbelieving subscribers to the *Beacon Journal* cancel their subscriptions by the dozens (how dare they print that!), but the president of the United States, the director of the FBI, and the attorney general of Ohio all rushed to the defense of the Guardsmen.

Both privately and publicly, all three of these high-level government officials took steps to make it appear as if the *Beacon Journal* had concocted a pack of lies and that the evidence to prosecute the Guardsmen never existed!

Recently declassified FBI files reveal that at 8:47 on the morning of July 24, 1970, President Nixon telephoned FBI Director J. Edgar Hoover to complain about the news leak, which was by now prominently featured in the Washington newspapers.

According to one memo that Hoover sent at noontime that day to six of his top aides:

> The President said that from what he has seen, although it was just a cursory examination of our report, it looks like the Guard had a lot of provocation. I said I thought they definitely had. The President said he told his people he was going to have it [the news story] "shot down" as he was not going to have this student business erupting, as basically, what do you expect the Guards to do . . . The President said . . . if I ever have an opportunity to "knock it [the story] down," and if I am asked, he hopes I say it is not true.

In a separate memo Hoover dictated to four of his aides a few minutes after writing that one Hoover characterized the request as an order. Hoover wrote:

> The President was quite disturbed about the article in the paper and directed me to take steps to have it "knocked down" insofar as the FBI was concerned. I told him I would see that this was done.

Other memos released by the FBI indicated that Hoover relayed this order to his top lieutenants, William Sullivan, Alex Rosen, and Thomas Bishop, who subsequently went to considerable lengths to carry out Nixon's order.

One memo, written by Bishop, the head of the Bureau's Crime Records Division (its public relations arm) to Sullivan, then the head of the Bureau's Domestic Intelligence Bureau, frankly states:

> As instructed by the Director on the morning of 7/24/70 my office has taken effective steps to "scotch" the story which originated out of Akron, Ohio . . . to the effect that the FBI has concluded the slaying of four Kent State students by Ohio National Guard was not necessary and not in order and six Guardsmen could be criminally prosecuted.

This memo indicates that the FBI issued a statement denying it drew any conclusions about the shootings, and

> furnished this statement to some friends at United Press International, the Associated Press, the *Washington Evening Star*, the *Washington Post,* the *Washington Daily News*, Scripps-Howard Newspapers, and radio stations in the Ohio-Pittsburgh area.
>
> In addition, Bishop has telephonically contacted the ASAC [Assistant Special Agent in Charge] of the Cleveland office (in the absence of the SAC) and instructed him to give this statement to the *Akron Beacon Journal,* to United Press International in Akron, and to the Cleveland newspapers. We also furnished this statement to the ASAC of the Cincinnati office and told him to give it to the papers in that area.

What the FBI did was seize on one relatively inconsequential error in the *Beacon Journal*'s story—the attribution of the information that the Guardsmen could be prosecuted, to the FBI, rather than the Justice Department—and implied the entire story was false.

This created a false public impression that the evidence against the Guardsmen did not exist.

Meanwhile, in Columbus, Ohio Attorney General Paul Brown pushed the same line: The information in the *Beacon Journal*'s story could not possibly be true. He told reporters he was unaware of any evidence that would tend to incriminate the Guardsmen.

Technically, that may have been true. There is no record that the Justice Department ever sent Brown any of its internal summaries of the evidence or recommendations indicating that the Department felt the Guardsmen should be prosecuted for what they did.

However, Brown refused to concede that such evidence might exist even after Attorney General John Mitchell, at the height of the fervor created by the leak, confirmed publicly that there were "apparent violations of federal law" involving both students and Guardsmen.

When a reporter brought Mitchell's statement to Brown's attention, the Ohio attorney general ingeniously insisted that Mitchell must have been misquoted, and claimed that no evidence existed against the National Guardsmen.

The Leak

Since the leak resulted in a concerted public campaign to discredit the *Beacon Journal* and had the effect of misleading the public about the nature of the evidence against the Guardsmen, the question of who leaked the Justice Department's memo to Ronald Kane—and why—is of some historical importance.

A story carried in the July 24, 1970, edition of the *Washington Post* quoted an unnamed Justice Department source as saying that Kane himself leaked the memo. This source, who raised the possibility that Kane sabotaged his own investigation, told the Post: "The pretrial publicity caused by making this memo public, in my judgment, has foreclosed the possibility of prosecution under Ohio law."

Another internal FBI memorandum, sent by one of Hoover's top lieutenants to another, supports that notion, and reconstructs the predicament the Justice Department had placed Kane in by trying to hand off the prosecution to him.

In this memo, Assistant FBI Director Alex Rosen reported to another assistant director, William Sullivan, the observations of Charles Cusick, the special agent in charge of the FBI's Cleveland field office. Cusick had outlined to Rosen the following scenario:

A: Kane talked about convening a county grand jury to investigate the disorders but did not do anything because he lacked sufficient manpower and funds.

B: The Justice Department, having concluded that the Guardsmen violated both federal and state laws, decided to dump the prosecution on Kane.

C: Assistant Attorney General Jerris Leonard met with Kane and tried to get Kane to commit himself to prosecuting the Guardsmen (which would relieve the Department of its responsibilities).

D: Kane "told Leonard, he would prosecute anyone, including National Guardsmen, if sufficient evidence is available."

E: "After Kane made such a commitment to Leonard, he obviously thought the matter over and realized the highly controversial issues which existed." Kane, who had some political ambitions in Ohio, knew that "nobody wants the National Guard prosecuted." Merely attempting a prosecution would have been politically suicidal.

F: When Kane realized that the Department was trying to pass a keg of dynamite to him, "Kane seized upon a scheme to outfox the Department of Justice inasmuch as it appears he [Kane] was pressured by Leonard into an untenable position."

G: Kane deliberately leaked the memo and the existence of the evidence against the Guard, and in doing so "turned the tables on the Department of Justice and dumped the entire thing in the Justice Department's lap."

What did Kane have to say about these allegations? In 1981, after he returned to private practice, Kane agreed to be interviewed for this book. He would not discuss Cusick's theory, but he did deny what the *Washington Post* had reported, and what two of my sources on the *Beacon Journal* later corroborated: that he did in fact leak the memo.

Kane told an entirely different story of what happened. He complained: "They took the investigation away from me."

Here Kane was referring not to the Justice Department, but to the state of Ohio, which "suddenly emerged in the picture" as soon as the story was published.

The state, he noted, "grasped control" of the investigation by convening a specially empaneled state grand jury in Portage County.

To support his claim that he really wanted to conduct the grand jury, Kane produced a letter he sent to Portage County Judge Albert Caris, dated July 31, 1970, asking Caris for authorization to reconvene a previous empaneled Portage County grand jury "for the purpose of a probe of the situation which occurred at Kent State University."

Kane said that he had sent the letter to Caris on a Friday afternoon, and that on the following Monday he discovered that the state of Ohio had stepped in and asked another judge in the same courthouse to convene a "special" state grand jury to be run not by Kane but by prosecutors specially selected by the Ohio attorney general.

Why did the state of Ohio, which had hitherto been silent when all this talk about conducting a grand jury was going on, suddenly step in the picture?

Some have speculated that the reason the state of Ohio suddenly convened the grand jury was because Kane had publicly threatened to subpoena Ohio Governor James Rhodes, who had called out the National Guardsmen and who had refused a request from Kane to close down the University. That request had been made when the two briefly met on the morning of May 3, and Kane could have embarrassed the governor.

A report in the September 17, 1970, edition of the *Akron Beacon Journal* quoted an unnamed Portage County political figure as saying Rhodes was going to any length to avoid having to testify himself. That may have been one reason the state took over the investigation.

The overriding reason, though, appears to have been that the state wanted to control who and what the grand jury investigated.

August 1970

The grand jury was now in the hands of the state of Ohio. And while Ohio Attorney General Paul Brown was publicly promising "the ultimate investigation" of the shootings, the *Akron Beacon Journal* noted that "state officials seem bent on vindicating the Guard's actions at Kent State."

In fact, it might not even be accurate to call the state grand jury investigation a "coverup" since Brown made public statements to the effect that indictments against the Guardsmen would not be considered.

To ensure that no charges would be brought, Brown appointed three conservative special prosecutors, one of whom was Seabury Ford, an attorney from nearby Aurora, Ohio. Although the Ohio attorney general would later deny knowing Ford's connections with the Ohio National Guard, the *Kent Record-Courier* reported on September 4: "He [Ford] served with the 107th Cavalry out of Cleveland in the 1920's. Troop G in Ravenna, part of the 107th, was part of the group" at Taylor Hall that fired the shots that killed the four students.

The Scranton Commission

While all these machinations were going on, the President's Commission on Campus Unrest came to Kent and held three days of public hearings.

Although the Commission subsequently issued a report that became one of the more important official documents in the case, it should be noted that the Commission's investigation was never intended to substitute for a full-scale criminal investigation (even though many believed that the commission was ploy on the part of the Nixon administration to head off a no-holds-barred inquiry and make it look like the shootings were thoroughly investigated, when in fact they were not.)

At the outset of the hearings the Commission's chairman, former Pennsylvania Governor William Scranton, described the goals of the Commission as follows:

• To identify the background causes of the disturbances on the campus;

• To examine the plans and preparations of local and University officials to handle such disorders; and

• To formulate recommendations to ensure that there would never be a recurrence of May 4.

In keeping with Scranton's promise not to interfere with any future judicial proceedings, the Commission did not, to quote spokesman Chris Cross, "subpoena any Guardsmen who shot people or any students who threw rocks."

The witnesses at the public hearings did include a fairly representative sample of students, professors, University administrators, and townspeople. All were given the opportunity to describe what they did that weekend, and to vent their frustrations.

At one point one of the student witnesses, James Woodring, Jr., started to testify how he watched an officer give what he thought was a hand signal to fire before firing himself into the crowd. Scranton quickly dismissed Woodring, reiterating that he did not want to "assess the guilt or innocence of any individual" or hear testimony that should be considered by a grand jury first.

At another point Commission staffers tried to obtain the testimony of two of the highest ranking officers in G Troop: Captain Raymond Srp and Lieutenant Alexander Stevenson.

After Srp and Stevenson were served their subpoenas, their attorneys rushed into the federal courthouse in Cleveland and obtained an injunction to block their testimony. The attorneys claimed that Srp and Stevenson's testimony would compromise their Fifth Amendment rights against self-incrimination.

The Commission decided not to fight the injunction. Joseph Rhodes, Jr., one of the Commissioners, told me the Commission was operating under a severe time constraint. By the time the courts had ruled on the issue, the Commission's mandate would have expired.

The Guardsmen's attorneys later attached a great deal of significance to their efforts to block the public testimony of these officers. Years later, a letter that Guard attorney William Ziegler sent to Guard General Dana Stewart surfaced which provided a summary of the efforts by Ziegler and his colleagues to prevent the Commission from obtaining the Guardsmen's sworn testimony.

Ziegler wrote that after he and his colleagues filed the injunction:

> The Commission ordered a withdrawal of the subpoenas and it proceeded without benefit of Ohio National Guardsmen as witnesses, except for the general testimony of General Del Corso and the limited testimony of General Canterbury. The court action proved to be a tremendous victory and in our judgment, one of the key landmarks in the overall defense of the officers and enlisted men of the Ohio National Guard in connection with this tragic incident. In our opinion, had [my law firm] not become involved, together with [attorneys C.D.] Lambros and [Delmar] Christensen, in early August, not only Colonel [Charles] Fassinger, but many other officers and enlisted men would have testified, and the direction of the entire proceedings would have been markedly changed, including possibly the results of the Ohio Special Grand Jury Proceedings.

September-October 1970

Approximately twenty guardsmen were subpoenaed before the state grand jury. However, it appears the only reason they were subpoenaed was for the sake of appearances. A careful reading of the transcripts of the Guardsmen's testimony suggests the Guardsmen were treated quite politely.

Instead of being asked "Why did you fire?" "How close were the students?" or "Why didn't you just keep on marching?" the Guardsmen were asked leading questions like: "Did you have reason to believe that some serious personal bodily injury could have come to you?" (An actual question asked of Guardsman Leon Smith).

Understandably, the Guardsmen, who did not want to be indicted, did not argue with the prosecutors when their defense was handed to them.

The grand jury's attitude toward the student protestors, though, was quite different. When it came to rioting and disrupting the public tranquility, the grand jury was far less tolerant.

Justice Department memos have now surfaced confirming unattributed reports in James Michener's book that the grand jury was bent on indicting literally hundreds of students and had to be restrained by the prosecutors.

Although one woman who served on the grand jury told me that the jurors never took a vote on whether or not to indict the Guardsmen, a Justice Department memo written by Robert Murphy (made available to me under the Freedom of Information Act) indicates that one of the state prosecutors, informed Murphy that one (and only one) vote was taken.

That vote was on whether or not to indict Sergeant Lawrence Shafer on assault charges. Shafer had admitted shooting a student identified as Joseph Lewis, Jr., who was giving Shafer the finger.

Shafer was exonerated by the grand jury by a vote to 15 to 0.

The grand jury voted to indict Lewis instead.

October 16, 1970

On October 16, 1970, the grand jury issued a lengthy report that condemned the students, the faculty, the administration, and the police department at Kent State . . . in fact, just about everyone except the Guardsmen.

The grand jury concluded that, on the basis that had been presented to them, the Guardsmen "fired in the honest and sincere belief . . . that they would suffer serious bodily injury had they not done so."

That conclusion, of course, flew in the face of the Justice Department's conclusion that the shootings were "neither 'necessary nor proper,'" and the conclusion of the Scranton Commission that the shootings were "unnecessary, unwarranted, and inexcusable."

The only individuals indicted by the grand jury—25 in all—were protestors, mostly students at the university, but also one professor, a few dropouts, and a few local drug pushers. The 25 individuals were indicted for offenses ranging from first degree riot to the burning of the ROTC building.

Late October-November 1970

The grand jury's report was immediately denounced by various factions of the University community and by equally appalled interested outsiders.

One of the sharpest critics of the grand jury was Ohio Senator Stephen Young, who said on the Senate floor that the grand jury was "conceived in fraud and fakery. Its sole purpose was to whitewash Governor James A. Rhodes for his abominable blunder in calling out the National Guard to police the campus of Kent State University."

During this period, reports also began trickling in that the grand jury had ignored this or that piece of crucial evidence, and that several Guardsmen who presumably could have provided damning evidence against their fellow soldiers, including Raymond Srp (who told the FBI it was not "a shooting situation"), were never asked to testify.

At the height of the furor special prosecutor Seabury Ford gave an interview in which he said the Guardsmen "should have shot" all the troublemakers.

"I think the whole damn country is not going to quiet down," Ford told a reporter, "until police are ordered to shoot to kill."

Meanwhile, Kent State student government leaders, professors, local clergymen, and KSU President Robert I. White (who was not upset that the Guardsmen were cleared—just that the grand jury blamed his administration for the tragedy) began demanding that the federal government step back into the picture.

In Washington, the Justice Department announced it would study the results of the "special" grand jury.

On November 17 Assistant Attorney General Jerris Leonard told reporters that a decision on whether to bring federal charges against the Guardsmen could be expected by the end of the year.*

---

*The findings of the special state grand jury were also studied by U.S. District Judge William Thomas, who considered appeals from the lawyers of the so-called Kent 25 to dismiss the indictments. Thomas allowed the indictments to stand, but he ordered that the grand jury's report be expunged from the record, and physically destroyed, for suggesting that the indictees were already guilty.

On November 15, 1971, just three weeks before most of the indictments were ultimately dismissed by the state of Ohio, the grand jury's report was burned in a wastebasket in a ceremony in the parking lot outside the Portage County courthouse while reporters and photographers looked on.

November 18, 1970

Contrary to Leonard's promise, there was to be no announcement from the Justice Department on whether or not there would be a federal grand jury.

President Nixon saw to that. Unknown to anyone outside the highest echelons of government, Nixon sent his chief domestic adviser, John Ehrlichman, to the office of Attorney General John Mitchell with a highly secret presidential memorandum making it clear "the President has decided that no such grand jury would be sought."

Interestingly, what has surfaced so far is not Nixon's original memorandum (which appears to have vanished), but a follow-up memorandum from Ehrlichman sent to Mitchell, dated November 18, 1970, and given a top-secret classification, "Eyes Only". The purpose of this memorandum was to remind Mitchell of Nixon's order.

It is very clear from this memo that Nixon was unhappy that Leonard was even publicly talking about a federal grand jury, and was trying to keep Leonard and the whole Justice Department in line.

The "Eyes Only" memo instructs Mitchell to "please ask Mr. Leonard to advise the President by letter or memorandum that he fully understands the President's instruction in this regard?"

The two memos raise some intriguing questions, not the least of which is: Why did Nixon personally intervene in the case?

Was it because he simply sympathized with the Guardsmen? Was it because he despised the students who were protesting against his war policies? Or did he simply have nothing to gain politically by prosecuting the Guardsmen, who were not only symbols of law and order to his constituents, but heroes in the eyes of many citizens?

The answer is: Probably all of the above.

However, it has also been suggested by some theorists that Nixon did not want the grand jury because grand juries are not always controllable, and because Nixon did not want to risk the possibility that a federal grand jury might venture into potentially sensitive areas (like the use of planted demonstrators on the campus that might be traced back to the White House or some other branch of the federal government.)

Whatever his motives were, it can be safely said that Richard Nixon took a special interest in the Kent State case from the very beginning— and his attitude toward a possible federal prosecution was consistent.

This is what we know about Mr. Nixon and Kent State:

(1) As we saw earlier, FBI Director J. Edgar Hoover reported that Nixon was "quite disturbed" when he discovered a prosecution of the Guardsmen was under consideration, that Nixon ordered Hoover to "knock it [that story] down," and that he directed the White House staff to do the same.

(2) We know that Nixon was "very upset" when the Justice Department subsequently defied his no-grand-jury decision and reopened the case. In 1978 NBC newsman James Polk reported that Nixon was "so upset they had to scrape the President off the walls with a spatula."

(3) We also know now that within just three days of the shootings, Nixon asked the Justice Department to provide him with a "summary of the nature and scope" of the investigation the FBI was conducting.

While that last item may seem innocuous enough, one wonders why Nixon also insisted that the FBI deliver to his chief domestic adviser, John Ehrlichman, not just summaries but same-day copies of the FBI's complete field report.

One would think that the White House had better things to do than to read 8,000 pages of raw investigative files, which included over 500 eyewitness accounts, laboratory analyses, coroner's reports, teletypes telling FBI agents what to investigate (which Ehrlichman specifically asked for), and sundry other minutiae that had not even been analyzed by Justice Department attorneys.

The White House did not try to keep its request for the FBI report a secret; however, to my knowledge, the only other time the Nixon White House demanded to see every little tidbit of information in an ongoing FBI investigation was in the Watergate case. In that instance the White House did so because it wanted to closely monitor the FBI's investigation. The White House's purpose was to control and direct the investigation, and to steer the FBI away from certain witnesses and incriminating avenues of inquiry—all to avoid the disclosure of White House involvement in the Watergate scandal and to conceal Nixon's dirty tricks operations.

Anyone who has studied the Nixon years has to acknowledge the possibility that, in shutting down the Kent State investigation, the Nixon White House had something to cover up.

And as we follow the Justice Department's unusual pattern of behavior over the next few years, we will see that many people voiced these suspicions.

As we will see in forthcoming chapters, one former high ranking Justice Department official wondered whether there was not a "skeleton rattling in this closet."

Dr. Glenn Olds, the next president of Kent State, also wondered what the White House had "hidden in the box."

October 1970-August 1971

During this ten-month period the Justice Department pussyfooted around, holding reporters at bay who were anxious for an announcement and claiming that Department attorneys had not yet reached a decision on whether or not to go ahead with the federal grand jury.

Attorney General John Mitchell told reporters to be patient. "The criminal justice system," he told the *New York Times* one month after Nixon had already ordered the case closed, "doesn't always work as fast as we might like."

Mitchell had two problems that prevented him from making a public announcement that there would be no federal grand jury. The first was that he had already gone on record as saying the Guardsmen had apparently violated federal laws. The second problem was that the Justice Department attorney assigned to head the investigation, Robert Murphy, and at least one other attorney in the Civil Rights Division, Robert Hocutt, had previously recommended that the a federal grand jury be convened.

What Mitchell needed at that point, to justify Nixon's decision, was an opposing view from someone else in the Department. It was needed in case Murphy's recommendation to prosecute the Guardsmen was leaked.

That second opinion was provided on March 9, 1971, when K. William O'Connor, the number two man in the Civil Rights Division and Murphy's immediate superior, sent division chief Jerris Leonard a memo recommending "closing the Kent State University investigation without prosecutive action." In this memo O'Connor recommended that the Justice Department close the case "because of serious evidentiary problems," including the lack of ballistics evidence to conclusively prove that a specific Guardsman holding a specific rifle killed or injured a specific student.

O'Connor seemed to take a very different view of the evidence from Murphy, and he seemed to sympathize with the Guardsmen, many of whom, he pointed out, were young, ill-equipped, poorly trained, and deprived of sleep.

Two weeks after O'Connor wrote the memo someone in the Justice Department leaked it to a friendly reporter, Ken Clawson of the *Washington Post*. On March 21, 1971, Clawson reported that:

> The government has virtually decided against convening a federal grand jury . . . Only final approval by Attorney General John N. Mitchell is needed to ratify a decision reached reluctantly by the Justice Department's Civil Rights Division, that the government should not enter the case.

The article repeated many of the arguments O'Connor made in his memorandum to Mitchell.

Undoubtedly the memo was leaked to see if anyone would protest the decision. And within a few days, there were protests against this trial balloon.

One was made by the Reverend John P. Adams, an activist and civil rights leader who was director of the Board of Church and Society of the United Methodist Church in Washington. Adams had been in contact with Arthur Krause, the father of Allison Krause, one of the students who was killed in Kent. And both Adams and Krause were upset by Clawson's report.

After reading the story in the *Washington Post*, Adams, who had tried to bring the families of the other victims together and to coordinate their efforts, set up a series of meetings in April with various Justice Department officials, including Jerris Leonard, in order to get more information about the decision and to see if anything could be done to persuade the Department to change its mind.

According to Adams, Leonard insisted that no final decision had yet been made about proceeding with a grand jury investigation and that he would listen to any arguments the victims wanted to make or consider any new evidence they had.

In May, Random House released *Kent State: What Happened and Why,* a massive book by James Michener that included an almost minute-by-minute rendition of those four days in May. While Michener's book did not change the decision of the Justice Department (which had been made six months earlier by Nixon), it did influence all subsequent public discussion about May 4.

While the book forwarded the dubious thesis that the shootings happened because unnamed, unidentifiable outside agitators willed it, the book also introduced new evidence which at the time seemed startling.

Michener intimated that the Guardsmen went into a strategy-like huddle on the practice football field about five minutes before the shootings (just before the troops marched back up to the Pagoda and Taylor Hall, where they about-faced and started shooting).

Michener wrote: "There is no acceptable proof of collusion on the part of officers of men," but it was "likely that some kind of rough verbal agreement had been reached among the troops when they clustered on the practice field."

On May 17, 1971, shortly after the book was published, Adams and Steven Sindell, Arthur Krause's attorney, met with the number two man in the Justice Department, Deputy Attorney General Richard Kleindeinst. At that meeting Sindell cited passages in Michener's book and asked Kleindienst if the Department had ever considered the possibility that the Guardsmen might have engaged in a murderous conspiracy to shoot the students at Kent.

According to Adams, Kleindienst claimed that the thought never occurred to the attorneys in the Civil Rights Division.

Adams then asked Kleindienst to delay a final decision "long enough [for us] to submit material concerning Michener's veiled hints." Adams reported that Kleindienst was amenable to this suggestion and even told them that if the parents had evidence they wanted Justice Department attorneys to consider, that it should be submitted in some type of "substantive" form to David Norman, the attorney who succeeded Jerris Leonard as assistant attorney general in charge of the Civil Rights Division.

After that meeting Adams turned to Peter Davies, who for the past thirteen months had been conducting an investigation of his own. Davies had studied all the official reports, collected a number of photographs, and even talked to one or two witnesses.

In response to Adams' plea for help, Davies produced a 227-page analysis of the shootings, entitled "An Appeal to the United States Department of Justice For an Immediate and Thorough Investigation of the Circumstances Surrounding the Shootings at Kent State University, May 1970" (which later became known as "An Appeal for Justice").

Davies later told me he wrote the report working almost nonstop for six days. In his report he seized upon Michener's claim that the Guardsmen huddled on the practice football field and took the idea that there was a conspiracy a few steps further.

Davies alleged that there was definitely a conspiracy to shoot and that Myron G. Pryor, the sergeant who was photographed out in front of the troops intently aiming a pistol, may have instigated it on the practice football field by telling the other Guardsmen he would give a signal to shoot (the signal possibly being the firing of a pistol) once the troops returned to the top of Blanket Hill.

Davies wrote:

> This theory is neither unrealistic nor improbable. In fact, it is the only theory which explains how so many guardsmen suddenly wheeled around like a flock of birds turning, why all their fire was directed in a certain area over 300 feet away when many more students were so much closer to them, and why the National Guard has gone to any length, no matter how bizarre, to try and justify the shooting.

Davies' report, which argued that "the parents and the American people have a right to know the answers to all these questions," was hand-delivered to the Justice Department on June 21, 1971. A month went by in which there was no formal acknowledgment of the report, so Adams arranged to have the report published in the *Congressional Record* and released it publicly in an effort to pressure the Justice Department to commit itself one way or the other on whether a grand jury should be called.

The release of the report resulted in considerable publicity, including a spate of editorials demanding that the Justice Department quit procrastinating and make an announcement.

Nineteen congressmen also signed a letter to Attorney General Mitchell asking that a federal grand jury be convened.

August 13, 1971

A few months earlier Justice Department spokesmen had promised an announcement at "the appropriate time" on whether a federal grand jury would be empaneled.

The "appropriate time" turned out to be quite "appropriate" indeed. In announcing that there would be no investigation on August 13, 1971, Mitchell waited until:

- Fifteen months after the shootings had passed;
- Ten months after he had received orders from President Nixon not to convene the grand jury;

- 4:00 on a Friday afternoon in August—a month and time that would ensure that press coverage would be at a minimum;
  - "Safely after Congress had left town for the summer recess"; and
  - Most Kent State students were away on summer break, not on campus where newsmen might find them.

Interestingly, in his announcement, Mitchell admitted he agreed with the Scranton Commission's conclusion that the shootings were "unnecessary, unwarranted, and inexcusable." Yet he insisted there was nothing the Justice Department could do.

He summarily dismissed Davies' 227-page report in one sentence, saying there was "no credible evidence" that the Guardsmen conspired to shoot the students and "no likelihood of successful prosecution of individual Guardsmen" on charges they deprived the victims of their due process rights.

In a letter to the *Washington Post,* Reverend John Adams noted that there was no way Mitchell could determine whether or not there had been a conspiracy without first convening a grand jury and taking sworn statements from witnesses. Similarly, Adams noted, there was no way of determining there was "no likelihood of successful prosecution" until a "successful investigation" had been held.

FIVE

The Struggle for Justice

It is my hope that this tragic and unfortunate incident will strengthen the determination of all on
the nation's campuses—administrators, faculty
and students alike—to stand firmly for the right
which exists in this country of peaceful dissent
and just as strongly against the resort of violence
as a means of such expression.

– President Richard M. Nixon, in a statement
responding to the shootings, May 4, 1970

Until the late summer of 1971, I was just an interested observer, watching developments in the Kent State case from a distance and occasionally writing about them.

I had spent the previous year at UCLA, where as a staff reporter for
the *UCLA Daily Bruin* I had covered the coverup and reviewed some of
the early exploitation books.

As I wrote in my review of James Michener's book, even though
Michener had raised the specter of conspiracy, "the Justice Department's
Civil Rights Division has decided against convening a federal grand jury
on the killings. That decision needs only final approval from Attorney
General John Mitchell. That is as good as saying the case is closed."

I was so convinced that there would never be a full investigation that
after I decided to take a break from my studies and returned home to

Ohio, I threw away a bulging file of newspaper clippings and a year's worth of notes.

Then, on October 6, 1971, I read a small item in the *Akron Beacon Journal.* It seemed that as soon as classes had resumed for the fall quarter two students on campus had struck up a petition urging President Nixon to overrule the no-grand-jury decision that everyone thought John Mitchell had made himself.

I was shocked that after a year and a half anyone still cared.

According to the story: "Dormitory counselors Paul Keane and Greg Rambo began circulating the petitions at noon Monday. By 2:30 they had . . . collected 800 signatures."

After reading the story I tracked down Keane and Rambo and asked them for an interview. We set up an appointment for the following week.

In the meantime the petition continued to circulate on campus until over 10,300 students and faculty members signed it, making it the largest response to any petition ever circulated at Kent State.*

When I met with Keane and Rambo, I told them I admired what they were doing, but that I thought they were crazy if they thought Nixon would investigate the killing of students who were protesting his Cambodian invasion.

But Keane was inspired. He told me of his great vision for the petition—how it seemed to combine all the right ingredients—that, for example, Nixon was now openly wooing the newly enfranchised 18-to-21-year-olds, and he could no longer afford to treat college students like dirt.

Moreover, Nixon himself had said after the shooting that he hoped the tragedy would teach students not to resort to violence but to use peaceful processes when they sought a redress of their grievances.

That is exactly what Keane and Rambo were doing: exercising their right to petition the government for a real investigation.

How, Keane asked, could Nixon now turn around and ignore college students who were trying to make the system work?

---

*That is not to say that everybody at Kent State wanted the federal grand jury. Kent's radicals opposed it, feeling that a federal grand jury would not seriously investigate the Guardsmen's conduct and would instead only indict more protestors.

Tom Grace, one of the radical students on May 4, even called Keane a fool for "begging from the hand that bit you" and told Keane "the only way to get justice is to pick up a gun."

To give the petition added respectability, Keane had deliberately picked his friend Greg Rambo, the president of the Young Republicans on campus, as cosponsor.

It also happened that the new president of Kent State, Dr. Glenn A. Olds, was a former Nixon campaign aide who had connections in the White House. Keane and Rambo wrested a promise from Olds to help deliver the signatures to his friends in the White House if a majority of students on campus endorsed the petition (as a majority did within two weeks).

As skeptical as I was, I was quite impressed, seeing these students my own age virtually come out of nowhere, maneuver their way into the White House, and for the next several months have both the national and local press eating out of their hands.

On October 20, 1971, Olds accompanied Keane and Rambo to Washington, where the three presented the signatures to presidential adviser Leonard Garment. Olds told Garment the issue of accountability was still very much alive on the campus and that he could not get on with "the creative or innovative work of the University" until this matter of unfinished justice was resolved.

After Keane and Rambo returned from Washington, I kept in close touch with them. They related their stories of meetings with White House and Justice Department officials, with senators and congressmen, and especially with newspeople, most of whom supported them (except for one UPI reporter who asked Rambo why he was bothering: "Kent State does not sell newspapers anymore").

I got caught up in the excitement of it all. Their adventures were certainly a departure from everyday life.

So, on November 1, 1971, after Keane asked me if I would help them, I readily joined the cause.

November–December 1971

After the petitions were submitted to the White House, several people in the Nixon administration made encouraging statements:

Attorney General John Mitchell (in a December 20, 1971, letter to Ohio Congressman William Stanton): "I assure you that the petition is receiving careful consideration."

KSU President Glenn Olds (quoting Nixon confidant Don Kendall, the president of PepsiCo and a mutual friend): "The petition is top priority on the White House agenda."

Presidential adviser Leonard Garment (in response to a reporter's query, November 14, 1971): "The matter of a grand jury is now under consideration here [at the White House] and at the Department of Justice. I'd hope [for a response] within the next couple of weeks."

Garment again (on December 9, after state prosecutors dismissed charges against the 25 individuals indicted by the state grand jury): "The dropping of the charges could speed up the Justice Department's decision."

The Dismissal of the Kent 25 Cases

While the White House was supposedly considering the petition, the trials of the 25 individuals who were indicted by the "special" Ohio grand jury began in Portage County on November 22, 1971.

However, the first five cases to be tried (or disposed of out of court) brought the state only one conviction on a misdemeanor charge and two plea-bargained guilty pleas.

Then, on December 8, state prosecutors dropped a bombshell. They announced they were dropping the charges against the remaining 20 individuals.

The reason given by the new Ohio attorney general, William Brown, was that there was insufficient evidence to convict any of the remaining defendants.

That explanation—if taken at face value—meant that the state grand jury made at least twenty mistakes in indicting twenty individuals it did not have enough evidence against, and that all the criminal investigations that preceded the grand jury investigation (by the FBI, the Ohio Highway Patrol, and the Ohio Bureau of Criminal Investigation) failed to gather enough evidence to convict more than a few people.

Press accounts at the time tended to focus on the reactions of the indictees, most of whom claimed that the dismissals meant that they and the other students had done nothing wrong. While it is certainly possible that some of the indictments may have been defective, one really has to wonder why the student indictments were dismissed. There were, after all, many photographs showing identifiable students participating in the disturbances at Kent State and throwing rocks at the soldiers on May 4.

More importantly, the FBI, according to the Justice Department's summary of the FBI report, felt it had identified 13 individuals who were involved in the attempts to burn the ROTC building on May 2 and prevent the firemen from extinguishing the blaze.

The chart on the following page shows how the indictments of the Kent 25 turned out.

January-July 1972

Contrary to Garment's statement, the dropping of the Kent 25 indictments had no effect on the White House or the Justice Department's supposed reconsideration of a federal grand jury.

January went by without a response to the petition, and there was some speculation at the time that the decision was being held up until Richard Kleindienst replaced John Mitchell as attorney general. That way, some thought, a new attorney general could reopen the investigation, without placing Mitchell in a position to reverse himself.

However, on February 23, when Kleindienst appeared before the Senate Judiciary Committee for his confirmation hearings as attorney general, Kleindeinst said he was not even aware that the original decision was being reconsidered and that if he was confirmed as attorney general he would not "second-guess" John Mitchell.

Keane and William Hershey of the *Beacon Journal* immediately called Leonard Garment, who cautioned them not to attach too much significance to what Kleindienst said. Garment led Keane and Hershey to believe that Kleindienst was probably just unaware of the review, and that the man he (Garment) was working with at the Justice Department was David Norman, the new assistant attorney general in charge of the Civil Rights Division.

Garment promised there would be "a review and a response [to the petition] in a formal fashion by the administration" within a few weeks, and implied that the announcement was being held up until Nixon returned home from his historic trip to China.

Nixon went to China—and came back—but there was still no response to the petition by early March. On March 10, Keane called David Norman, the man who was supposed to be aware of the "review." According to Keane, Norman seemed to be only vaguely familiar with the

The Kent 25 Cases

Indictee	Charged With	Results
Jerry Rupe	Arson; first degree riot; striking a fireman; interfering with a firemen at an emergency scene	No witnesses were able to positively connect him with the fire. Convicted only on a misdemeanor charge he conceded to: hampering the firemen's efforts to douse the blaze.
Peter Bliek	Arson; first degree riot	Charges dropped in the absence of witnesses.
Larry Shub	Attempt to burn; first degree riot	Pled guilty to reduced charge of second degree riot. No trial held.
Thomas Fogelsong	First degree riot; interfering with a fireman	Same as Shub.
Mary Helen Nicholas	Interfering with a fireman	Confession ruled inadmissable. Charges dismissed.

Charges Dismissed Against

Richard Felber, Professor Thomas D. Lough, Craig Morgan, Douglas Cormack, Alan Canfora, Kenneth Hammond, James M. Riggs, Joseph B. Callum, Joseph Lewis, Jr., Ronald Weissenberger, Jeffrey Hartzler, John J. Gerbetz, Thomas D. Miller, Michael Steven Erwin, William Arthrell, David O. Adams, Rosemary Canfora, Ruth Gibson.

Sentencing

Rupe's six-month sentence ran concurrently with a separate 10-to-20-year sentence he was already serving on drug possession charges; so he did not spend any extra time in jail as a result of his activities at Kent State. Shub received probation. After the remaining 20 prosecutions were dropped, Fogelsong's attorney quietly withdrew his guilty plea and the state of Ohio agreed to enter a plea of "nolo prosequi" ("we will not prosecute you further") on his court records.

The end result: Not one person indicted by the "special" state grand jury went to jail as a result of any crime he or she may have committed.

petition and legal briefs that the petitioners had sent to the Justice Department.

Norman said: "We're getting a new attorney general in here and he might want to consider the petition after he is confirmed." However, Kleindienst had already said he would not reopen the case if he was confirmed.

It was clear the students were getting a real runaround.

In April the Justice Department's excuse for not responding to the petition was that the decision was now being held up by the Senate Judiciary Committee, which had not yet confirmed Kleindienst's confirmation as attorney general pending the outcome of its hearings on the ITT scandal.

The implication was that Kleindienst needed to be confirmed before making any decision. However, there was some testimony that Kleindienst, as acting attorney general, was making policy decisions in other cases during this period.

By May, the petitioners had given up hope of even receiving the courtesy of a response to their petition. Others had to press for an answer. During April, May, and June, Arthur Krause, the father of slain student Allison Krause, and Peter Davies, kept pressuring Garment for an answer. They besieged him with letters and phone calls.

On June 13, a reporter asked Kleindienst if the Kent State petition matter had ever been resolved. Kleindienst said he had always been opposed to a federal grand jury and that he could not even understand why anyone was asking the question.

But Krause still was not certain that Kleindienst's remarks at the press conference constituted the administration's formal response to the petition. After all, Garment had promised a public announcement.

Several months earlier, Garment had even told Rambo that he would give the students one day's advance notice of any announcement if the students promised not to leak the news to reporters.

By the end of June there still had not been a formal response from the White House, and Kleindienst was finally confirmed by the Senate. Finally, on July 6 Garment responded to a letter sent to him four months earlier and signed by the parents of the four slain students. In his response Garment echoed Kleindient's comments at the press conference that no one had shown Kleindienst "sufficient new evidence or information" to convince him to reverse Mitchell's decision.

Keane and Rambo only received carbon copies of Garment's letter and for a time were not sure that it was the administration's formal response to the petition.

Krause, though, was. He said sending them carbon copies of a letter was the Nixon administration's way of "telling the petitioners to go to hell."

In reaffirming the decision, the Nixon administration seemed to repeat its behavior of the previous year.

It became clear that the way the case was closed previously could not be viewed in isolation. A pattern of behavior seemed to emerge. That pattern suggested that the Nixon administration was going out of its way to bury the case.

Consider the following parallels:

ITEM: Garment acted exactly as Mitchell had a year earlier in trying to discourage any questioning of the no-grand-jury decision. Garment made no formal announcement.

The White House also mailed Garment's letter so it was timed to arrive during the middle of the week of the Democratic National Convention. At that point (and two and a half years after the shootings) who was supposed to pay attention?

ITEM: The letter was mailed during the dead of summer again—again during Kent State's summer break, and when students were not on campus to mount a vigorous protest.

ITEM: Garment and Kleindienst also ducked numerous subsequent requests from the petitioners and the parents of the dead students for personal meetings to explain the rationale behind the decision. Again . . . the secretiveness.

ITEM: The administration made the students wait an inordinate period of time before responding to the petitions.

The only difference in the delay between the first time the grand jury was ruled out, and the second time, was one month. Whereas John Mitchell had made the parents of the dead students wait ten months before making their announcement, the White House and Garment made the students wait only nine.

At one meeting in July 1972, KSU President (and former Nixon campaign aide) Glenn Olds told Keane and KSU student body president

Bob Gage that the White House was acting in such a peculiar manner that he (Olds) believed the White House "had something hidden in the box."

After reading Garment's letter, Keane, fearing that the petitions might end up in one of the now-infamous Nixon administration shredders, wrote to Garment asking that he return the 10,000 signatures.

In contrast to the previous nine-month delay, this time Garment responded promptly, returning the 25-pound package within ten days.

The petitions, of course, would be resubmitted the following year after Nixon started to go under because of Watergate.

However, in August of 1972, student body president Robert Gage perhaps best summed up the frustration of many students at Kent.

"All we can do now," he sighed, "is hope that some Guardsmen on his deathbed tells the truth."

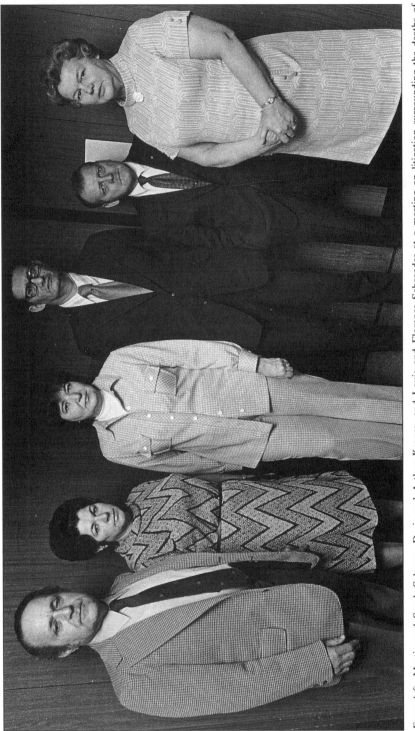

From left, Martin and Sarah Scheuer, Doris and Arthur Krause, and Louis and Florence Schroeder at a meeting on litigation surrounding the deaths of their children. Mrs. Elaine Miller was unavailable for the photo. (Photo by Greg Santos.)

Peter Davies. (Photo by *Akron Beacon Journal.*)

Weed-strewn and rock-cluttered, the informal memorial garden for the four slain students is cleaned by Paul Keane (left) and Greg Rambo, who then planted four memorial plants. (Photo by Greg Santos.)

SIX

The Struggle for Justice
(Continued)

> Kent State, the bitter climax to the campus rebellion, is about to pass into history.
> – *Time* magazine, December 20, 1971

Certainly if the Nixon administration and the state of Ohio had their way, the Kent State shootings and all the issues of equal justice and accountability they raised would have quietly faded into history.

However, they did not. Kent State was one of those issues that seemed to have a life of its own.

As the Cleveland *Plain Dealer* put it, it absolutely refused to "stay quiet in its grave."

Kent State refused to remain buried not because the ACLU or any political organization kept demanding that the Guardsmen be prosecuted, or because the "eastern establishment" suddenly wanted to do something about civil liberties, as an aide to Governor Rhodes once remarked.

Nor did it magically reopen as a consequence to the Watergate scandal, as one KSU professor seemed to imply.

It is true that the investigation never would have been reopened had Nixon's crimes not been exposed, destroying his ability to control the Justice Department. Eventually Justice Department officials defied Nixon's orders and reopened the investigation on their own.

However, the system did not automatically work by itself. It was not as if the Department suddenly woke up three years after the fact and realized: "Gee, we forgot about Kent State."

The Justice Department had to be forced (yes, forced) into reopening its investigation.

And that is why there was eventually a grand jury and a prosecution of the National Guardsmen.

Without that constant pressure on the Justice Department, it seems highly unlikely that the federal prosecutors would have reopened the investigation on their own initiative, as one of the prosecutors would later claim.

The pressure on the Justice Department to reopen the case was unrelenting, and it was one of several important reasons why the Department was ultimately forced to convene the grand jury.

There were, of course, other reasons. Among them:

• There were renewed questions about a possible conspiracy to shoot the students. Davies' book was published in September 1973, and his charges that the shootings were deliberate received considerable attention at the time;

• A U.S. House Judiciary Subcommittee suddenly took an interest in charges that Terry Norman, an undercover operative for the FBI, may have started the shooting—a charge that linked the FBI itself to May 4;

• The Subcommittee, which also had oversight responsibility for the Department of Justice, threatened to investigate, and possibly hold public hearings to examine the Department's reasons for closing the case;

• There was new blood within the Justice Department itself; including a new attorney general and a new head of the Civil Rights Division, both of whom were receptive to demands that the investigation be held; and

• A Justice Department attorney made a crucial slip of the tongue that rekindled both the national and local media's interest in the case.

Ultimately, though, the case was reopened because the people who demanded the grand jury were incredibly persistent, resourceful, and talented public relations practitioners who knew how to effectively raise questions, capture the imagination of the press, and keep the issue alive.

By the time the third anniversary of the shootings rolled around, very few people, including myself, realistically believed a grand jury would be held. At that time the student newspaper, the *Daily Kent Stater,* was the only newspaper in the country still calling for an investigation.

Leonard Schwartz, an ACLU attorney, speaking at a panel discussion on the eve of the anniversary, predicted: "We're never going to see a federal grand jury in our lifetime . . . It's an impossible dream."

THE STRUGGLE FOR JUSTICE (CONTINUED)   131

That "dream" became a reality because there were just enough dreamers around who ignored the conventional wisdom, who refused to get discouraged in the face of great odds, and who believed they were doing the right thing.

I. F. Stone later wrote: "Convocation of the grand jury shows that no cause is ever hopeless if there are men around with enough heart to keep fighting. I never dreamt the case would be reopened. Above all it is a tribute to Arthur Krause and Peter Davies that we are finally getting the grand jury. It is an extraordinary victory for a tiny handful of dedicated people and a moral lesson for all of us."

"Tiny handful" was an apt phrase. Other than Arthur Krause, Peter Davies, Paul Keane, and Greg Rambo, there were only a few individuals who were consistently active or who made significant contributions to what journalist Bill Moyers called in one of his PBS Journals "the struggle for justice."

There was the Reverend John P. Adams of the United Methodist Church in Washington. He arranged the meetings between the parents' attorneys and the Justice Department. He distributed Davies' conspiracy report, acted as a counselor and go-between for the parents, and worked behind the scenes in many other important ways.

Another person who made a significant contribution was Dean Kahler, the most seriously wounded survivor of the shootings. Dean was shot in the spine and will spend the rest of his life in a wheelchair.

There were also Krause's two attorneys, David Engdahl and Steven Sindell, who made many contributions beyond handling the victims' legal affairs. Engdahl and Sindell wrote numerous articles drawing attention to the business of unfinished justice. At one point they even filed a suit in the U.S. District Court in Washington, accusing the Justice Department of acting in bad faith in closing the case and asking a federal judge to compel the Department to conduct a grand jury.

Later, the parents of the other dead students became active in seeking the grand jury by speaking out, writing letters to editors, and making pleas for an investigation of their children's deaths on radio and TV.

However, by and large, these were the eight individuals who played the most significant roles in getting the Guardsmen prosecuted.*

----

*None of the other wounded students and no one on the Kent State faculty pushed for the investigation.

Of the main players, two merit special mention. One is Paul Keane. Keane was the one who really squeezed the maximum mileage out of the petitions, engendering approximately forty articles in national and local newspapers as well as numerous radio and TV interviews over a two-year period. He concocted schemes which, in his own words, "forced the press to report me."

One of his gimmicks was to form Pop's Snow Squad, a volunteer snow shoveling service for a 72-year-old Kent school crossing guard. The squad was staffed by student volunteers to get up in the wee hours of the morning to shovel five blocks of sidewalks in town, enabling "Pop" to get to work.

The University loved the publicity because the Snow Squad demonstrated that not all Kent State students were radicals. Jim Bruss, the director of the University's news service, said the Snow Squad was one of the best stories ever to come out of Kent State.

CBS News' "On the Road" reporter Charles Kuralt thought so, too. Kuralt made the Snow Squad his Christmas story in 1972, and even today cites Keane as an example of American decency.

It was no coincidence that the crossing guard, "Pop" Fisher, was one of the few Kent residents who spoke out against the shootings and who blasted Governor Rhodes for even calling out the Guard. And it was no coincidence that Kuralt found out about the story. Keane had asked me to write to Kuralt and plug the Snow Squad.

In one of his other escapades Keane joined student radicals protesting the Kent 25 trials—only he took a different tack. Borrowing a trick he learned from his friend, tax crusader Vivien Kellems, Keane resorted to sheer eccentricity to capture the attention of the press.

Dressed in a three-piece suit, Keane stood outside the Portage County courthouse in subzero weather with a sign saying: $137,000 of *your* TAX MONEY is being WASTED."

While radicals yelled "Ho, ho, Ho Chi Minh," Keane built a snowman to hold up his tax sign. The mayor of Ravenna came out of his office to offer Keane a bowl of chicken soup and somebody (undoubtedly Keane!) tipped off the *Akron Beacon Journal* about that.

During the first week of May 1972, Keane called Garry Trudeau, the creator of "Doonesbury," and asked him to write a comic strip to run on the second anniversary of May 4. Trudeau complied, and the editorial content of the strip, chiding Mitchell for not convening the grand jury, caused the *Beacon Journal* to withhold it, thus creating a furor over censorship and keeping May 4 in the news.

Keane was also responsible for establishing the Kent State archives at Yale and for pressuring the Kent State administration into setting aside a special room in its main library—a room known as "The May 4 Resource Center." The University resisted the idea originally, then tried to hide the Center in a closet-size out-of-the-way room on the third floor of the library, but Keane demanded that they put it on the first floor.

(One KSU professor, referring to the University's renowned insensitivity to the victims and its long-time indifference to preserving the memory of the event, once asked another: "Does Kent State have a conscience?" The other answered: "Yes, Paul Keane.")

The other person deserving special mention is Peter Davies. From the day of the shootings, Davies launched into a holy crusade—a never-ending battle for "truth and justice" the American way.

Only he did not look like Superman. He was not much taller than a jockey, had a middle-aged receding hairline, and was painfully shy in person.

More than any other individual, Davies was responsible for getting the Guardsmen prosecuted.

He also significantly shaped and influenced the public's view of the shooting, as well as the resultant public debate.

Davies was a stubborn man . . . a dedicated man . . . and a self-righteous one, too. As the title of his book reflects, he always thought he knew *The Truth About Kent State.*

Davies was a 40-year-old Staten Island insurance broker who had immigrated to England in 1957 because he felt his native land was becoming too socialistic. He had a wife, three young sons, and his own business selling insurance.

It is easy to understand why the parents of the dead students, or young, idealistic students like Keane and Rambo became involved in this issue. Davies was different, though. Before May 4, 1970, he had no connection with the University. In fact, like most Americans, he had never even heard of Kent State. He did not know any of the victims. He was old enough to be their father, yet, as a reporter for *Life* magazine put it, he "plunged almost heedlessly into the investigation, neglecting both his business and family . . . He spent evenings, weekends and at least half of each working day doing research . . . In expenses and insurance business lost, this personal investigation cost Davies thousands he could ill afford."

Davies had an especially strong emotional reaction to the death of Allison Krause. He spoke and wrote about her frequently. Once he sent a letter to his friends saying that he would never give up trying to get justice, that in some strange way he felt Allison's presence, and that Allison's death had somehow changed his life.

I later learned that Davies' obsession with Allison Krause was part of a pattern. In 1965 Davies launched into what *Life* called "a quixotic public dispute when a New York secretary was convicted of carrying a concealed weapon after pulling a tear gas pen from her purse to fight off an attacker. Davies joined enthusiastically in a public deluge of protest, and the girl was let off. Davies felt he had helped."

In 1974, Davies also rushed to the defense of Patty Hearst after she participated in the robbery of a Hibernia, California, bank. After examining bank photographs Davies theorized that Hearst was forced to participate in the robbery because her weapon seemed to be strapped on in such a way that she could not discard it without first taking off her jacket.

He suggested that the Symbionese Liberation Army, which had kidnapped her, dressed her in that way so that, if she refused to participate in the robbery, the SLA could shoot her.

Never one to consider less conspiratorial explanations when more sinister ones were available, it apparently never occurred to Davies that perhaps Hearst dressed in that manner so her machine gun could not be spotted when she walked into the bank.

Davies lost a number of supporters in the news media when Hearst herself issued a communique to a radio station insisting that she willingly joined in on the robbery and denounced her father, newspaper magnate Randolph A. Hearst, as a pig.

Davies' papers in the Yale archives give a clue to his obsessions. In a letter to a friend, Davies reported that, as a 17-year-old boy in England, he had happened to be in a burlesque theater when a dancer, whose face had been bloodied by a razor, was being carried away on a stretcher. Davies believed that she and the other dancers were attacked by hoodlums from a bookmaking ring who were apparently trying to collect a debt from the owners of the show. The hoods victimized the girls, and Davies was horrified by what he had witnessed. He said he was haunted for life.

Although we always felt that his conspiracy theory deserved to be investigated by a grand jury, Davies' obsession with Allison Krause constantly made Rambo and me wonder how much his emotions crept into his theories.

I was particularly disillusioned when I discovered that at the time he wrote his conspiracy report, he had never set foot in Ohio, much less visited the campus.

By the time his book was published two years later, Davies had spent only fifteen minutes on the campus. This was significant because part of his theory was based on the Guards' relationship to certain physical objects on the campus, and the peculiar topography of the hill.

Despite his shortcomings, Davies' motives were altruistic. He was sometimes criticized for exploiting the shootings for financial gain, a criticism that was completely unjustified.

He had contempt for the student photographers—"the vultures," he used to call them—who tried to get, and often succeeded in getting, exorbitant fees for the use of their pictures.

When NBC commissioned its docudrama on the tragedy, the network paid James Michener and another author, neither of whom shared Davies' insatiable thirst for justice, $400,000 for the right to use their books.

NBC eventually relied most heavily on Davies' work, and when I asked the executive producer on the program how much the network had paid Davies, the producer answered, "Nothing."

Davies had not asked for a cent.

SEVEN

Reopening the Investigation

> I want the American people—I want you to
> know—beyond a shadow of a doubt that during
> my term as President, justice will be pursued fair-
> ly, fully and impartially.
> – President Richard M. Nixon, promising to get to
> the bottom of the Watergate scandal, in a
> nationwide address, April 30, 1973

> It's our turn to receive some of the same justice
> they are handing out.
> – Florence Schroeder, mother of William
> Schroeder (one of the four fatalities),
> May 1, 1973

To understand how the Justice Department was forced to reopen its investigation, let us go back to the spring of 1973 and look at the climate
in Washington.

It was a time when the most sensational allegations were made daily
against the president, the vice president, the director of the FBI, two of
Nixon's attorneys general, his lawyers, his chief of staff, his chief domestic adviser, and many other top officials in the White House.

Telltale tracks leading from the Watergate burglary to the Oval Office made it clear that the Nixon administration was thoroughly corrupt.

On April 30, 1973, Nixon appeared on national television and announced that he had accepted the resignations of his chief of staff, H. R. Haldeman, his chief domestic adviser, John Ehrlichman, his attorney general, Richard Kleindienst, and that he had fired his turncoat counsel, John Dean.

Nixon also announced two other changes: Leonard Garment, the presidential counselor who handled the petitions, assumed John Dean's job as Nixon's legal counsel, and Elliot Richardson moved over to the Justice Department to become Nixon's third attorney general.

The change of personnel gave some renewed hope that there might be a reevaluation of what everyone thought at the time was the Justice Department's decision not to convene the grand jury.

On May 1 the parents of the slain students, accompanied by their attorneys, took the occasion to renew their grand jury demands.

In Kent, Keane and Rambo decided to resubmit the petition. Keane figured that if Nixon's aides kept Watergate a secret from him, as Nixon was claiming, maybe they never told him about the petition.

On that day Keane called me and asked if I would help him draft a press release to announce they were going to resubmit the petitions to the White House.

"It's a good publicity stunt," I told him, "but you are crazy if you think it's going to get you anywhere."

Keane did not have anything to say to that, but he did prevail on me to get together with him and Rambo at the Kent Motor Inn. (By that time, Keane had already graduated from Kent.)

Keane also asked Dean Kahler, the student who was paralyzed in the shootings, to join in this effort. In his wheelchair, Kahler was a powerful symbol of the shootings, and Keane wanted to take advantage of any publicity edge he could get.

Keane, Rambo and I then hammered out a press release, which all of us (except perhaps Keane) realized was utterly ridiculous at the time. In the release we accused John Mitchell and Richard Kleindienst of a "premeditated obstruction of justice," and asked that Nixon make the decision on whether to convene the grand jury himself and not send the petitions back to the Department of Justice.

Keane wanted Kahler to read the statement at a press conference and then break down and cry in front of the cameras, but Kahler did not respond to Keane's coaching. In fact, Kahler never seemed to show any trace of anger or bitterness toward the people who were responsible for his condition.

On May 3 Keane and Rambo invited a small entourage of reporters over to President Olds' office, where the two had earlier scheduled a meeting to ask Olds if he would again take them to Washington. Keane and Rambo tried to corner him in front of the press.

Olds refused to be pinned down publicly, but he privately telephoned Elliot Richardson, an old acquaintance, and asked Richardson to reopen the investigation. Olds also warned Leonard Garment that, if the White House did not agree to meet with the petitioners again, Kahler would appear outside the White House gates. Kahler had threatened to bang on the gates with his wheelchair if Garment did not agree to meet with them.

On May 9 Keane, Rambo and Kahler left for Washington, even though at that point they had been unable to arrange a definite appointment with anyone in the White House. When they arrived the students were able to meet with Leonard Garment's deputy, Bradley Patterson, and Deputy Assistant Attorney General K. William O'Connor. Although the students did not know it at the time, O'Connor was the Justice Department official who originally had recommended that the Department close the case "without prosecutive action."

Keane, Rambo and Kahler again submitted the 10,000 petitions and the accompanying legal briefs and (according to Keane), Patterson apologized profusely for not answering the petitions the first time they were submitted. He said, "Leonard wanted to meet with you, but he was too busy Watergating."

Then, after accepting the petitions, Patterson left for another meeting he had to attend, leaving the students in the room with O'Connor. As they were talking, Keane asked O'Connor why the Justice Department could not just convene the grand jury. That was when O'Connor made his fateful slip by conceding that the Justice Department *already* had enough evidence to prosecute the Guardsmen.

Having said that, O'Connor added he still opposed empaneling a grand jury because he felt any resultant prosecutions were doomed to fail. According to Keane, O'Connor cited an analogy of another shooting incident in which a law enforcement officer shot a protestor who had his hands in his pockets, who was obviously defenseless and posing no threat to the sheriff. Despite that clear-cut evidence, O'Connor said the Justice Department was unable to persuade a grand jury to return an indictment against the sheriff.

A brief but civil argument ensued in which the students pleaded with O'Connor. They told him not to prejudge what might happen during a grand jury and said in effect: "Why don't you give the system a chance?"

But O'Connor stuck to his guns. The students left the meeting angry and dejected.

May 11-17, 1973

Although O'Connor still opposed the convening of a federal grand jury, he did at least provide an impetus to reopen the case.

As soon as the students left the meeting with him, they headed straight for a press conference that had been arranged by the Reverend John P. Adams to announce the concession O'Connor had made: that there was enough evidence to prosecute the Guardsmen.

In Ohio and elsewhere the statement made front page news. When reporters called O'Connor to see why he still opposed a grand jury, he seemed to backtrack somewhat and cite more reasons why he felt a grand jury would be an exercise in futility. For example, in an interview with the *Washington Post,* O'Connor called the evidence against the soldiers "pretty thin stuff." O'Connor also claimed that, in all probability, the government would never be able to secure convictions sustainable upon appeal.

O'Connor also told the *Daily Kent Stater:* "The most any Guardsmen could be indicted for would be a misdemeanor," and suggested that would be like issuing a traffic ticket to the Guardsmen.

It seemed to me that O'Connor was dead wrong when he suggested the Guardsmen could only be prosecuted for misdemeanors. He did not mention a provision in the law passed by Congress in 1968 providing for felony prosecution under the statute he was referring to, Section 242 of the U.S. Code (the deprivation of civil rights law).

On May 16 I called O'Connor to confirm that Section 242 was indeed the same statute O'Connor was alluding to. As I later wrote in a letter to Keane:

> I pointed out that the statute was amended in 1968 to be a felony, so he replied: "If death results." I countered: "There was death at Kent State." Then he said the problem would be that a specific Guardsman would have to be linked to a specific student and that intent would have to be proved.

Of course, no one in the Justice Department had ever before said that the Guard could only be prosecuted for misdemeanors. O'Connor's comment to the *Daily Kent Stater* sounded like just another excuse not to hold the investigation.

O'Connor also did not do a very good job convincing many of the newspapers. After he made his statement and gave his explanations there was still a spate of editorials calling for the federal grand jury to be held.

May 25-30, 1973

This time the White House did not wait very long to answer the petition. Circumstances dictated that they act fast.

Not only were they faced with renewed demands for the grand jury, but a high-level Justice Department official had just publicly admitted that there was sufficient evidence to indict the Guardsmen. Moreover, a new, independent-minded attorney general was coming in and he could very well ignore Nixon's directive.

On May 25, the same day Elliot Richardson's nomination as attorney general was being voted on by the Senate, the White House rushed out its response.

Leonard Garment sent a letter to Keane, Rambo, and Kahler, saying: "The answer on convening a Federal Grand jury is negative," and citing "all the reasons Mr. O'Connor gave you."

The letter stated:

> Of all these reasons, I think one stands: It was our unanimous judgment if a Grand Jury were convened, it would either bring no indictments, or indictments which would only result in acquittal, either or both of which would be counterproductive to the objectives you yourself are pursuing.

Garment, in his letter, tried to offer some consolation by saying that "law enforcement officers nearly everywhere . . . are now better trained and more inclined to act with the maximum possible restraint in handling civil disturbances. Let this be the lesson of Kent State."

The *Daily Kent Stater* saw the lesson differently. It editorialized:

> Mr. Garment, the lesson we have been taught involves a morally bankrupt Administration, a dismissal of civil liberties, and a slap in the faces of people who tried to force the system to work.
>
> No, we will not forget.

June 9, 1973

The commencement exercises held at Kent on June 9, 1973, seemed to underscore the "apparent reality" that the Kent State case was forever closed.

Not only had the White House denied a grand jury for a third time, but (with very few exceptions) the last of the students who were on campus in 1970 were graduating with the class of 1973. With a new generation of students coming in, there would not be anyone around to ask again for a real investigation.

However, none of the people who were pushing the hardest for the investigation were prepared to give up even after this third strike.

Peter Davies later said: "Believe it or not, we [Arthur Krause, John Adams and Davies] were determined to go to 1976," when a new president would be in office and possibly overrule Nixon's decision.

Keane wrote to Leonard Garment again and demanded that Garment return the boxful of petitions a second time.

In what seemed like wishful thinking, he sent me a note saying: "If Nixon is impeached, we can use these signatures again."

June 13, 1973

On June 13 we learned that the prospect of an investigation had not been ruled out at all—despite the letter Garment sent reaffirming Nixon's decision.

Elliot Richardson, who had just been confirmed as attorney general, sent a letter to KSU President Olds saying that the new head of the Civil Rights Division, J. Stanley Pottinger, was "taking a fresh look at the Kent State issue" to determine if Attorney General John Mitchell had acted properly in closing the case. And Richardson had approved this new review of the decision.

Two days after this information was made public, it became apparent why the Justice Department had experienced this sudden change of heart. The House Judiciary Subcommittee on Civil Rights and Civil Liberties, chaired by Congressman Don Edwards, had finally responded to requests from Davies, the Kent State student government, and others to conduct an investigation into the Justice Department's handling of the case.

As Pat Englehart, who directed the *Beacon Journal's* coverage, put it: "The Justice Department is running scared shit."

June 15, 1973

On June 15, 1973, Pottinger held a press conference in which he confirmed that he was reviewing the Justice Department's files on the case. Pottinger claimed that he had actually begun reviewing the FBI files back in April before anyone had even asked Elliot Richardson to reopen the case, and that his review was triggered by a letter "from an investigative reporter who claimed to have new evidence."

As Pottinger told it: "I asked the staff, 'What is this?'. . . I was reminded that we were approaching the third anniversary. I was also told that we should expect a number of inquiries from parents, from citizens, from congressmen, from investigative reporters, from a whole panoply of interested parties. I felt that I had better . . . familiarize myself with this case."

That explanation seemed reasonable enough, but it did not explain why, if he was still reviewing the files in mid-May, the White House shut the lid on Kent State before Pottinger's review was complete.

Pottinger suggested that there was just a breakdown of communications between the White House and Justice Department and that what happened was that Garment's office called his office to see "if we had any grounds to reopen the Kent State case." Pottinger's office told the White House no, because at that time Pottinger was still reviewing the file; his review had not been completed yet.

However, that still did not explain why the White House ignored Pottinger's ongoing review and rushed out a letter falsely claiming there was a unanimous decision not to hold a federal grand jury. The White House could have waited until Pottinger had completed his review or stalled for time (as it did in both 1971 and 1972). Instead of telling the petitioners: "Hold on. Pottinger is reading the reports and making up his mind," the White House sent out a letter which emphatically stated: "No! You can't have the grand jury! Everyone agrees with us. Now, get lost."

It appeared that the real reason the White House rushed out the letter was to discourage Pottinger and Richardson from reopening the case by presenting them with a *fait accompli,* thus putting Pottinger and Richardson in a position where they would be disinclined to consider a decision made three times.

Nathan Lewin, a highly respected Washington attorney and columnist for *The New Republic,* also suspected that Pottinger was not telling the whole story on another point: his own motivation for reopening the case. Lewin had served as the deputy attorney general in the Civil Rights Division during Lyndon Johnson's presidency, holding the position one notch below Pottinger's in the Department hierarchy.

Lewin wrote in *The New Republic* that "it was most unusual for a new division head to reexamine decisions fully considered by his predecessors." In this case, the Kent State investigation had been closed by not one but two previous heads of the Civil Rights Division.

Lewin wrote that:

Suspicious minds may wonder in light of the recent revelations of the role that partisan politics played in Mr. Mitchell's Department of Justice, whether there is not a skeleton rattling in this closet, and whether the renewed interest in Kent State was designed to head off some startling disclosures as to how or why the case was initially quashed. What makes the circumstances all the more suspicious is that the August 1971 decision [not to prosecute the Guardsmen] was so plainly out of keeping with what the Civil Rights Division was doing at the time in less publicized cases and so completely unjustified as a matter of law that it is difficult to believe that it could have been reached in good faith.

In his article Lewin cited a number of instances in which the Civil Rights Division had prosecuted law enforcement officials for official misuse of power "even after the Kent State investigation was closed," and asked:

Why, in light of this consistent policy, did Mr. Mitchell refuse to call together a federal grand jury that could hear sworn testimony in the Kent State case? Did the explanation that there could be "no successful prosecution of individual Guardsmen" mask some aspect of the case—apart from the evidence of guilt or innocence—that made prosecution impossible? The recent disclosure that Terry Norman, identified in the published FBI reports as a "freelance photographer" who was carrying a weapon, was an undercover infiltratormay simply be the tip of the iceberg. Might there have been other embarrassing information that the prosecution would have been compelled to disclose if it had indicted the Guardsmen?

June-July 1973

Between June 15 and August 3 the public and media pressure on the Justice Department to reopen its investigation remained steady, although by no means overwhelming, as Pottinger continued his review.

The House Judiciary Subcommittee pursued its preliminary investigation, sending staff members to Kent to interview various individuals, including Rambo, Kahler, and me, about various experiences we'd had with Justice Department officials.

The Subcommittee, the *Akron Beacon Journal,* and Trudy Rubin of the *Christian Science Monitor* also began new investigations of the incident involving Terry Norman.

At this point, reporters were still trying to figure out if Norman had any involvement in the shootings itself.

We knew this much. We knew that only a few moments after the Guardsmen fired, Norman had been involved in a fight with some students. During the scuffle Norman drew a .38 caliber pistol, which he had kept concealed under a sports coat, brandished the weapon at the students, and then ran across the length of the Commons to police and National Guard lines, where the pistol was confiscated.

We knew that as he was being chased a man clutching a briefcase (later identified as Harold Reid) yelled: "Stop that man! He has a gun. He fired four shots!"

Since Norman was the only person other than a Guardsman known to have been armed on May 4, he figured prominently in speculation immediately after the shootings that he may have been the so-called sniper the Guard tried to blame the shootings on.

In fact, a few students had told the FBI that Norman had fired his gun "at students just prior to the time the Guardsmen fired." Investigators had initially discounted those claims, largely on the basis of assurances by KSU Detective Tom Kelley, who examined the pistol and reported it "was fully loaded and had not been fired."

Kelley and former KSU Police Chief Donald Schwarztmiller also denied they had any working relationship with Norman. However, as we discovered in the summer of 1973, the campus police had lied about that. Kelley ultimately admitted that Norman had not only taken pictures for him on May 4, but that Kelley had even provided Norman with three rolls of film.

Kelley's claims that Norman's gun had not been fired also were undermined when two witnesses surfaced whose stories suggested that Norman may have fired his gun at some point.

Neither of the witnesses had actually seen Norman fire his gun, but both were standing by the burned down ROTC building after the shootings. These witnesses had watched Kelley take possession of Norman's gun and open the barrel. One of the witnesses, the Guard's public information officer, Sergeant Michael Delaney, claimed he overheard Norman say: "I had to shoot."

Both Delaney and NBC newsman Fred DeBrine insisted that they both overheard Kelley blurt out: "My God! He fired four times. What the hell do we do now?"

Most of the investigations conducted at this point focused not only on Delaney and DeBrine's stories, but on Norman's work as an undercover informant. Some newsmen were convinced that, after leaving Kent State, Norman went on to perform undercover assignments for the Washington, D.C. police.

One of the main reasons the Subcommittee and the newspapers suddenly became interested in Norman was because FBI *provocateurs* surfaced in several other highly publicized cases involving political protest.

The thought occurred to quite a few people that Terry Norman may have been a government *provocateur* too.

Late July 1973

During this period the House Subcommittee investigators also took advantage of a unique opportunity to question the FBI about its investigation of Norman's activities and their then-rumored relationship with him.

In mid-June Nixon had to nominate a new FBI director to replace L. Patrick Gray, who was forced to resign from office for destroying crucial Watergate evidence. Nixon's nominee was Clarence Kelley, the chief of police of Kansas City, and Kelley's nomination had to be approved by the Senate Judiciary Committee.

At the request of Pat Shea, an investigator for the House Judiciary Subcommittee, Senator Birch Bayh of the Senate Judiciary Committee submitted a list of questions about Terry Norman to Kelley.

Shea wanted to know, among other things:

• Did Terry Norman ever work for the FBI as an informant?
• Was he specifically working for them on May 4, 1970?
• Did the FBI ever interview him after May 4?, and
• Were any ballistics tests ever conducted on his gun?

On July 24, Kelley responded to the list of questions. He insisted that Norman had not been working for the Bureau on May 4. That answer, however, was undoubtedly not true. Later, a statement that Norman gave to the KSU police surfaced in which he specifically said he had been taking pictures "for Detective Tom Kelley of the Campus Police Department and Bill Chapin of the FBI Akron office."

FBI Chief Kelley did concede, however, that one month before the shootings, the FBI had used Norman to spy on a neo-Nazi group "for which he received a cash payment of $125."

Kelley also insisted that the FBI had never run a ballistics test on Norman's gun to determine if it had been fired.

That statement was also untrue. FBI files released in 1977 proved that a lab test had been conducted, which demonstrated that Norman's gun had indeed been fired since it had been last cleaned.

Unfortunately, there was no way of telling from the test where Norman had fired the gun, or if he fired it on May 4.

In any event, news stories about Kelley's answers to these questions were reprinted all over Ohio, and perhaps the luckiest break of all in the reopening of the case happened as a result.

The stories triggered a reaction by National Guard Captain John Martin, who had commanded some of the troops on Blanket Hill. Martin had long been troubled by Norman's role. He decided to write to Bayh and share what he knew about the incident.

Martin wrote:

On May 4, 1970, I was in command of Company A, 145th Infantry, of which 54 men were involved in the "skirmish line." It was through my men that Terry Norman returned after the shooting incident in which four students were killed. Although I did not personally apprehend him, the incident came immediately to my attention and I attempted to gather all the information I could on the matter. Without any formal investigative capabilities, I was only able to gather statements from my own men and tried to relate these to the official investigative bodies which I came in contact with.

Along with this letter Martin sent Bayh eyewitness accounts from two of his men who watched Norman surrender his gun. And one of the soldiers, Sergeant Richard L. Day, thought he heard Norman admitting shooting a student who started to beat him up.

Amazingly, Martin also reported that:

The FBI seemed to show no interest whatsoever in these statements whenever I reported them . . . I always wondered if the gun which the FBI checked was actually the one Norman turned over on May 4 [to the Kent State police].

On August 3, Bayh held a press conference in which he released Martin's letter and the accompanying statements from the Guardsmen.

Bayh added his own charge: that Terry Norman may have been "the fatal catalyst" for the shootings.

Bayh also accused the FBI of running a "shoddy show" for not fully investigating Norman's role on May 4.

Two hours after Bayh made his accusations, Pottinger held a press conference of his own in which he announced the Justice Department would now conduct what he called "an additional investigation" of the shootings. That meant that Pottinger would not just review the FBI files, but that Department lawyers would also start asking questions and interview people outside of their offices.*

August 2, 1973 (The Crewdson Connection)

One of the strangest incidents in the aftermath of the shootings also began to unfold on the afternoon before Pottinger announced his "additional investigation."

The incident is one of those wild cards that somehow seems to fits into the larger mosaic of the Justice Department's behavior. But exactly how it fits—and what it means—remains a mystery even today.

---

*As for Terry Norman, Bayh's charges resulted in sensational front-page stories that kept Norman in the local and national headlines for about a week. Most of these stories tended to cast doubt on the possibility that he did anything to initiate the Guard's volley. For instance, the *Akron Beacon Journal* published Norman's statement to Ohio Highway Patrol investigators in which Norman denied firing his weapon, and an eyewitness account that for the first time supported Norman's claim that he only drew the pistol after the shootings and after a student jumped him. This interview was particularly important, because it was conducted with the student who admitted lunging at Norman. The student, Thomas Masterson, said he vented his own anger over the shootings on Norman.

Sources close to Norman (probably his lawyer) also suggested that the Ohio Guard was trying to set up Norman as "a fall guy" in the investigation in order to divert attention from the action of their own soldiers.

The story, at least for me, began about 5:00 P.M. on August 2, when I received a telephone call from Peter Davies, who told me he was in "a state of shock."

Davies said he had just had a "wild conversation" with a reporter for the *New York Times,* who Davies had called to tip him off about Pottinger's press conference scheduled for the next day.

Since what Davies related to me was essentially the same as what he later wrote in an article for *The Village Voice* ("Another White House Horror Story," November 8, 1973), I am going to quote directly from his article.

But I am only going to quote the statements I was subsequently able to confirm were said.

Davies wrote:

> I had an amazing, and deeply distressing, phone conversation with a highly respected Washington correspondent with the *New York Times.* What he said literally left me momentarily stunned. This man had long been sympathetic toward my efforts in this issue and, on occasion, was extremely helpful. To compound my confusion was the fact that I had initiated the telephone call for the purpose of informing him about the forthcoming news conference the next day, August 3.
>
> As best as I can recall, his remarks went something like this: I know about the Pottinger press conference. As a friend I have to suggest that you let Kent State die. There is information in the hands of the government which could cause the parents of the dead students far greater pain if revealed by a full investigation than the pain they are suffering now from (having) no investigation at all. . .
>
> Despite my pleas, and a follow-up phone call, he adamantly refused to elaborate. All he said was that his advice was based on his "judgment" of what he had seen or been told by government officials.

The conversation was very strange, and it was difficult to imagine what kind of information the reporter could be referring to.

The Justice Department had been acting as if it were covering something up—but what could the "pain to the parents" be that this reporter was alluding to?

What kind of information could hurt the parents that much? And even if there was damaging information in government files about one of the students, why would the information reflect on the others?

I was even more confused the following day when Pottinger announced his "additional inquiry." I suspected that the Department was only taking this step because Senator Bayh had forced their hand with his accusation against Terry Norman, and that the Department really wanted to close the investigation again, but now had to stall for time.

Then that afternoon, August 3, another bizarre incident happened that somehow seemed related to the conversation Davies had with the reporter. I was sitting in the student government offices in Kent, serving as a press agent for Paul Keane, Greg Rambo, and Dean Kahler, answering reporters' inquiries, and giving them our reactions to Pottinger's announcement.

While I was doing this I noticed that Kahler was carrying on a very odd conversation with a reporter on another line. Kahler seemed to be struggling with some of the questions; so I picked up the phone and introduced myself.

The reporter at the other end identified himself as Don Shuble of WBBM Radio in Chicago. Shuble asked if anyone had investigated the background of the four students who were killed. He had heard a rumor that one of the fatalities was a secret government *provocateur.*

A few days later I talked to Davies again. This time he identified the *Times* reporter he had talked to as John Crewdson.

I had never heard the name before, but I found out soon afterward that his beat was the Justice Department and the FBI and that he was very good.

At the time all I knew from Davies was that Crewdson was relatively young, extremely intelligent, and that he had previously expressed an interest in Davies' conspiracy theory and the allegations Davies had made against Sergeant Pryor.

Later, after a little research, I found that Crewdson had an impressive journalistic resume.

In June of 1973, for example, Crewdson, along with a colleague, Christopher Lydon, was the first journalist to get his hands on the infamous Huston Plan documents. Those documents, which had been smuggled out of the Nixon White House by former Nixon counsel John Dean, revealed that in 1970 Nixon ordered a series of illegal actions by government agencies to combat growing protests and domestic violence against the Vietnam War.

In December 1973 Crewdson revealed the contents of a secret internal FBI report suggesting that former FBI Director L. Patrick Gray may have lied when he swore under oath that he knew nothing about 17 "national security" wiretaps Nixon ordered in 1969 after news of the secret

Cambodian bombings leaked. That confidential report had apparently been leaked to Crewdson by an official very high in the FBI.

Later that same month Crewdson revealed "a personal memorandum from the late J. Edgar Hoover" disclosing that White House Chief of Staff "H. R. Haldeman prompted the Federal Bureau of Investigation and the White House to issue a misleading explanation of the bureau's controversial explanation of Daniel Schorr," a CBS newsman Nixon was trying to intimidate.

In April 1974 *Sixty Minutes'* Mike Wallace cited Crewdson's reporting on the air while interviewing Watergate dirty trickster Donald Segretti. Somehow Crewdson had managed to obtain copies of the secret interviews the FBI had conducted with Segretti. Those files were supposed to have been sacrosanct.

Still later, Crewdson revealed that, despite claims by the FBI that its notorious COINTELPRO program, designed to disrupt and destroy the New Left, had ended, the FBI was continuing to use COINTELPRO-type techniques to harass domestic radicals (including the burning of automobiles, assaults, and illegal wiretaps).

Crewdson's government sources were so good ("golden was the word used by *Esquire* magazine in an article about the *Times'* coverage of Watergate) that the FBI launched an investigation of him. They wanted to know who was leaking to him all these secret documents.

Years later *New York Times* editor Harrison Salisbury would write in his book *Without Fear or Favor:* "In normal times these stories [the Segretti stories and the Huston Plan story] might have won Crewdson a Pulitzer Prize. But this [1973] was no normal year." The prize went instead to the *Washington Post* for their Watergate coverage.*

Crewdson's uncanny access to secret FBI files was indeed impressive, and given his interest in Kent State, it seemed quite possible that his sources in the FBI might have given him secret documents about the students killed on May 4.

In pondering the possibilities, I dismissed the rumor that one of the fatalities could have had a secret connection with the government. That seemed ridiculous on its face.

---

*Crewdson did win a Pulitzer Prize in 1981, in the category of national reporting, for his articles on illegal aliens and immigration. The Pulitzer was not the only journalistic prize he won—just the biggest one.

Besides, Shuble did not have any solid information, and some of his other questions—like, did some of the National Guard commanders have a secret connection with the CIA—made it easy to dismiss what he had to say.

Unfortunately, Crewdson would not talk for the record, and that left me playing annoying games.

Davies played them, too. Only the inferences he drew from his conversation were highly conspiratorial. For example, in the *Village Voice* article, Davies wrote that after talking with Crewdson, he (Davies) phoned Roy Meyers, a reporter for the *Cleveland Press,* who subsequently phoned Crewdson himself. Davies wrote that in the Crewdson-Meyers conversation, Crewdson clarified his "pain to the parents" remark to really mean "pain to the nation."

On the basis of that Davies suggested that Crewdson was privy to some information about a White House plot to shoot students.

Meyers, however, told me Crewdson never said anything about "pain to the nation" and "that was just the interpretation Peter was making of it."

Without any satisfactory answers from Crewdson, all I could do was consult other journalists to see what they thought of this strange incident. Most seemed skeptical that Crewdson knew anything. For example, David Hess, a reporter for Knight Newspapers, thought that Crewdson would have written a story himself if he'd had any solid information. He also thought that if there was any damaging information in government files about any of the victims, the Ohio special grand jury would have "jumped on it."

Pat Englehart, the *Beacon Journal*'s state editor who directed the newspaper's coverage of May 4, was more blunt. In typical newsroom language, Englehart said: "If that son of a bitch knows anything, what kind of a fucking newspaperman is he if he doesn't write a story? The idea that he knows the story of the century, but that he's sworn to secrecy and ain't going to tell anybody is pure bullshit. I'll give him a big, fat zero."

Similarly, John Dunphy, the *Beacon Journal* reporter who subsequently covered the grand jury and the Guardsmen's trial, suspected that Crewdson's statements might just be "meandering bullshit" he said journalists privately engage in.

However one interprets Davies' strange conversation with Crewdson, it should be noted that no information ever surfaced at the trials, or in the FBI reports that were subsequently made public, that caused any pain or embarrassment to the parents of the victims.

August-October 1973

For the next three months, the Justice Department quietly went about its "additional investigation," deliberately keeping it low key.

Few details about the scope or goals of the investigation were made public. However, recently released FBI files do reveal that Department attorneys asked the FBI to investigate several previously unexplored leads.

I can find no record that the Justice Department asked the FBI to pursue what I consider to be the most intriguing lead: a report in James Michener's book that a Guardsman who recognized a student, James Nichols, waved Nichols out of the line of fire just in the nick of time. (Nichols' story suggested the Guardsmen knew something was about to happen.)

The Department did ask the FBI to investigate a report in the *Pittsburgh Forum* that Sergeant Lawrence Shafer bragged that he had taken direct aim at fatality Jeffrey Miller. The FBI found the supposed source of the story—an acquaintance of Shafer—in Jacksonville, Florida, but the man denied talking to the reporter and gave no indication that Shafer had even made such a claim.

The Department also asked the FBI to follow through on a number of leads regarding the Terry Norman affair, some of which had been reported in the press. Interestingly, the Cleveland office of the FBI seemed to balk at this request. In an October 19, 1973, memo to FBI headquarters, the Cleveland office protested that the entire matter had been previously investigated.

That was not true. During my investigation of the Norman incident that summer, I learned, for example, that the FBI had never interviewed six witnesses who had seen Norman surrender his gun to the campus police. Some of these witnesses claimed that Norman admitted firing a shot or thought they heard Detective Tom Kelley say the gun was fired.

If I was able to find these witnesses as a recent college graduate (then 22 years of age), one would assume the FBI could have done the same if it wanted to.

Another major development during this period was the publication of Peter Davies' book *The Truth About Kent State*.

In the book, which Davies' publishers watered down considerably in order to avoid a lawsuit, Davies repeated the theory, first offered in his 1971 conspiracy report, that the shootings were deliberate.

There were indications that the Justice Department was now taking Davies' conspiracy allegations seriously. The Department reinterviewed two of the wounded students and asked them if they had seen any Guardsmen huddle on the practice football field before the shootings.

The huddle—in which the Guardsmen supposedly talked about shooting students—was, of course, the cornerstone of Davies' theory.

October 20-November 1, 1973

Just as the investigation began picking up steam, it was almost shut down again as a result of Watergate-related developments in Washington, D.C.

On October 20, the battle over the Nixon tapes came to a head when Nixon fired Special Watergate Prosecutor Archibald Cox, rather than yielding to Cox's demands for access to Watergate tapes. Both Attorney General Elliot Richardson (who had reopened the Kent case) and his deputy, William Ruckelshaus, resigned as an act of conscience rather than carry out Nixon's orders to fire Cox.

With Richardson out of the picture, the future of the Kent State investigation began to look cloudy. It would all depend on whom Nixon chose as his new attorney general.

Would the nominee be someone who would allow the investigation to go forward? Or would Nixon try to cut it off again?

November 1973

It did not take very long to find out the answer. On November 1 Nixon chose as his new attorney general the one man in the country most likely to terminate the new probe.

That was Ohio Senator William Saxbe, who, coincidences of coincidences, had all sorts of connections with the people now under investigation.

What kinds of connections?

• Saxbe was a friend and political ally of Ohio Governor James A. Rhodes, who called out the Guard and who gave them undetermined orders while Rhodes was on campus;

• Saxbe himself was a long-time National Guard commander. He had once commanded in a unit in the 107th Armored Cavalry, which the Justice Department was now investigating;

• He was still a colonel in the National Guard reserves; and

• He was, by his own admission, intimately acquainted with the two generals in the Kent Affair, Sylvester Del Corso and Robert Canterbury (although he denied it at first).

Saxbe not only had always opposed a federal grand jury investigation, but he had even opposed a fact-finding congressional investigation in which no criminal penalties were involved.

He seemed willing to shrug off the killings as "an emotional response that we too often get in our perfect society," as if violations of federal laws were unimportant.

Fortunately, he was also a man who spoke his mind.

When reporters asked him if he planned to continue the "additional investigation," he immediately said he was inclined to terminate it.

Had Saxbe kept his mouth shut, he probably could have very quietly scuttled the Department's probe. Instead, he played right into the hands of those pressing for a grand jury. He compounded his error by taking a gratuitous swipe at Elliot Richardson, calling the new investigation "cruel and unjust."

After Saxbe made his remarks, everyone who had ever asked for the grand jury, and many others, insisted that Saxbe disqualify himself.

Benson Wolman, the executive director of the Ohio ACLU, told reporters that "an examination of campaign and other records in Columbus indicates that leading figures in the Kent State investigation have close personal and political ties with Saxbe. Thus there will be a conflict of interest if Saxbe is given access to materials being prepared for a potential grand jury, and a still greater conflict if he is part of the decision-making process."

There was also a spate of newspaper editorials demanding that Saxbe keep his hands off the case. As the *Akron Beacon Journal* saw it:

It would be a disaster for Saxbe to shut down the Justice Department investigation at this time . . . The only way Senator Saxbe can avoid the appearance of a cover-up for his friend, ex-Governor Rhodes, is to let the Justice Department follow its full course—and then give a full disclosure of the findings.

The *New York Times* viewed the issue in the context of the crisis of confidence in the Justice Department itself after Watergate:

> The case remains a test of the Justice Department's determination to make a clean break with a past of politics, accommodations, coverups and potential conflicts of interest.

But perhaps the most sharply worded editorial appeared in the *St. Louis Post-Dispatch,* a newspaper that previously had not paid much attention to the aftermath of May 4:

> The history of the Kent State investigation has been an extended chronicle of justice denied and perverted, as when an Ohio grand jury exonerated the Guardsmen and indicted 25 demonstrators. But now it appears that the government may at least be serious about getting at the truth . . . It is, therefore, unthinkable that Mr. Saxbe should be considering scuttling the investigation if he is confirmed. At the very least, such an action would have a devastating effect on the morale at the Justice Department, which was just beginning to gain its self-respect under Mr. Richardson. And beyond this, it would reconfirm the impression held by millions not only here but abroad that the United States lacks the moral courage to face squarely the question of why four young persons were shot to death by soldiers protesting . . . the invasion of Cambodia.

December 1973

Saxbe's confirmation hearings before the Senate Judiciary Committee were scheduled to be held on December 12, 1973. The parents of the dead students, who did not know what to expect from Saxbe, began to worry.

A delegation of them, led by Arthur Krause, went to Washington personally to try to convince Senator Edward Kennedy, the chairman of the Senate Judiciary Committee, to urge Saxbe to disqualify himself because of his conflict of interest.

Those of us in Kent waited to see how Saxbe would handle this ethical dilemma. Would he disqualify himself from the decision-making process? Or would he continue to insist he could make unbiased decisions about his political friends and about soldiers in a cavalry unit he once commanded?

Then, about 9:00 P.M. on December 11, the night before his confirmation hearings were scheduled, I received a call from Paul Keane. He said that "Bob Downing of the *Beacon Journal* just called me. The Justice Department convened a grand jury a half hour ago."

The government had closed for business about four hours earlier, and I was wondering what was going on. Whatever was, the Department did announce that Pottinger had approached the acting attorney general, Robert Bork, and received permission to ask a federal judge in Cleveland to convene the federal grand jury the following week. The Justice Department was not going to wait until Saxbe was confirmed.

Clearly, the Justice Department, in convening the grand jury at this unusual hour the night before Saxbe was scheduled to appear before the Senate, was trying to present Saxbe with a *fait accompli.* This was a very clear slap in Saxbe's face.

In addition, it appeared from our vantage point that the Civil Rights Division of the Justice Department, which had previously been ordered to stay away from Kent State by Nixon, was telling Nixon it would not listen to him anymore.

The Justice Department was going to go ahead with the investigation—and this time Nixon could not stop it.*

---

*There is some question as to whether Saxbe disqualified himself from the grand jury proceedings. The news media generally reported that he did, but Steven Sindell, Arthur Krause's attorney, suspected differently. Following the trial and a conversation with chief prosecutor Robert Murphy, Sindell told me: "Murphy made certain comments which led me to believe he was not free to pursue charges against higher-ups."

Murphy angrily denied the suggestion and told me that "the day-to-day decisions of the grand jury, if you will, were mine."

Saxbe's Senate Judiciary Committee testimony seems unclear: "If, however, they have, *as a result of this grand jury, further proceedings,* it is my intention to remove myself from any participation" [emphasis added]. This sounds like he only intended to disqualify himself from any trail that resulted from the grand jury—not from the grand jury process itself.

EIGHT

The Prosecution of the
National Guardsmen

The grand jury convened on December 18 when Federal Judge Frank Battisti swore in 23 jurors in his Cleveland courtroom.

Battisti instructed the jurors that the grand jury was convened primarily to investigate the shooting of students at Kent State University on May 4, 1970.

He then related a brief history of the grand jury as an institution and explained that its purpose was to determine whether any crimes had been committed and whether there was probable cause to indict anyone.

Battisti also stressed that the grand jurors had to maintain absolute secrecy about their deliberations.

That, of course, did not prevent the leaks, most of which came from the defense attorneys.

Most of the actual sessions were held in an eleventh floor office in the Williamson Building, a busy office building in downtown Cleveland. Consequently, witnesses and jurors were removed from the glare of the press.

Reporters from several local newspapers and television cameras crews did, however, stake out the lobby of the Williamson Building to look for familiar faces, but only a few faces were recognized.

Those lying in wait were at least able to glean bits and pieces about how the investigation was running. They were able to determine that the

160 FOUR DEAD IN OHIO

grand jury began by examining photographs and investigating the Terry Norman incident. John Dunphy of the *Beacon Journal* reported that Assistant Attorney General J. Stanley Pottinger flew in from Washington specially to interrogate Norman.

Norman was not indicted by the grand jury. Later, when I asked Pottinger what we should conclude about Terry Norman, Pottinger answered simply: "Terry Norman has been cleared."

From accounts quoting the Guardsmen's lawyers, it appeared that the Justice Department was pursing its investigation in a methodical way. After dismissing the Terry Norman incident (and finally subpoenaing several important witnesses that the FBI overlooked in its original investigation), the prosecutors subpoenaed the Guardsmen who were at Kent State on May 4, 1970.

The prosecutors first called the men in C Company, 145th Infantry, the unit that was diverted from the main Guard contingent 17 minutes before the shooting started.

After that the Department attorneys questioned the soldiers of Company A, 145th Infantry, the troops that had done most of the firing into the air.

Finally, the attorneys questioned the men in G Troop, 107th Armored Cavalry, the troops that had done most of the firing into the crowd.

In early February word leaked out that many G Troopers had invoked their Fifth Amendment rights against self-incrimination. Included in this number were seven of the eight Guardsmen who were eventually indicted.

Sergeant Myron Pryor (not one of the eight) did testify. He denied that he was part of a conspiracy, and he denied firing his own gun.

Late February

In late February Adjutant General Sylvester Del Corso, the highest ranking officer in the Ohio National Guard in 1970, and the staunchest defender of the Guard's actions—at least publicly—testified before the federal grand jury. Although it was not reported until two years later, the prosecutors or the grand jurors themselves asked Del Corso sixteen separate times if he considered the shootings justified.

Each time he was asked Del Corso said no.

Just before the grand jury hearings ended, former Ohio Governor James A. Rhodes appeared, boldly claiming that he was volunteering his testimony and appearing of his own free will.

Technically, he was telling the truth. However, prosecutor Robert Murphy later told me that, had Rhodes waited a few more days, the Justice Department would have subpoenaed him, too.

The Indictments

On March 25, 1974, the Justice Department submitted its lists of recommendations to the grand jury. These recommendations were supposed to be kept in the strictest of secrecy, but I was told by two sources who were in a very good position to know that the Justice Department asked the grand jury to indict the Guardsmen on a charge of conspiracy.*

The grand jury rejected this recommendation, and I was unable to learn why. However, I suspect the grand jury balked at the recommendation *(a)* because the principal "shooters" themselves refused to testify, *(b)* their leader, Sergeant Pryor, who was accused of starting the conspiracy, denied there was one, and *(c)* there was no "smoking gun."

The evidence presented to the grand jury was only circumstantial.

On March 29, after four days of deliberations, the grand jury did indict eight Guardsmen under Section 242 of the U.S. Code, the statute guaranteeing the victims the right not to be summarily executed without receiving due process of law.†

Ironically, it was the same statute prosecutor Robert Murphy wanted to use to indict the Guardsmen almost four years earlier.

The indictments alleged that the eight Guardsmen named, "acting under the colors of the laws of the State of Ohio, aiding and abetting each other, did willfully assault and intimidate persons who were inhabi-

---

*These statements were supported by the Guardsmen's attorneys, who, based on what was reported back to them about the nature and direction of the prosecutors' questions, were convinced that the Justice Department was trying to prove the existence of a conspiracy at Kent. "There is no question about it," said C. D. "Gus" Lambros, Sergeant Myron Pryor's lawyer.

†The eight were Lawrence Shafer, James Pierce, William Perkins, James McGee, Barry Morris, Ralph Zoller, Matthew McManus and Leon Smith. All but McGee had pleaded the Fifth Amendment before the grand jury.

tants of the State of Ohio . . . by willfully discharging loaded [weapons] at, over, into, and in the direction of [the victims], and did thereby willfully deprive said persons of the right secured and protected by the Constitution and the laws of the United States not to be deprived of liberty without due process of law."

In plain English, that meant the victims' rights were violated when they were summarily killed or wounded by the militia without first being arrested and brought to trial.

After the indictments were announced, many newspaper and magazine columnists, as well as television commentators, reminded the public that the Guardsmen must be presumed innocent until proven guilty.

Many of these pundits also repeated the platitude, "The American system of justice ultimately prevailed."

One did not hear this platitude, though, from those who worked so hard to get the Guardsmen indicted.

"Anybody who thinks the system worked is nuts," said Paul Keane, who could only think of the "tremendous price people paid for justice" in terms of their time, energy, and out-of-pocket expenses.

Peter Davies had a similar view. "The system," he noted drily, "is supposed to work on its own."

The Pretrial Hearings

Seven months intervened between the handing down of the indictments and the beginning of the trial. During this period, the Guardsmen's attorneys tried to have the indictments dismissed.

The attorneys filed challenges to the admissibility of every statement their clients had given to any investigative body, whether it was the FBI, the Ohio Highway Patrol, the National Guard's Inspector General's office, or the special Ohio grand jury.

Had the attorneys succeeded, the government would have had to drop its case because the indictments rested heavily on the Guardsmen's own admissions that they had fired into the crowd.

Pretrial hearings on these issues were held beginning in late September. Federal Judge Frank Battisti ultimately ruled that all these statements were properly taken from the soldiers—except for the after-actions reports the Guardsmen gave to their own superiors.

These hearings had no effect on the trial itself; however, they did produce some rather intriguing testimony, including some startling allegations against the FBI.

During the hearings each of the indicted Guardsmen swore that the FBI agents who took their statements assured them that they need not worry about anything. Some Guardsmen suggested that the FBI had only gone through the motions of the investigation to make some people happy. Guardsman Ralph Zoller, for example, testified that he was under the impression that the FBI "was more or less on our side."

The prosecutors, led by Robert Murphy, countered these allegations by calling as witnesses each of the FBI agents who had interviewed the Guardsmen. Each FBI agent disputed the Guardsmen's claims.

That turned the hearing into a "swearing contest," with no outside evidence to support either side. Judge Battisti eventually sided with the FBI because each of the Guardsmen had signed statements warning them: "Anything you say may be held against you in a court of law."

Battisti also agreed to suppress the after-actions statements the Guardsmen had provided to their superior officers on the basis of some testimony that was also quite surprising. A captain named Brent Robertson, who was assigned to take the shooters' statements, testified that he was specifically instructed by Colonel William Spain of the Guard's legal staff *not* to advise the shooters that they had a constitutional right to remain silent.

Robertson testified that he considered the command most unusual, that he asked Spain "Are you sure," not once but twice, that Spain repeated the command, and that he (Robertson) secured the statements without advising the shooters of their rights.

Robertson's testimony strongly suggested that the Guard's Inspector General's office deliberately tried to protect the Guardsmen in advance of any proceedings by ensuring that any statements they gave would later be declared inadmissible in court.

Opening Statements

The trial began on October 29, 1974, after a jury was sworn in.

The composition of the jury greatly pleased the lawyers for the National Guard.

One of the lawyers, C. D. "Gus" Lambros, thought "the jury was perfect." Another giggled: "They've got more goddamn guns than the National Guard!"

In his opening statement, prosecutor Robert Murphy announced almost immediately that there would not be any major surprises in the government's case. That in itself was surprising since the Justice Department had recently completed a three-month-long grand jury investigation in which 179 witnesses were called.

The investigation had been billed as one of the most comprehensive in the history of the Department's Civil Rights Division, and some followers of the case had assumed it would result in some kind of breakthrough.

Murphy did, at least, concisely recap the evidence that the Justice Department had known about for years. The photographs and the testimony, he said, would show that "there was no massive rush of students toward the Guardsmen . . . No student was shot within sixty feet . . These thirteen people were shot from a distance of sixty to six hundred feet . . . Only two of the thirteen were shot in the front."

When Murphy was finished, the three principal defense attorneys each took turns presenting their arguments, taking up three times the amount of time Murphy got.

C. D. "Gus" Lambros, who represented James Pierce, Ralph Zoller, and Barry Morris, went on the attack immediately, portraying the crowd as crazy, frenzied rioters who were not exercising legitimate constitutional rights. In his portrait, the shootings were just a simple issue of the Guardsmen defending themselves against a charging crowd of demonstrators going nuts.

When Lambros was done, Bernard Stuplinski, a shrewd former U.S. Attorney, got up and took a far more subtle tack. "It was a tragedy, a regrettable tragedy," Stuplinski acknowledged. "But this regrettable incident occurred not because of any action of these eight men but because of the action of other people."

Stuplinski blamed Governor Rhodes, the University administrators, and the commanding officers who placed the troops in a vulnerable position.

In other words, he blamed everybody but the Guardsmen who pulled the triggers.

After that, the third and final attorney, Edd Wright, representing Leon Smith, delivered his arguments to the jury.

A small-town lawyer, Wright was less flamboyant than his associates and would have been happy to disassociate Smith's case (which was by far the weakest one) from all the rest.

Like Lambros and Stuplinski, Wright argued that the students were not exercising their rights for a redress of their grievances and that they were just rioting.

"Leon Smith," he argued, "assaulted no one. He was assaulted himself."*

October 30-November 7, 1974

For six days Murphy and his two assistants, Robert Hoyle and Paul Lawrence, presented the evidence they had. They called 33 witnesses, most of them students who had photographed the events.

The prosecutors also called to the witness stand the nine students who were wounded. The victims described what they were doing on the afternoon of May 4, 1970, and the extent of their injuries.

Virtually all of these witnesses testified that the Guardsmen were never in any serious danger, suggesting that there was no reason to shoot.

The defense attorneys tried to poke holes in the credibility of these witnesses' testimony by showing that the witnesses were not paying attention, that they were underestimating the number of rocks thrown, or that they were contradicting previous statements they had made to the FBI.

Ironically, one of the wounded students, John Cleary, proved to be one of the best witnesses for the defense. Cleary was confronted with statements he had given to the FBI in 1970 saying the Guardsmen looked panicky and that the rocks thrown at them were large as softballs.

Under intense grilling, Cleary meekly claimed that he was under medication when he made those statements and that his memory was better now—four and a half years after the fact.

The Justice Department also introduced into the record the statements the Guardsmen had given to various investigative bodies. These statements clearly indicated that most of the defendants had aimed at specific individuals in the crowd.

_____

*Of course, when Murphy subsequently introduced Smith's statement to the Ohio Highway Patrol, that argument went down the drain. Smith was specifically asked by the Patrol if he was injured, and he replied, "I had a rock hit my boot but it only scratched the leather."

On November 7, as Murphy prepared to wrap up his case, Judge Battisti directed some remarks to him that the *Akron Beacon Journal* termed "highly unusual."

Battisti advised the prosecutors that they should have their arguments ready the following day in the event the defense attorneys made a motion for a directed acquittal (which is what defense attorneys routinely do after prosecutors rest their cases. In the overwhelming majority of instances the motion is denied.)

Battisti even told Murphy, "I might have something in writing."

It appeared that Battisti had already made up his mind to dismiss the charges against the National Guardsmen.

November 8, 1974

When Murphy went to court on the morning of November 8, he did not believe that Battisti would throw the charges out.

Before resting his case, Murphy introduced his final exhibits: a tape recording of the shootings made by KSU student Terry Strubbe, which he (Murphy) considered his strongest piece of evidence, samples of the types of rifles and bullets used in the shootings, and additional statements previously made by the Guardsmen on trial.

Battisti then excused the jury from the courtroom and the defense made their expected motion to dismiss the charges for lack of evidence.

The courtroom was hushed when Battisti asked Murphy to tell him what he had just proved. After the exchange began, it became apparent that the judge and the prosecuting attorney had fundamentally different views as to what constituted "specific intent," and that Murphy had not proved the type of specific intent that Battisti was looking for.

When Murphy acknowledged this, Battisti said: "We really don't have to go much further." The judge then called the jury back into the courtroom and read excerpts of an 18-page opinion he had prepared the night before.

The opinion stated: "The government has presented no evidence directly bearing on the intention of those Guardsmen . . . who fired weapons."

Battisti ruled that, even if the government's argument was correct, they had failed to prove the charges beyond a reasonable doubt, and that he was required by law to acquit the soldiers himself.

He had already prepared copies of his opinion for the press.

Reactions

One of the more interesting epilogues to the trial was the almost uniformly cynical reaction of the parents, the student petitioners, and just about everyone who had asked that the prosecution be held.

These people, who had expressed strong and often naive faith in the judicial processes, were suddenly asking the most amazing questions, such as:

"Who bought off the judge?"

"Did the Justice Department throw the trial?"

"Why weren't any of the Guardsmen called to testify about what they had done?"

Student petitioner Greg Rambo, for example, noted that "the Justice Department never wanted the grand jury in the first place." He considered the proceedings to be an elaborate charade on the Department's part.

Rambo also suspected that the prosecutors would never "cross their boss," Attorney General William Saxbe, who, Rambo noted, had long opposed the prosecution.

He thought Murphy and his assistants just went through the motions "to make it look good."

I also heard a number of people wonder whether there was a connection between the acquittal and James A. Rhodes' reelection as governor of Ohio only four days earlier.

Peter Davies was particularly suspicious. He told me that the Justice Department must be covering up something "big and horrible," and that "this absolutely smells."

Davies also accused the Department of going through a fancy charade to prevent the congressional subcommittee from holding public hearings into the Department's handling of the case and ultimately discovering what the Department was really trying to hide.

As Davies saw it, the prosecutors were able to conceal information about White House involvement in the shootings "by avoiding charges against those most likely to blow the whistle on higher officials" and by indicting only low-echelon Guardsmen on charges the Department knew would never stand up in court.

Davies was far from alone in suspecting this. Several professors at Kent suggested that the trial was a continuation of the coverup.

While one must keep in mind that the Department did go to extraordinary lengths to bury the case—and had to be forced to undertake the prosecution—there are some reasons to believe that the charges made by Davies and others are misdirected.

One was that Murphy was never part of the coverup. While his superiors in the Justice Department and in the White House stood in the way of the prosecution, Murphy was one of the few men in the Justice Department who always wanted the opportunity to bring charges against the soldiers. He recommended doing so within six weeks of the shootings. (In fact, even after it became clear that his initial recommendations would be rejected, Murphy tried to convince his superiors to pursue a civil suit against the Guardsmen and the officers. That, too, was overruled by Attorney General John Mitchell.)

Murphy's commitment to the prosecutions was clear to others who dealt with him directly. The defense attorneys insisted he was "no slouch" and that he fought bitterly over the introduction of evidence in the privacy of Judge Battisti's chambers.

While the defense attorneys might have a stake in arguing that Murphy tried his best (after all, if he did and failed, that might make the evidence look more favorable to them), they were not the only ones defending Murphy.

David Engdahl, one of the attorneys for the parents of the slain students, reported that Murphy was frustrated and depressed over Battisti's decision. Moreover, Pat Shea, the investigator for the House Judiciary Subcommittee that pressured the Justice Department into reopening its investigation, said it was clear to him that Murphy wanted to pursue the evidence vigorously.

I watched Murphy fight back tears after the acquittal. He was clearly upset.

Years later, he even brought his daughter to Kent State on a vacation to give her a tour of the campus. He told a reporter he wanted to explain why "her father had been away for a long time" during the trial.

The federal grand jury testimony of Pfc. James McGee, which was introduced into the record, also supports the notion that Murphy had his heart in the prosecution. The transcript shows that the prosecutors vigorously challenged McGee's story that his life was in danger, tried to show that he exaggerated the distances between him and the student he admitted firing at, and asked him about communications among the Guardsmen during the alleged huddle on the practice field.

Murphy, of course, was not able to interrogate any of the other defendants, who pleaded the Fifth Amendment before the grand jury.

One of the most serious charges that Davies made was that Murphy protected Sergeant Myron Pryor, the man Davies believed instigated the conspiracy. Pryor had not been indicted by the grand jury, and that led Davies to charge that Murphy, in an attempt to divert attention from higher-ups, went easy on Pryor.

There were, however, several indications that the Department had indeed tried to nail Pryor, even though they ultimately came up empty-handed.

Pryor's lawyer, C. D. "Gus" Lambros, confirmed speculation in the press that Pryor was a key target of the grand jury, and said that the prosecutors "zeroed in" on Pryor while trying to prove Davies' charge against him.

According to Lambros, when Pryor testified before the federal grand jury, Assistant Attorney General J. Stanley Pottinger and his deputy, K. William O'Connor, flew in specially from Washington to take turns trying to crack Pryor. Lambros called this "a gathering of the eagles."

Murphy himself confirmed part of Lambros' account. Although he did not come out and say so, I got as much corroboration from Murphy as one might ever get from a federal prosecutor.

Late one night after the trial I reached him by phone in his office in Washington. I asked him if he had tried to indict Pryor and he reluctantly conceded: "I suppose."

(He sounded tired and may not have realized what he was saying. Federal prosecutors are not supposed to divulge such information.)

Some of the other criticisms of the prosecution may be more valid. One surprise was that the Department did not call any other Guardsmen as witnesses against the eight defendants.

In the Justice Department's summary of the FBI report, which Murphy coauthored in 1970, he noted: "Six Guardsmen, including two sergeants and Captain [Raymond] Srp of Troop G, stated pointedly that the lives of the members of the Guard were not in danger and that it was not a shooting situation."

Why did not Murphy call any of these Guardsmen? When I interviewed him after the trial, he seemed defensive on this point and said that his tactics were to demonstrate the eight men on trial acted differently from the Guardsmen who refrained from firing.

If that was his intent, he certainly did not communicate it to anyone in the courtroom.

There was also a question as to why Murphy did not present any evidence concerning the most serious accusation against the soldier. In the summary of the FBI reports, Murphy wrote:

> We have some reason to believe that the claim by the National Guard that their lives were endangered by the students was fabricated subsequent to the event. The apparent volunteering by some of the Guardsmen of the fact that their lives were not in danger gives rise to some suspicions.

Most of his suspicions, though, had been based on an interview that a Guardsman (who insisted on anonymity) gave to a Knight Newspaper reporter in 1970. The Guardsman, who was identified only as a 23-year-old married machinist, was quoted as saying that he had "just closed my eyes and shot . . . shoulder-level toward the crowd." He admitted he did not feel he had to save his life: "It was an automatic thing. Everybody shot, so I shot. I didn't think about it. I just fired."

More importantly, the Guardsman said: "The guys have been saying that we got to get together and stick to the same story, that it was our lives or them [sic], a matter of survival."

Murphy knew of only one Guardsman who matched this man's description—defendant Ralph Zoller—but Zoller gave the FBI a different version of his role from the one reported in the newspaper version.

Was the source of the newspaper story Zoller? After the trial Murphy told me that he could never find out who this anonymous Guardsman was and that it was quite possible that the Guardsmen never existed.

However, David Engdahl, one of the attorneys who represented the victims in the subsequent civil trial, noted that the Guardsman could have been someone who lied to the FBI to protect himself, but who gave a more candid and realistic interview to a newspaper reporter who guaranteed his anonymity.

Engdahl felt that the Guardsman in question may have existed, but that Murphy simply could not find him.

The Ruling

Judge Battisti's acquittal—which caught many courtroom observers off guard—also received a fair amount of criticism.

Assistant General J. Stanley Pottinger told me he considered Battisti's decision "an aberration" and said that Battisti "was wrong as a matter of law. In virtually all other cases that I am aware of, the courts have not construed the intent provisions as narrowly as Judge Battisti did."

The *Akron Beacon Journal*'s David Hess later wrote: "While the judge's interpretation of the law was a bit narrower than the law's language might have allowed, the fact remains the law is quite narrow. By fixing its sights on the intent of the alleged violator, the law largely misses the consequences of the violator's deed."

That assessment was echoed by defense attorney Michael Diamant, who said the trial was not so much about what happened at Kent State, but "whether a certain particularized element of truth was present."

That element was specific intent, and it is interesting to consider what evidence would have been needed to prove a violation of the statute, at least according to Battisti's interpretation of it.

In his opinion Battisti ruled that it was not enough for the Guardsmen to have an "evil motive" or a generalized "bad purpose." Yet he seemed to contradict himself in his own opinion when he wrote:

> Normally, such proof of such "willfulness" will not be difficult in a case brought under 242, since in the typical case it can easily be inferred from the egregious circumstances surrounding the alleged acts. Typically, a 242 defendant has pre-existing malice toward his victim, deprived him of his rights at close range with weapons designed to beat or maim, continued his assault for some time, and acted without provocation.

Battisti claimed "none [of these factors] are present in the instant case." Yet that was not true.

Just before the acquittal (and after Battisti's opinion was written) Murphy had introduced into evidence a tape recording demonstrating that the Guardsmen continued their assault for some time—13 seconds.

He also introduced the statements that each Guardsman had given to Ohio Highway Patrol investigators. In each of the statements the eight defendants were specifically asked: "Were you provoked into firing?" Three (Ralph Zoller, Barry Morris, and James McGee) said they were, but four others (Lawrence Shafer, William Perkins, James Pierce, and Leon Smith) admitted they were not. The eighth man, Matthew McManus, had to stop and debate the question.

Most of the students, of course, were not shot at close range. They were shot at distances that should have aroused suspicions about the Guardsmen's intentions.

Only on the issue of preexisting malice did Murphy fail to introduce any evidence. He had no proof that the Guardsmen harbored any ill will against the students.

That, however, might have been inferred from the rocks that had been thrown at the Guardsmen or the very fact that the students were protesting the war in Vietnam. Most of the country had ill will against these demonstrators.

Interestingly, even as he acquitted the Guardsmen, Battisti seemed to agree that the Guardsmen deserved to be prosecuted. He felt, however, they were being prosecuted on the wrong charges in the wrong court-room:

> Very different considerations would obtain if this were a trial of eight Guardsmen in a state court on charges, for example, of shooting with intent to injure or maim. In that situation, the issues of justification, of possible excessiveness of force, of provocation, or self-defense, might be relevant.

Battisti did not feel any of these issues were important here and later returned to the theme of state prosecutions by writing:

> It is entirely possible that state officials may yet wish to pursue criminal prosecutions against various persons responsible for the events at Kent State. This opinion does not pass on the propriety of such prosecutors, if any.

The ultimate irony of Battisti's opinion was that it was precisely the state of Ohio's refusal to prosecute the Guardsmen—and to enforce the law—that resulted in the four-and-a-half-year-long struggle to get the federal prosecutions.

According to one report, the defense attorneys, after reading Bat-tisti's suggestion that the state prosecute the Guardsmen—and knowing that James A. Rhodes, who had called out the Guardsmen, had just been reelected governor of Ohio—"left the courtroom laughing."

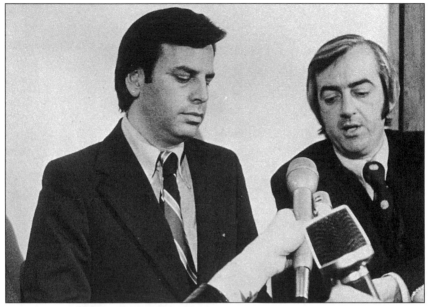

Assistant Attorney General J. Stanley Pottinger (left) and federal prosecutor Robert Murphy announce the indictment of the eight Guardsmen. (Photo by Cleveland *Plain Dealer*.)

Following their acquittal, Guardsmen Barry Morris, William Perkins, James Pierce, Matthew McManus autograph a trial exhibit photo of them shooting students. (Photo by Wide World Photos.)

NINE

The Civil Trials

May your life be filled with lawyers.
– Mexican curse

The acquittal of the National Guardsmen did not end the major litigation stemming from the shootings at Kent State.

Six months after the Guardsmen walked out of the federal courthouse as free men, a second trial was held in Cleveland.

This trial considered wrongful death and injury claims that had been filed by the parents of the four slain students and the nine students who were wounded and survived.

The defendants in this case included not only the eight Guardsmen who were prosecuted, but every other Guardsman who admitted firing, each of their commanding officers, Dr. Robert I. White, the former president of Kent State, and James A. Rhodes, who in October 1974 had been reelected governor. As such, Rhodes was Ohio's nominal commander-in-chief.

Although this trial came on the heels of the criminal prosecutions, it had no direct bearing on the criminal case. In the civil trial the Guardsmen were again charged with due process violations, but this time were being judged by a different standard of proof.

In civil cases, plaintiffs only need to prove charges with a preponderance of the evidence, whereas in criminal prosecutions charges must be proved beyond a reasonable doubt.

The soldiers and officers were charged with many other offenses. (For a breakdown of who was sued for what, see the accompanying chart.)

These suits had first been filed in 1970, when Arthur Krause, the father of Allison Krause, alleged that the defendants (43 in all) were responsible for his daughter's death.

Over the course of the next year, the other victims had filed their own claims. Eventually these suits were consolidated by the courts.

The reason why the suits were not tried until May 1975, more than five years after the event, was because for most of the first four years the lower courts held that the defendants could not be sued under the doctrine of sovereign immunity. That legal principle, a carry-over from pre-sixteenth century feudal England and characterized by the slogan "the king can do no wrong," meant that no one acting as an agent of the state of Ohio could be sued for damages without giving their consent.

Naturally, no one gave their permission to be sued.

On April 17, 1974, the U.S. Supreme Court, in a landmark ruling, held that this immunity could only be used as a defense at a trial, and not as a defense to block a trial from being held.

The ruling paved the way for the victims to present their evidence in court and try to secure compensation for their losses.

(Combined, the suits of these thirteen plaintiffs sought $46 million in damages.)

The civil trial was scheduled to be held after the criminal proceedings ran their course and after a lengthy discovery period in which depositions were taken from the defendants and witnesses.

In preparing for this trial, the attorneys for the victims deposed approximately 100 individuals, many of whom, like the National Guardsmen, had never been subjected to cross-examination before.

In many respects, the civil trial was more important than the criminal prosecutions. The trial lasted for fifteen weeks and provided the most comprehensive airing of testimony.

Many new photographs and exhibits were introduced. We also heard expert opinions about the evidence.

Much of the testimony was new. Some of it was unexpected, and in many instances witnesses contradicted each other or their own previous statements to the FBI or other investigative agencies.

This chapter recounts some of the highlights of the trial. While I could provide a detailed rendition of what happened over the three months, the reader would only get hopelessly confused and overwhelmed by the sheer weight of the often contradictory facts.

The lawyers for the victims never seemed to appreciate this. In fact, while the lawyers for the defense did everything they could to take the jury's minds off the central issue of the trial—the use of excessive force by the soldiers—the plaintiffs' attorneys inadvertently hurt their own case by failing, in the words of the *Plain Dealer,* "to present a clear and simple case focusing on only a few issues."

Spring 1975

Even before the trial, while the suits were still in the so-called discovery phase, I began hearing reports that the different attorneys who represented the various victims could not get along with one another, that strong egos were in collision, and that the attorneys were at odds over trial strategy.

The main point of contention seemed to be who would be chosen as chief counsel for the plaintiffs. At one point it had been settled that former U. S. Attorney General Ramsey Clark would lead the trial team. However, some of the wounded students and David Engdahl, one of the attorneys who had represented the attorneys from the start, claimed that another of the victims' attorneys tried to nullify the agreement so that he (the other attorney) could be ensured of a more significant role during the trial.

According to Engdahl, Clark bowed out because he thought the competitiveness was "highly destructive and damaging to the interests of the clients," and that he did not want any part of this squabbling.

Just one week before the trial began, the victims agreed on a compromise candidate to be chief counsel. That was Joseph Kelner, a New York City-based attorney who represented the family of fatality Jeffrey Miller.

Kelner had a distinguished background as a trial attorney that included a term as president of the American Trial Lawyers Association.

Kelner was chosen, I was told, precisely because he had not spent much time on the pretrial work and was not involved in any of the divisive fights between the Ohio-based attorneys.*

---

*Author Peter Davies, who volunteered his services as a researcher for the victims, later charged that "Kelner was out of it in more ways than one." As Kelner obliquely conceded in his account of the trial, *The Kent State Coverup,* he had never been to Kent State before. He also apparently had not reviewed any of the 100-odd depositions taken by the other attorneys, and he came to rely heavily on the advice of Galen Keller, the team's principal paralegal, partly because he did not know which attorney to trust.

Civil Suit Defendants

State Officials

1. James A. Rhodes,
   Governor, Ohio

Charged With

1. Failure to ensure, as commander-in-chief of the militia, that the National Guard complied with Department of the Army regulations governing the use of weapons and training; thus substantially increasing the likelihood that civilians would be killed or injured in a confrontation.

2. Gave the Guardsmen authority to resort to lethal force through his bellicose remarks at the press conference on May 3.

3. Ordered that all rallies, peaceful or otherwise, be broken up, in violation of the students' First Amendment freedom of assembly rights.

4. Illegally imposed martial law after the fact to justify the no-rally ban.

5. Failed to sign the proper proclamations when the Guardsmen were ordered into Kent State.

2. Dr. Robert I. White
   President, Kent State

1. Ordered that the fateful May 4 rally be broken up.

National Guard Officers and Noncommissioned Officers

3. Sylvester Del Corso,
   Adjutant General, ONG

1. Same as Rhodes #1.

2. Personally directed or authorized his subordinates to order that all rallies, peaceful or otherwise, be prohibited.

3. Failed to exercise sufficient control over his troops.

4. Robert Canterbury
   Assistant Adjutant General,
   ONG

1. Same as Del Corso #2 and #3.

2. Botched the dispersal mission by not watching where the troops were marching, by ordering the troops to lock and load their weapons, and by committing into action Guardsmen whose acute nearsightedness was not corrected when they took their glasses off and put their gas masks on.

5. Charles Fassinger
Lieutenant Colonel
Same as Canterbury.

6. Major Harry Jones
Same as Canterbury.

7. Captain Raymond Srp
Same as Canterbury.

8. Captain John Martin
Same as Canterbury.

9. Captain Ron Snyder
Same as Canterbury.

10. Lieutenant Alexander
Stevenson*
Same as Canterbury.

11. Lieutenant Howard Fallon[†]
Same as Canterbury.

12. Lieutenant Dwight Cline
Same as Canterbury.

13. Sergeant Myron Pryor[§]
Same as Canterbury.

14. Sergeant Okey Flesher
Same as Canterbury.

Enlisted Guardsmen Who Admitted Firing at Specific Students or Generally Into the Crowd

15. Pfc. James McGee

16. Sergeant Barry Morris

1. Violated rights of the victims to enjoy due process of law (in other words, the right not to be summarily executed).

17. Sergeant Lawrence Shafer

2. Assaulted the students.

18. Spec. 4 James Pierce

3. Meted out cruel and unusual punishment.

19. Spec. 4 Ralph Zoller

20. Spec. 4 William Perkins

4. Used excessive force when other alternatives were available (e.g., the bayonets attached to rifles)

5. Aided and abetted one another.

---

*Stevenson denied firing, but the plaintiffs tried to prove he did so by introducing Captain Srp's testimony that his weapon was fired.

†Fallon denied firing, but the plaintiffs tried to prove he did so by introducing the Company A sign-out sheet which indicated the weapon assigned to him was fired.

§Pryor denied firing, but the plaintiffs tried to prove he did so by bringing to the stand four witnesses who claimed they saw him fire. One Guardsman, Barry Morris, also claimed to have seen Pryor fire on the practice football field several minutes before the shooting.

Guardsmen Who Claimed They Fired in the Air But Whose Statements Suggest Someone May Have Been Hit as a Result

21. Sergeant
Matthew McManus

22. Spec. 4. Leon Smith

1. Violated rights of the victims to enjoy due process of law (in other words, not to be summarily executed).

2. Assaulted the students.

3. Meted out cruel and unusual punishment.

4. Used excessive force when other alternatives were available (e.g., the bayonets attached to their rifles)

5. Aided and abetted one another.

Guardsmen Who Admitted Only to Firing into the Air or the Ground and Not at Human Beings

23. Sergeant
Dennis Breckenridge

24. Spec. 4 Lloyd Thomas

25. Pfc. Rudy Morris

26. Spec. 4 William J. Case

27. Pfc. Joseph Scholl

28. Pfc. Rodney Biddle

29. Sergeant James Brown

30. Pfc. James W. Farriss

31. Pfc. Robert Hatfield

32. Spec.4 Robert James

33. Pfc. Roger Maas

34. Pfc. Lawrence Mowrer

35. Pfc. Ronnie Meyers

36. Pfc. Paul Naujkos

37. Pfc. Philip Raber

38. Pfc. Richard Shade

1. Fired negligently, thus increasingly the likelihood that someone might be struck by a ricochet or falling bullet.

39. Pfc. Paul Zimmerman*

40. Sergeant William
     F. E. Herschler[†]

41. Sergeant Richard Love

42. Spec.4 Richard Lutey

43. Pfc. Richard Snyder

NOTE: The following Guardsmen were dismissed as defendants during the trial: Dennis Breckenridge, James K. Brown, William Case, James W. Farriss, Robert Hatfield, Lonnie Hinton, Roger Maas, Rudy Morris, Ronnie Meyers, Paul Naujkos, Phillip Raber, Joseph Scholl, Richard Shade, Richard Snyder, and Paul Zimmerman.

NOTE: Kent State President Dr. Robert I. White was also dismissed as a defendant by the Sixth Circuit Court of Appeals in 1977 in its appeals ruling. The court ruled that even though no overt acts of violence had occurred on May 4 before the Guard broke up the crowd and shot the students, authorities could legally disperse the rally since the previous days' rallies on campus had all turned violent.

White was dismissed as a defendant because the only testimony against him was General Robert Canterbury's claim that White asked him to disperse the crowd of students on May 4.

---

*Zimmerman was out of the country during the trial.

[†]Herschler denied firing, but the plaintiffs tried to prove he did so by introducing a statement by Sergeant Matthew McManus that Herschler fired eight rounds into the crowd.

Kelner's selection, however, did not stop the internecine squabbling among the attorneys. According to Engdahl, Kelner's specialty was in negligence claims, and all throughout the trial he resisted attempts to emphasize the constitutional or deprivation of civil rights aspect of the case that Engdahl, a constitutional scholar, and the ACLU attorneys who represented some of the wounded students, considered to be more important.

Mid-May 1975

The principal attorneys for the defense, Burt Fulton and Charlie Brown, gave a clue as to how they were going to conduct their defense when they interrogated potential jurors. Fulton and Brown repeatedly asked the jurors whether they were affiliated with or sympathized with the radical Weather underground or the SDS—two organizations that evoked strong emotions but that, as far as anyone knew, had nothing to do with anything that happened at Kent State.

Of course, the jurors had no way of knowing that, so just by asking these questions and others in a related vein, the defense attorneys legitimized the possibility that revolutionaries or subversives were responsible for the tragedy.

(As we shall see, this strategy of creating straw men and trying to shift the jurors' focus was a consistent thread throughout the trial.)

May 28, 1975

The defense's opening statements closely paralelled those delivered in the criminal trial—with a few exceptions.

Since the state of Ohio was paying for the defense of all 43 defendants in this trial, the defense attorneys could not play one party against another, as the lawyers for the Guardsmen in the criminal trial had done.

The defense attorneys had to find somebody else to blame for the shootings. That "somebody else" was the students, including the ones who were shot by the Guardsmen, regardless of whether they were demonstrators or innocent bystanders.

Charlie Brown, in his opening statement, virtually screamed that "burning, looting, rioting and terrorism were . . . the order of the day . . . This was not a Mayday picnic, but an insurrection!"

On the other hand Joseph Kelner, the chief counsel for the plaintiffs, tried to draw a distinction between his clients and the rest of the protestors. Kelner conceded that the acts of violence that occurred during May 1-4, 1970, were inexcusable, but argued that his clients should not be blamed for what others did.

Kelner argued that:

• His clients still had a right to peaceably assemble on May 4;

• The Guardsmen did not have to shoot and had other alternatives available;

• There was an order to fire; and

• The Guardsmen covered up what they did after the fact, not knowing that their versions would be contradicted by numerous photographs.

Late May-June 1975

One day early in the trial, several of the reporters gathered over lunch and agreed that the plaintiffs would lose the case.

According to Sandra Bullock, the reporter for the *Kent Record-Courier,* this consensus was reached not because of the evidence, but because Kelner, who was constantly repeating questions and talking in condescending tones, was alienating the jury.

Nonetheless, the plaintiffs at least got off to an impressive start. They produced witnesses like photographer Howard Ruffner, whose photos showed plenty of empty space between the students and the Guardsmen; Professor Charles Brill, who compared the volley to his experiences on a firing line; and other witnesses who saw few rocks being thrown at the soldiers or who saw Guardsmen brutalize or bayonet students the night before the tragedy, thus suggesting a predisposition to use excessive force.

Defense attorneys Fulton and Brown tried to find discrepancies in the witnesses' stories and tried to distract attention from the Guardsmen's behavior by closely questioning the plaintiffs' witnesses about the ROTC fire and the other acts of violence that occurred in Kent on the days before the shootings.

Kelner objected to these repeated questions, stating that he had already stipulated that people other than his clients had instigated acts of violence. Kelner argued that repeated questioning about these prior events would be prejudicial to his clients.

Kelner recognized that all this minute questioning about the ROTC fire and other pre-May 4 events would double the length of the trial, bury the jury in "an avalanche of detail," and cause the jurors to wonder whether his clients had participated in the previous rioting.

On June 1 Kelner petitioned Judge Donald Young to severely limit the scope of the defense's questioning. Judge Young took the matter under advisement.

In response to the plaintiffs' objections, Judge Young proposed what seemed to be a reasonable compromise. Young indicated he would cut off the defense attorneys' incessant questioning about all the events that took place before May 4, 1970, if the plaintiffs were willing to drop one of their claims in the suit: that Governor Rhodes, in sending the Guardsmen to Kent, failed to sign the proper legal proclamations.

Since this claim was probably the least important of all the claims the plaintiffs made at the trial, the plaintiffs would have been well advised to accept Young's offer.

However, it appears that Kelner did not understand what Judge Young was proposing. Kelner apparently thought that Young was telling him that if he did not want the trial to get bogged down in the avalanche of detail, the plaintiffs would have to drop all of their claims against Rhodes.

The transcript of the trial shows that Kelner kept arguing with Young, but in the end refused to accept the offer.

For the rest of the trial the defense lawyers were virtually unrestricted in their questioning of the witnesses.

Early June 1975

On June 4 one of the most important witnesses testified for the plaintiffs. He was Harry William Montgomery, an ex-Marine and KSU student whose testimony strongly suggested that the Guardsmen were given an order to fire.

Montgomery testified that he had kept his eye on Sergeant Myron Pryor before the shootings because Pryor was bringing up the rear of the troops and because Pryor was carrying a .45 caliber pistol. Montgomery testified that he had carried a .45 in Vietnam and that he "identified" with the pistol.

As Montgomery told it, he watched the Guardsmen reorganize at the crest of Blanket Hill, then watched as Pryor tapped three or four other Guardsmen on the back or hindside, and finally saw all the Guardsmen turn about-face simultaneously.

In his cross-examination, defense attorney Burt Fulton virtually ignored the suggestion that Pryor gave an order to fire. Fulton failed to find any significant contradictions in Montgomery's testimony.*

On June 5, the plaintiffs called Sergeant Lawrence Shafer to the stand. He thus became the first Guardsman to testify publicly about his role in the shooting.

Shafer insisted that he fired because his life was in danger and that he fired at a student who was charging him, and who was only thirty feet away.

Shafer conceded that he did not fire in panic and that he intended to hit the student. He further testified that the night before the shooting, while manning a command post on campus, he had struck a Vietnam veteran with his rifle. Shafer testified that the veteran was bad-mouthing him and that he was not about to take "any guff" from this student veteran.

The second Guardsman called was William Perkins, whose nervousness and memory lapses made him look silly. Perkins claimed that there were a hundred students closing in on him, some coming as close as thirty feet.

Other Guardsmen who testified told similar stories, but they were repeatedly challenged.

One Guardsman, Larry Mowrer, testified he felt ashamed for even firing a rifle in the air, as if even that was not necessary.

June 16-17, 1975

Even though the plaintiffs' primary contention was that Sergeant Myron Pryor had initiated the shootings by giving an order to fire, that did not stop them from introducing testimony that undercut their own arguments.

On June 16 Kelner called another Guardsman, Richard Love, who had given his superiors a statement that he heard a verbal order on Blanket Hill to turn around and face the students. Love thought the order had been issued by Major Jones.

---

* When Montgomery testified to seeing the signal, a friend of the wounded students was watching the reacton of Governor Canterbury and the other Guardsmen who were in the courtroom. According to this friend: "They didn't seem shocked, outraged, or anything."

The next day Kelner produced yet another witness, a KSU graduate student named Robert Pickett. Pickett was called because he could testify to acts of brutality by Guardsmen on the night before the shootings, thus bolstering the pattern-of-excessive-force argument.

When testifying about the shootings, Pickett did not have anything to say about Sergeant Pryor, but he did testify that he saw Major Jones wave his baton before the Guardsmen fired (suggesting again that it was Jones, not Pryor, who gave the order to fire).

After the trial, I asked plaintiffs' attorney David Engdahl half-facetiously if the plaintiffs were trying to sabotage their own case. Engdahl denied this, but he explained how these screw-ups happened.

Part of the problem, Engdahl explained, was that the different attorneys for the victims kept promoting their own pet theories, which often conflicted with those of the others, instead of having the trial team agreeing on one theory of what happened and presenting the jury with a simple, cohesive picture.

Engdahl said that even during the trial itself "we went back and forth on the theories." Kelner did not know which attorney to trust because he came into the trial cold, and as Engdahl saw it, "was basically ignorant of the facts."

After the trial Chris Jindra of Cleveland's *Plain Dealer* similarly wrote: "Lawyers for the plaintiffs spent weeks trying to prove that 1st Sergeant Myron Pryor fired the first shot with his .45 caliber pistol. Then, amazingly, they put on the stand a sound specialist who testified the first shot came from a .30 caliber rifle."

Defense attorney Burt Fulton later told me that when the sound specialist testified he almost fell out of his chair.

June 18, 1975

The courtroom was packed when Sergeant Myron Pryor finally took the witness stand.

Pryor had quite a few charges to answer, and his testimony took up the better part of the day.

Pryor denied everything. He portrayed himself as a clerk who normally pushed papers at the Guard armory and who only accompanied the troops as a last minute favor to Captain Raymond Srp.

As Pryor told it, he did not give a signal to fire, he never fired his weapon, and all he did was follow the example of the men under his command by turning with them, and then crouched and aimed his gun at the students (without firing) for 11 seconds.

Pryor refused to be shaken from his testimony, even when Kelner tried to ridicule his testimony that he just stood there like a cigar store Indian.*

June 1975

Throughout June principal defense lawyers Fulton and Brown continued their strategy of trying to discredit the victims by associating the innocent bystanders and the ones who played only minor roles in the demonstration (like throwing a rock) with the more radical students.

As plaintiffs' attorney David Engdahl put it: "They tried to paint them all with the same radical [brush]."

The defense team tried to establish contributory negligence—the argument that the victims contributed to their own injuries by their own negligent actions. This defense was supported when some of the victims conceded that they had heard a Kent State policeman advise them that the May 4 rally was illegal and warn them: "Please disperse for your own safety." Moreover, two of the students, Dean Kahler and Alan Canfora, conceded throwing rocks at the soldiers.

Judge Donald Young gave the defense considerable latitude. He allowed Fulton and Brown to explore issues such as plaintiff Robby Stamps' political beliefs and his trips to a psychiatrist after the shootings.

Stamps later complained: "They weren't put on trial, we were."

Young also allowed the defense to plant outrageous suggestions in the minds of the jurors. For example:

• In grilling wounded student Alan Canfora, defense attorney Fulton kept saying "allegedly shot in the wrist," or your claim to have been shot," as if Canfora had faked his injury.

• When innocent bystander and wounded student John Cleary took the witness stand, defense attorney Brown tried to suggest that an object protruding from Cleary's jacket was a lead pipe he was going to throw at the Guardsmen. Actually, Cleary identified it as "a cardboard [cover]

---

* Arthur Krause was so angry with Pryor's testimony that he let out a loud groan and stormed out of the courtroom.

that goes over a tear gas cannister" that he had "picked up on the Commons as a souvenir." At the time of the shooting Cleary was trying to take a Polaroid snapshot and was no threat to the Guardsmen.

• When plaintiffs' witness Charles Deegan corroborated witness Harry William Montgomery's story that Sergeant Pryor seemingly gave a signal to fire by the tapping the Guardsmen closest to him, Fulton tried to shift the blame for the shootings on Deegan. Noting that Deegan had earlier in the day half-joking counted cadence to the soldiers, Fulton asked: "Did you give any orders like 'stand and turn' or 'stand and shoot?'" (as if the soldiers would take orders from a demonstrator.)

In effect, Fulton also put Deegan on trial by asking if he did "anything that could have created the incident," and then questioned Deegan's denials in a tone of voice suggesting he was lying.

June 30, 1975

One of the biggest bombshells of the trial was dropped when the captain of C Company, 145th Infantry, Ron Snyder (known as "Cyanide" Snyder to his men), admitted he had lied when he earlier claimed to have confiscated a gun from the body of Jeffrey Miller, one of the slain students, and brass knuckles from a demonstrator Snyder had clubbed in an unrelated incident about fifteen minutes before the shootings.

Snyder admitted that when investigators from the Ohio Highway Patrol interviewed him in 1970, he produced a "throwdown" (planted) pistol from his own desk, as well as his own brass knuckles, and that he repeated these false claims under oath when he subsequently testified before the Ohio special grand jury.

Under cross-examination, Kelner tried to flush out some of the details of why Snyder felt it was necessary to fabricate these stories. Snyder had earlier told the federal grand jury that after the first civil lawsuit was filed in June 1970, he and the other Guardsmen were worried about the legal difficulties they might be in, and Snyder told his captain: "Well, hell, I got the answer to this thing. We got self-defense."

Snyder then showed his captain the planted pistol and the knuckles, "and the next thing I knew, everybody had the information" and he found himself locked into the story.

Characterizing Snyder's testimony as powerful evidence that called into question the validity of the Guard's entire defense at the trial, Kelner tried to question Snyder about the motivation behind his lies and why he finally told the truth about the gun and brass knuckles to federal prosecutors.

He did not get very far. Judge Young ruled that under the existing rules of evidence, Snyder's federal grand jury testimony was inadmissible.

Young also prevented Kelner from pursuing this line of questioning, ruling that "things that happened after" the shootings were beyond the scope of the trial.

Kelner protested, and later claimed that Young's ruling prevented him from exposing a coverup among the Guardsmen.

In fact, in his book on the trial, Kelner wrote that he considered Snyder's testimony to be "the big break I was looking for, one that could crack the case wide open for us."

Was it?

I had the opportunity to read Snyder's suppressed federal grand jury testimony, which was read into the court record out of the hearing of the jury and newsmen. Although Snyder's testimony showed he was personally willing to go to great lengths to protect himself and smear the dead, that was all it showed. It required a gigantic leap to believe that just because Snyder was a perjurer, he was directing the cover-up among the principal shooters.

Snyder, after all, was not directly involved in the shootings. He and his men in C Company were on the other side of Taylor Hall when the firing broke out, and there was no indication he had any contact with the officers or men of G Troop or Company A, the men who did most of the firing and who had been claiming self-defense two months before Snyder concocted his so-called answer to the Guardsmen's problems.

July 1, 1975

Major Harry Jones followed Captain Snyder to the witness stand and denied that he had given a signal to fire or that the hand signals he admitted giving the troops ("Hurry up" or "Stay in formation") could have been misconstrued as such a signal. Jones also testified that he felt his own life was in danger.

However, had Judge Young allowed the plaintiffs to introduce Major Jones' testimony before the federal grand jury into evidence, the jury would have heard Jones tell a different version.

Jones had secretly told the grand jury: "It's my honest opinion that it [the shooting] should not have happened. As I see it, from where I was standing and from what I know about the incident, it was against the concepts and procedures that we had trained in."

The reason Young gave for refusing to allow this testimony into evidence was: "I'm not going to let every Tom, Dick, and Harry express his opinion on the ultimate issues in the case." (In other words, whether the Guardsmen were justified in firing.)

This was one of the most extraordinary rulings during the trial. Jones was not just any Tom, Dick or Harry.

He was one of the highest ranking officers on Blanket Hill that day, and the officer closest to the troops that fired.*

Meanwhile, the local newspapers began running news analyses about one of the more annoying sidelights of the trial: the constant bickering between the lead counsels for the plaintiffs and the defense.

John Dunphy of the *Akron Beacon Journal* criticized "the juvenile outbursts by the chief attorneys in the case," and perhaps thinking of Cicero's famous legal maxim ("When you have no basis for an argument, abuse the plaintiff"), suggested "that defense attorneys Burt Fulton and Charlie Brown committed their outbursts as a tactical trial strategy to rattle the other side."

The defense attorneys—particularly Fulton (who later said he liked to have fun in a trial)—mercilessly teased Kelner about his manner of questioning. "Is that the way you do it in New York?" Fulton and Brown would ask when objecting to his questions.

Judge Young admonished the lawyers—usually to no avail.

_____

*In his book Kelner charged that the exclusion of this highly damaging federal grand jury testimony was evidence that Judge Young was biased against the plaintiffs. However, as defense attorney Burt Fulton told me after the trial: "Young's a pretty liberal guy." He had a reputation of being an advocate of civil liberties, and after the trial both defense and plaintiffs' attorneys agreed that if Young was biased, it should have been for the plaintiffs.

Why then did Young rule so often against the victims (which was one of the reasons Kelner claimed he lost the trial?) Fulton told me: "They [the plaintiffs] could have had him in his hip pocket, but they pissed him off so." Fulton said he agreed with comments by David Engdahl that Kelner alienated Young by "crossing swords" with him repeatedly on procedural matters, by constantly repeating questions, and by bickering over issues that ultimately were not that important.

"Ironically," Chris Jindra of the *Plain Dealer* wrote, "when the lawyers quarrel, the seven men and five women on the jury appear bored."

Mid-June to Mid-July 1975

During this period the plaintiffs intermittently called to the stand the four other Guardsmen who admitted firing at the students: James Pierce, Barry Morris, James McGee, and Ralph Zoller. However, the plaintiffs diluted their case against the four by intermingling their appearances on the stand with the appearances of more than half a dozen other Guardsmen who also fired, but who fired into the air or into the ground away from the students.

There was little reason to believe that any of these "small fry" Guardsmen hurt anyone, but the plaintiffs pursued claims of negligence against them, suggesting they acted negligently by merely discharging their rifles and that someone could have been hurt by ricochets or falling bullets.

Many of these "small fry" Guardsmen testified that they were frightened or that they feared for their lives, which only served to undercut the victims' case.

They also put the plaintiffs' attorneys in the defensive position of having to challenge their testimony.

After the trial, some of the wounded students told me the reason these Guardsmen were called was because certain lawyers on the plaintiffs' team had grudges against certain soldiers. Lieutenant Alexander Stevenson and Howard Fallon were two Guardsmen cited specifically.

According to these plaintiffs, the lawyers also fought among themselves over who would get to cross-examine a "big" shooter as opposed to just a "little" one.

David Engdahl agreed that the strategy of pursuing claims that these "small fry" Guardsmen was "bad judgment" on the lawyers' part. He told me: "A strategy decision had been made before the trial to put all these shooters on the stand. The motivation for it, I am afraid, was the insistence of people like Galen Keller (Kelner's paralegal) that those bastards ought to be put on the stand and made to squirm. And they were. They had their purgatory.

"But while we got the satisfaction of seeing them uncomfortable on the stand, it was not the best strategy as far as winning the case. It cluttered up the record with a whole lot of little crap, prolonged the trial very much, and did not help our liability case, which would have been more effectively put together with much more sparse testimony."

July 22, 1975

Most of the questions posed to Guard Adjutant General Sylvester Del Corso concerned his policies regarding the arming of the troops, the extent of training the soldiers had, and whether the Ohio National Guard's practices of dealing with civil disorders complied with the stringent standards set down by the Department of the Army.

The really interesting aspect of Del Corso's testimony, though, came after Kelner asked him his opinion, as the highest ranking National Guardsman in the state of Ohio, whether or not the shooting could be justified.

Del Corso had been asked that very same question sixteen separate times when he testified before the federal grand jury a year earlier. And sixteen times Del Corso answered he could see no justification for the shooting.

However, when Kelner tried to get Del Corso to repeat this before the jury, Del Corso's lawyers jumped to their feet and reminded Judge Young that he had earlier disallowed the introduction of federal grand jury testimony because of the existing rules of evidence. Young then ruled that Kelner could not ask Del Corso this "ultimate question" unless Kelner first qualified Del Corso as an expert witness for the plaintiffs. And that meant Del Corso would have to agree to be a witness for the plaintiffs.

To get that crucial testimony, Kelner offered to drop all claims against Del Corso. The offer was relayed to Del Corso, who was advised by Judge Young that he ought to consider retaining private counsel because the attorneys representing him also represented the Guardsmen he would testify against, thus presenting the lawyers with a conflict of interest.

It is not known whether Del Corso followed Young's advice, but after thinking over the offer, the general, like a good soldier, refused Kelner's offer and decided to either stand or fall with the rest of the soldiers.

The result: The jury never heard the opinion of the highest Guardsmen in the state of Ohio that there was no way to justify the killings.

Early August 1975

Because the plaintiffs' attorneys were unable to communicate to the jury that the adjutant general of the Guard considered the shootings unjustifiable, the attorneys tried to find other experts to offer the same testimony.

One was a former Army colonel named Edward King, who had commanded troops in Korea and Germany after World War II (some twenty years earlier).

King's lack of recent command experience made him a less-than-perfect expert witness, but as Engdahl put it, he was the only "straight Army type we could find who had any kind of credentials at all and who was willing to testify" against the soldiers.

King testified that:

• The shootings were improper;

• The Guardsmen could have used a rifle butt stroke instead of shooting (King demonstrated that jabbing motion to the jury and testified the method had proved effective in previous riots);

• Ohio National Guard procedures allowing individual soldiers to routinely lock and load their weapons before going into crowd control duty without being ordered to do so contrasted with "good standards and procedures;"

• The company commanders never should have sent Guardsmen who were nearsighted into riot control situations, since the Ohio National Guard had not complied with regulations requiring gas masks to be fitted with corrective lenses. (Ten of the 33 Guardsmen who testified at the trial admitted they usually wore glasses, but were unable to wear them under their gas mask on May 4. One lawyer once told me that some of the Guardsmen could not see "as far as the end of their rifles."); and

• The Guardsmen fouled up by yielding high ground to the students, by letting soldiers from different units intermingle with one another (thus preventing the officers from effectively controlling the men), by not ensuring that enough tear gas was brought along, and by allowing Guardsmen to swap weapons with their buddies (King explained that each rifle had a different sight setting).

Many of King's criticisms were supported by the expert testimony of James Ahern, a former police chief of New Haven, Connecticut, who had considerable experience in keeping demonstrations under control.

During the weekend before the tragedy, Ahern had handled, without casualties, potentially more explosive demonstrations at Yale.

July 29, 1975

The last major defendant to be called by the plaintiffs was James A. Rhodes, the white-haired governor of Ohio.

Once sworn in, Rhodes compared the situation at Kent to a "state of war."

However, as commander-in-chief of the Ohio National Guard, Rhodes insisted he gave no orders to crush the insurgency.

Mid-August 1975 (The Defense's Turn)

Since the defense attorneys had already cross-examined the plaintiffs' witnesses and tried to make all of them look like liars, the defense's case was relatively short and simple. They tried to reinforce the impression that Kent had been in the throes of an insurrection in May of 1970, that no one in authority had done anything wrong, and that the Guardsmen, emperiled by maniacal students, had to kill to save their own lives.

The defense witnesses included:

• A policeman who testified about the window-breaking in downtown Kent on Friday, May 1, and the injuries sustained by a few members of the Kent police department;
• A shoe store owner who testified about the damage to his property and about his fears for his own personal safety;
• Colonel Donald Manley of the Ohio Highway Patrol, who called the protestors the most vicious and aggressive people he had ever encountered; and
• Paul Locher, a student from Ashland College visiting Kent that weekend, who claimed the students "were out for blood."

After that the defense turned their attention to the events of May 4. They also offered the jury another theory to latch on to—just in case the jury did not want to buy the self-defense stories.

Even though none of the Guardsmen had testified that they had seen a sniper or that they even suspected anyone was firing at them, the defense attorneys tried to suggest that an unknown gunman had fired at the Guardsmen.

To support this, the defense called Joy Hubbard Bishop to the stand. She was a sophomore at Kent State in 1970, and she had watched the action from the roof of Johnson Hall. She testified that, as the Guardsmen approached the Pagoda, she watched a man walk up behind them, draw a pistol from a briefcase, and fire it in the air "two to five seconds" before the troops turned and fired.

Parts of Bishop's story closely resembled the episode that involved Terry Norman, the Kent State student and undercover photographer who had been seen on Blanket Hill with a pistol and whom some students suspected may have been involved in the gunfire. On May 4 he was wearing a tan sports coat, which could easily have been the yellowish-gold sports coat Bishop saw her mystery man wearing.

Norman did not carry a briefcase on May 4. However, one of the men who subsequently chased Norman from the scene did, and Bishop could have been just confused on that point.

There were, however, some serious problems with Bishop's story:

(1) Bishop had previously talked to Professor Jerry M. Lewis of Kent, and while Lewis agreed that Bishop claimed to be able to identify the man who fired the first shot, Lewis said Bishop told him the man was a Guardsman with a .45, not a civilian wearing a sports coat.

(2) At the time Bishop witnessed this incident she was standing on the roof of Johnson Hall next to her roommate, Pat Frank Rivera, and Rivera's boyfriend, Bruce Phillips. Neither Rivera nor Phillips saw the man in the sports coat, and significantly, both Rivera and Phillips said later that Bishop never mentioned the man either at that time or later that day when Rivera and Phillips gave Bishop a ride to her hometown of Canfield, Ohio.

Had Bishop seen the man who started the Kent State shootings, one would assume that she would have mentioned it to her friends.

After Bishop testified, Rivera, her former roommate, told reporters: "I don't think she's lying. I think she's just confused."

David Engdahl agreed, and during a break in the proceedings he joked about Bishop's testimony with Dick Waltz, a young attorney on the defense team who had recently graduated from law school and who was on friendly terms with Engdahl, a professor of constitutional law.

Engdahl said he told Waltz: "'I thought Joy Bishop was a red herring. But she turned out to be a real turkey.' Waltz chuckled and then came back at me with this. He said, 'You know, on law school examinations, there [are] always one or two red herrings in the questions to throw the students off track.'"

"Waltz said, 'That kind of stuff doesn't foul up the A students and it usually doesn't screw up the B students, but it really plays havoc with the C students.' I said, 'Yeah, that's right.'

"Then he smiled and said: 'There aren't any A or B students on that jury.' And I responded: 'I understand your strategy.'"

August 14, 1975

While the defense wrapped up its case by calling some other witnesses whose testimony seemed mostly redundant, two other incidents affecting the jury occurred outside the courthouse. In one, a juror, Douglas Watts, was dismissed because he told a coworker he considered the plaintiffs communists ("misguided leftists" was the phrase Watts conceded he had used).

Watts was excused because he had talked about the case out of court.

In an unrelated and more disturbing incident, another juror, Richard Williams, reported to the jury that on his way home an unidentified burly man pinned him to a wall and threatened to beat him up and blow up his house if he did not vote in a certain way. (Which way was never specified by Williams.)

Judge Young promptly called in the FBI and sequestered the jury.

"I've had blood on my hands from ignoring previous threats in other cases," he told the jury.

August 22, 1975

On August 22 Judge Young, who had previously advised the jury that they would have as many as 50 variations of verdicts to choose from, read 76 pages of instructions to the jury.

To give an idea of how long and complicated the charge was, the charge was so long that it was roughly twice the length of any chapter in this book.

It was so complex that none of the 16 lawyers involved in the litigation caught some of the errors in the convoluted multiple choice questions Judge Young presented to the jury. It was the jurors, trying to figure out what the charge meant, who caught them.

The jurors retreated to the Sheraton-Cleveland Hotel to deliberate the evidence. It would take them six days to reach a verdict.

They did not ask to be supplied with any of the trial transcripts, but they did ask to see a somewhat indistinct eight millimeter movie of the shootings that had been taken by a student from a nearby dorm, maps of the campus, some of the photographs, and a magnifying glass.

August 27, 1975

On Thursday, August 27, 1975, the jurors trooped back into Judge Young's courtroom to announce that they had finally arrived at a decision.

Some of the women on the jury appeared to have been crying. When the plaintiffs looked into their eyes, they knew they had lost the trial.

The clerk then read the jury verdict sheets, which named all the slain students and all the wounded students. After naming each one the clerk read: "We the jury . . . find in favor of the Defendants."

Some of the wounded students lost their cool, yelling, "They're still murderers!" or "The trial's a sham," while some of the other plaintiffs either started crying or sat there stunned.*

September-October 1975

The plaintiffs did not waste any time announcing that they would appeal the verdict on the grounds that Judge Young's rulings had denied them a fair trial.

They asked Judge Young to overturn the verdict himself, but Young refused, saying he believed the jury had arrived at a proper decision.

Adding insult to injury, Young also ruled that the parents of the dead

---

* After the trial the jurors, for the most part, refused to discuss how or why they reached their decision, although one juror, Richard Williams, said he thought he heard the words "Lay down your guns, we've got you surrounded" on the Strubbe tape recording of the shootings. No one else was able to hear those words.

Chris Jindra of the *Plain Dealer* reported that the jurors spent more time debating whether or not to assess damages against former KSU President Robert I. White than they spent debating the role of any other defendants. In fact, Jindra reported that the jurors came closest to blaming White.

That surprised not only White's lawyer, who argued that White was "a small oak in a large forest," but plaintiffs' attorney David Engdahl, who told me after the trial: "There wasn't any evidence against White."

students and the nine wounded student had to pay the lawyers for the Guardsmen and Governor Rhodes over $72,000 to cover court expenses.

Commented Benson Wolman, the executive director of the Ohio ACLU: "It somehow offends one's sense of decency. It's like the state, having licensed people to kill and having justified it, has now chosen to charge the survivors."

Late 1975 to Mid-1977

As Kelner noted in his book on the trial: "The thirteen plaintiffs turned the appeal over to the American Civil Liberties Union, which offered to advance funds for expenses and provide the [staff]."

The lawyer chosen to head the appeals team was Sanford J. Rosen, a San Francisco attorney who had previously worked on an unrelated lawsuit in which KSU students who lived in dormitories successfully sued the University and law enforcement officials for illegally searching their rooms after the shootings. The authorities, attempting to justify the shootings, conducted the warrantless search in a futile attempt to find student weapons.

Rosen appealed the civil verdict on several grounds, claiming that Young denied the plaintiffs a fair trial by:

• Terrifying the jury by making his "blood on my hands" speech and by not dismissing threatened juror Richard Williams;
• Refusing to allow the plaintiffs to use the federal grand jury testimony so damaging to the Guardsmen;
• Allowing the defense attorneys to dwell on pre-May 4 activities; and
• Allowing the defense to closely question various victims about their personal political beliefs, in effect putting the victims on trial.

On June 21, 1977, Rosen delivered his oral arguments before the Sixth Circuit Court of Appeals in Cincinnati.

Later, Rosen said he was not optimistic about the outcome. Most appeals courts, Rosen noted, will go out of their way to avoid overruling district level judges and ordering new trials.

September 12, 1977

To the surprise of Rosen and many of his clients, the appeals court ruled that the plaintiffs had indeed been denied a fair trial.

In ordering a retrial, the court, in its opinion, sidestepped most of the issues raised by the exclusion and inclusion of certain evidence. Instead, it focused on the threat to juror Williams, which the court described as "an attempt to pervert our system of justice."

In its opinion the court stated:

Every litigant is entitled to a verdict which is free from improper influence. It was an error for the trial judge to determine ex parte and without personal interrogation that a juror who had been threatened and assaulted and told that his home would be blown up could continue to serve, unaffected by these incidents. The threatened juror should have been questioned by the court to hear his version of the reported incident and to learn whether he had discussed them with other jurors, including the possibility that he disclosed the way in which his assailant was attempting to cause him to vote . . . Unless the court was completely satisfied after questioning him that there was no possibility that the threatened juror would be affected in the performance of his duties that juror should have been excused.

1977 to 1978

Once the Sixth circuit Court of Appeals paved the way for the second trial, the plaintiffs' attorneys began arguing among themselves again over which attorney would lead the second trial team.

Kelner lobbied to be reinstated, while the ACLU pushed for its own candidate, Rosen, who had never tried a case before a jury before.

I was able to obtain the letters that the various attorneys sent to the victims in November 1977, just before the decision was made. David Engdahl, who sided with Rosen in this battle, sent the KSU victims a remarkable seven-page, singled-spaced letter in which he said, "It is time for all of us lawyers to try to be totally honest with you."

Engdahl itemized several "extremely serious mistakes" which he alleged Kelner made at the first trial and suggested the victims had been poorly served by their attorneys.

That charge was echoed by Rosen, who in his own letter, told the victims, "At the first trial, the case was not so much won by the defendants as lost by the plaintiffs."

Engdahl, in his letter, reminded the clients that Kelner's eleventh-hour selection as lead counsel was a "desperation measure," and, referring to what he called Kelner's lack of preparedness and lack of understanding "of the theory of the case," wrote: "During the trial, one of the defense counsel confided in me that Joe Kelner, as plaintiffs' lead counsel, was the defendants' major asset in the trial."

Kelner's letter to the victims asking that he be retained as lead counsel was sent before Engdahl's, so Kelner did not have much opportunity to respond to Engdahl's charges. However, Kelner did warn the victims that they would be inviting disaster if they picked Rosen, an ACLU attorney, as their chief attorney, because: "In the eyes of many prospective jurors the ACLU itself is regarded as a radical organization."

And criticizing the other attorneys he had to work with, Kelner wrote that "the inept performances of inexperienced lawyers led to open laughter and derision by the jury."

The victims would lose again, Kelner warned, if they allowed themselves to be represented by an attorney like Rosen, who had never tried a case before a jury.

On December 4, 1977, the victims selected Rosen to head the second trial team. One of his first decisions was not to invite back any of the lawyers who participated in the first civil trial, with the exception of David Engdahl.

Rosen also asked the National Jury Project, led by sociologists at Columbia University, to poll potential jurors in northeast Ohio in order to assess his chances of winning the second trial. The conclusions of that study disturbed Rosen. Even though eight years had passed since the killings, the study showed, as Rosen put it: "There was a high degree of probability that we weren't going to win."

October 1978

Rosen, at least, was pleased with some of the pretrial rulings issued by Federal Judge William Thomas, who was assigned to preside over the second trial. Thomas' rulings in several key instances were diametrically opposite to positions that Judge Young took in the first trial. For example, Thomas ruled that the plaintiffs could make use of the federal grand jury testimony; ask witnesses their opinions about whether the shootings were justified or not; and prohibited the defense attorneys from asking the victims about their political beliefs unless the defense attorneys could demonstrate some direct relevance.

Even with these rulings, Rosen later said he was still "honestly pessimistic" about the chances of winning the trial.

Earlier he had initiated discussions with the defense attorneys about the possibility of settling the suits out of court. At the time the discussions went nowhere.

December 9-18, 1978

By the time a jury was selected for the second trial there were rampant rumors of a tentative compromise settlement.

Both the *Plain Dealer* and the *Akron Beacon Journal* quoted sources close to both sides as saying that an agreement had been reached on the amount of damages to be awarded to the victims and that the only stumbling block was the wording of a statement to be signed by all the defendants.

Rosen had wanted an outright apology, and defense attorney Burt Fulton made it clear to him that "was totally out of the question."

The newspapers also reported at the time that the settlement had to be approved by the Ohio State Controlling Board, which had already allocated $380,000 to the defense attorneys to cover their costs at the trial. However, the state board temporarily tabled debate on the issue. Rosen said later "the snag was the Ohio politicians and legislators" who first need to send up trial balloons to see how much flak they would get from their constituents before paying money to the victims of the Kent State killings.

December 19, 1978-January 3, 1979

While the State Controlling Board waited to test the waters, Judge Thomas ordered that the second trial get underway.

Opening statements were virtually a repeat performance of arguments delivered at the first trial, and no new arguments or witnesses were presented.

On December 21, 1978, Judge Thomas recessed the trial in order to conduct hearings on a truckers' strike in northeast Ohio. That gave the State Controlling Board more time to consider the settlement.

When the trial resumed in January 1, there would only be one more day of testimony from witnesses.

January 4, 1979

On January 4, 1979, Judge Thomas announced that a settlement had been reached and approved by the Ohio legislators. The terms of the agreement:

The plaintiffs agreed to drop the lawsuits and all future claims against the Guardsmen and Governor Rhodes in return for a lump sum of $675,000 in damages to be divided among the 13 victims. The money was to be provided by the state of Ohio, and not by the individual defendants.

Almost half of the sum, $350,000, went to Dean Kahler, who was permanently crippled, to compensate him for his pain and suffering and to meet any future medical expenses.

The other eight wounded students were awarded damages from $15,000 to $42,000, depending on the nature and severity of their injury.

The parents of the four students who were killed each received $15,000 to compensate them for the loss of their children.

At the same time, the defendants signed "a statement of regret" that was so nebulously worded that anyone could interpret it any way they wanted to.

Thus, Rosen was able to tell reporters that the defendants had apologized for the shootings. At the same time Charles Shanklin, Governor Rhodes' attorney, was able to state: "The Governor is not guilty of anything. Nor are any of the defendants."

The statement read:

In retrospect, the tragedy of May 4, 1970, should not have occurred. The students may have believed that they were right in continuing the mass protest in response to the Cambodian invasion, even though this protest followed the posting and reading by the University of an order to ban rallies and an order to disperse. These orders have since been determined by the Sixth Circuit Court of Appeals to have been lawful.

Some of the Guardsmen on Blanket Hill, fearful and anxious from previous events, may have believed in their own minds that their lives were in danger. Hindsight suggests that another method would have resolved the confrontation. Better ways must be found to deal with such confrontations.

We devoutly wish that a means had been found to avoid the May 4 events culminating in the Guard shootings and the irreversible deaths and injuries. We deeply regret those events and are profoundly saddened by the deaths of four students and wounding of nine others which resulted. We hope that this agreement to end this litigation will help to assuage the tragic memories regarding that sad day.

The Settlement

I do not know of anyone who was thrilled by the settlement. Exhaustion and fear of losing the second trial seemed to be the prime motivating factor for both the plaintiffs and defendants.

The settlement was a way of ending the litigation safely and without further emotionally traumatizing any of the parties.

Dr. Thomas Hensley, a professor of political science at Kent, provided the best analysis of the settlement. Hensley wrote:

> A fundamental stimulus for settling out of court was fear of losing the case. The plaintiffs' chief attorney, Sanford Rosen, described the trial outcome as a "crapshoot." That was probably too optimistic. It was unlikely that any juror selected would have been initially sympathetic to the parents of the students. For example, the Kent State Jury Project, involving random telephoning of registered voters in Northeast Ohio, found that a majority of the respondents rejected the plaintiffs' basic argument that the Guardsmen fired upon the students without provocation. Jury selection in the 1979 trial reinforced strongly the situation facing the plaintiffs . . . Even assuming that twelve truly impartial jurors were selected, a most unlikely probability, the plaintiffs still faced enormous obstacles. The 1975 jury had voted 9–3 against the plaintiffs, and Rosen and his colleagues had no major new evidence to introduce. Most critically, the plaintiffs' attorneys still lacked the major piece of evidence they need, an explanation as to why the Guardsmen fired. Rosen, in his opening statement, admitted "we do not know . . ." But the lawyers for the defendants had an answer. The Guard fired because they were in serious danger of death or injury from the riotous students.

Hensley characterized the decision to settle out of court as "eminently reasonable" under the circumstances and cited other considerations that had to be taken into account "even assuming the plaintiffs could win the case."

As Hensley pointed out, it was extremely difficult to predict how much money might be awarded in damages since there were few guidelines or precedents to follow in deprivation of civil rights lawsuits like this one.

In fact, when I interviewed Rosen, he told me it was "absolutely possible" that even if he had won the trial, the jury might have returned with only a token award, as small as one dollar.

"There were no guidelines," Rosen said, "because this was not a personal injury case, despite what Joe Kelner might think."

Some of the other defense attorneys, including Robert Blakemore, who represented former Kent State President Robert I. White, felt that the plaintiffs might have done better had their attorneys not tried to turn Kent State into a test case for constitutional issues.

Kelner was also among those sharply critical of the settlement, dismissing the $675,000 award as a pittance. In his book Kelner argued that "any experienced trial lawyer would have hung his head in shame."

In a sense, Kelner's criticism of the award was justified. If you compare the amount of damages awarded to the Kent State victims to the amount of damages awarded to victims in most negligence suits, the award of $675,000 divided thirteen ways was embarrassingly low.

Coincidentally, an article that appeared in the *New York Times* just one month before the first civil trial started noted that there was a nationwide trend for settling personal injury and damage suits in the millions.

In fact, just to cite one example, a few months after the first trial was held, a 31-year-old Detroit woman was awarded $260,000 by a jury because her dentist's drill bit slipped. She lost the sensation in her lower lip, and received the award because she could no longer enjoy kissing her husband.

Did the settlement ultimately serve the interests of justice? I posed that question to Rosen. His answer was: "There is no such thing as justice. We just try to serve the needs of our clients."

Although it could be argued that the "statement of regret" he insisted on was, if anything, an embarrassment to his clients, and the victims might have won the first trial had they had a more sympathetic judge and attorneys who'd had their act together, it is difficult to quarrel with the assessment that, in 1979, the settlement was the right choice under difficult circumstances.

Yet one is also left with the nagging feeling that someone should have been held accountable for the shootings. After the first trial the *New York Post* published an editorial that addressed this issue. The *Post* editorialized:

> It is true there has been a verdict in the Kent State trial . . . The civil trial consumed scores of days. Dozens of witnesses, prominent and humble, were heard. The printed transcripts made stacks [of] thousands of pages. And yet, in the end, the record seems tragically empty . . .
>
> It is as though the decision had been reached that the dead and injured were victims of some unfortunate, unforseen accident, that they had been struck by a runaway car or had perished in a fire, and that no one could honestly be charged with blame.
>
> That judgment may satisfy some Americans who are, perhaps understandably, weary of five years of reading, hearing and wondering about the Kent State tragedy. It does not satisfy the sense of justice, which never tires.

And because of that the Post made one final and prophetic judgment: "Kent State will remain an open and disturbing case indefinitely."

TEN

Some Final Thoughts About May 4

If you have ever read any of the books on the Kennedy assassination, you know that they almost always end on an optimistic note.

One otherwise thoughtful book ended with Chaucer's famous quote, "Murder will out" (an optimistic wish that history would take care of itself), and several books have pleaded for a new investigation of the assassination.

This despite the fact that more than three decades have passed since the crime was committed, that many of the witnesses are dead, unavailable, or cannot be trusted to remember anything at this point, and that even if a new investigation were held, no one would know where to begin.

Despite the advice of some in the publishing world, I will resist the temptation to end this book with a similar plea. I cannot imagine what a new investigation of the Kent State killings would accomplish.

If the investigations that were held a generation ago were unable to yield "the smoking gun" or any of the other elusive hidden truths that many in Kent are still looking for, it is extremely unlikely that another investigation will.

Still, there is one important piece of unfinished business. Kent State remains an unsolved murder, and there are four or five Guardsmen—the men who were on the left flank of the firing line—who have to know why the Guardsmen fired under such extremely suspicious circumstances.

These men declined to reveal their identities to the FBI, and since we can only guess who they might be, we do not even know if they have ever been questioned by authorities, or if they were, what stories they told.

These four Guardsmen should know which witnesses told the truth, which witnesses perjured themselves, and whether there was, as the circumstantial evidence strongly suggests, an order to fire on the students issued by one of the officers.

This is probably wishful thinking on my part, but I would like to see these Guardsmen come forward and provide those answers. Some may be reluctant to do so because it might mean thrusting themselves in the public eye, but even that is not necessary.

Even if all the Guardsman did was record what he felt history should note and placed that record in a time capsule in the Kent State archives, that might be helpful in fulfilling an obligation to history.

Unless that happens, there will never be a final chapter in this case.

APPENDIX I

Excerpts from the John Ehrlichman Interview

In November 1970, John Ehrlichman, President Nixon's chief domestic adviser, hand delivered to Attorney General John Mitchell a presidential memorandum ordering Mitchell to close the Justice Department's investigation of the Kent State case. Until my interview with Ehrlichman on February 18, 1982, no one who served in the Nixon White House had been willing to discuss Nixon's intervention in the case.

GORDON: Why did Nixon send you over to Mitchell's office with the secret memo to crush the grand jury?

EHRLICHMAN: I am not sure it happened that way. My recollection is that after a conversation with Governor Rhodes, Nixon decided to try to forestall a grand jury.

GORDON: That is very interesting. Did you talk to Rhodes yourself?

EHRLICHMAN: No. No, I did not. But I know Nixon did.

GORDON: Do you know why Rhodes did not want the federal grand jury?

EHRLICHMAN: No, I don't know.

GORDON: Are you saying then it was not really Nixon's idea—it was Governor Rhodes' idea not to have the grand jury?

EHRLICHMAN: I don't know about that. But I know that it came out of a conversation between Rhodes and Nixon.

GORDON: Did you ever speak with Nixon about his attitude toward prosecuting the Guardsmen?

EHRLICHMAN: Yes . . . He [said he] did not want to prosecute them.

GORDON: Did he say why?

EHRLICHMAN: Well, he felt that they were enforcing the law and that this incident had occurred in the chain or stream of law enforcement process and the evidence was very ambiguous, very unclear, and therefore he felt that if any prosecution took place it ought to be at the state level or not at all.

GORDON: The Justice Department at that time was supposedly considering a prosecution, and you had dealt with them.

There were recommendations from the Justice Department to the effect to prosecute the Guardsmen.

Was he aware of those?

EHRLICHMAN: I don't think so. I don't think so. I don't know.

GORDON: I didn't quite understand why Nixon had to even tell Mitchell not to convene the federal grand jury because it seemed to me automatically Mitchell would not as a "law and order" issue.

EHRLICHMAN: I do not know. I think once Nixon had decided on his own, he did not want to leave it to some mischance.

Our experience with Mitchell in his administration of the Justice Department was not entirely a happy one, and I think by that time Nixon had a pretty healthy skepticism about how well Mitchell would perform in any given pattern. So he [Nixon] was leaving very little to chance.

GORDON: This memo that came out, the "eyes only" memo [Ehrlichman's memo to Mitchell of November 18, 1970] alludes to the president's memorandum [Nixon's original memorandum] to Mitchell on the subject. Do you recall what was in that memorandum?

EHRLICHMAN: No, I don't.

GORDON: Well, since then it's vanished. The Justice Department says it has no record of having such a memo.

EHRLICHMAN: Huh. Well, the chances are that it is still in Nixon's archives.

GORDON: Were you with Nixon when the shooting happened? I wanted to find out what his gut reaction was.

EHRLICHMAN: No, I do not believe I was. I do not recall . . .

GORDON: Was anybody surprised at the White House that it happened?

EHRLICHMAN: Oh, I think we were all surprised in the sense that—

Let me go back. The context is this: that Nixon decided to do the Cambodian incursion, so-called. He called me in and said, "Look, I'm going to have to lay aside domestic matters for a period of perhaps ten days and you are going to have to bring me all the decisions you want made right quick. Otherwise they are going to have to be deferred for a week or ten days."

So I went back and tried to anticipate what our problems were going to be over the period of the next couple of weeks. And I came back to him and got a number of decisions and some guidance on things that were going to come up.

The expectation was that he was not going to have to devote any attention at all to domestic matters, although in the planning process I think it was anticipated that there would be a certain amount of domestic protest.

The Kent State shootings derailed that assumption that he was going to be able to stay out of domestic affairs. His involvement was inescapable at that point in coping with the aftermath of Kent State, so . . . when you ask, was it a surprise? It was unanticipated, certainly. Our planning did not involve anything of that kind.

GORDON: A *Newsweek* article said that Nixon's reaction came dangerously close to saying the students deserved [to be shot]. Do you think that would be a fair statement? Did that reflect his thinking?

EHRLICHMAN: There certainly is a flavor of that in it. And I think that may have been his initial reaction to the events.

GORDON: That the students deserved it?

EHRLICHMAN: That they brought it on themselves, so to speak, by resorting to violence. Because that, you see, was the initial report: that the Guardsmen had been either fired upon or pelted with rocks or something to which they reacted.

GORDON: Did [Nixon] consider the victims bums?*

EHRLICHMAN: No. See, that "bums" business was related to an incident in Stanford, where a professor from India had all of his research papers destroyed in a fire which was the result of a protest and Nixon's remark was directed specifically to that incident and to the people who cost that man his life's work. But it very quickly lost its context.

---

*Three days before the shootings, Nixon, speaking extemporaneously at the Pentagon, denounced antiwar protestors as "bums." Nixon said: "You know, you see these bums, you know, blowing up the campuses. Listen, the boys on the college campuses are the luckiest people in the world—going to the greatest universities—and here they are burning up the books, storming around like this, I mean—you name it. Get rid of the war and there'll be another one. And then, out there, we got kids who are just doing their duty, and I've seen them. They stand tall and they're proud."

GORDON: You mean he was not referring to all students as bums?
EHRLICHMAN: Oh, no.
GORDON: Or all protestors?
EHRLICHMAN: No. Definitely not.
GORDON: This brings up the subject of what [Nixon's] attitude was toward the people protesting the Vietnam War. [Nixon's chief of staff] H. R. Haldeman gave an interview in 1972 [to the "Today" show] and he said critics of Nixon's Vietnam policies were aiding and abetting the enemy—almost the definition of being traitors.

Was that Haldeman talking or Nixon talking?
EHRLICHMAN: That was Haldeman talking.
GORDON: But did Nixon feel that way?
EHRLICHMAN: I think the way Nixon felt was that there were two political elements in this country on the war, one who supported him and one who opposed him, and it was very important to him at any given time where the numerical superiority lay between those two elements.

When we had two or three hundred thousand people out on Pennsylvania Avenue marching along with signs and flags and so on—
GORDON: Are you talking about right after the shootings?
EHRLICHMAN: No, I'm talking about—we had six or seven of those New Mobe and antiwar demonstrations in Washington over the years we were there. As those were going on the papers were headlining, "Three Hundred Thousand March," Nixon could look in his pocket at the polls which showed that tens of millions of people in the country supported him. So his attitude toward the protestors was one of rather comfortable tolerance because he knew that somewhere between 60 and 70 percent of the American people were for him. So, you know, he was not about to let foreign policy be made on the streets.
GORDON: In Nixon's memoirs he mentioned he could not get the photographs of the dead students out of his mind. He even mentioned that the father of one of the girls who was killed said, "My child was not a bum."
EHRLICHMAN: [Arthur] Krause.
GORDON: Yes. Did Nixon have guilt feelings afterwards?
EHRLICHMAN: No, I do not know about it if he did.* And I'm not sure that he ever talked to Krause. I talked to Krause frequently . . . He used

*In *The Haldeman Diaries,* Nixon's chief of staff H. R. Haldeman told a different version. Haldeman wrote that Nixon was very disturbed by the killings and "afraid his decision [to invade Cambodia] set it off."

to call me . . . He would call and ask what the federal government was doing [about a federal grand jury]. And he was very emotional and several times he broke down and cried and simply could not continue the conversation. It was very touching.

GORDON: After the memo came about [Nixon suppressing the federal] grand jury, he [Krause] was accusing Nixon of distortion and lying and misleading him.

Krause wrote a letter to the editor of the Op-Ed page of [the *New York*] *Times* and accused Nixon of "deceptions, omissions and outright distortions of historical facts" in his book.

EHRLICHMAN: Well, you know that (chuckles), I guess we all have a point of view on Nixon's book.

GORDON: How would you assess this event within his [Nixon's] presidency?

EHRLICHMAN: That is one of those thumb-suckers . . . I think that at the time it was a major event. It tended to magnify—well, magnify is not the word—it tended to increase the degree of the protests, if not the kinds of protest we were getting. And it appealed to a great many people who were on the fence. It shocked and dismayed them. And it had a very direct impact on the White House because almost immediately delegations of protestors, particularly young people, began coming to Washington, and for some reason they felt that the pinnacle of their climb was to have an audience at the White House, and preferably with the president. So we were getting a tremendous influx of protestors and we were coming in face-to-face contact [with them]. A great many of us dropped what other duties that we had to talk with them, and to try and explain the president's position and to act as a conduit between them and the president.

So it put the White House into a very close individual contact with the protest for the first time.

GORDON: When you testified at the Senate Watergate Committee, you said that Nixon was not "paranoid, weird or psychotic on the subject of demonstrators." What was Nixon on the subject of demonstrators?

EHRLICHMAN: As I said, he was pretty cool about it by and large. He did not like it, certainly. He would make his dislike clear. They were his enemies as far as the conduct of foreign policy was concerned.

But at the same time he looked at his hole card and he knew he had the American people with him in the main. So it was as if he were a poker player in a card game sitting there with a fat hand.

Sure, the other people around the table were trying to get his money, but he knew he had the winning hand.

GORDON: There were some people who accused Nixon of calculatingly exploiting demonstrators.

EHRLICHMAN: I think perhaps that is a fair comment. I think he thought the demonstrators inflamed or infuriated the average middle American and to the extent that he could encourage that he felt that was to his advantage.

GORDON: You wrote in your book that once during the 1968 campaign Nixon told the Secret Service to go beat up on these demonstrators—

EHRLICHMAN: He told me. (Chuckles) He told me to have the Secret Service—

GORDON: Okay. And then the last time there was a leak of White House tapes, journalist Seymour Hersh [revealed that] Nixon told Haldeman to get Teamster thugs to beat up on protestors.

EHRLICHMAN: Yeah. Yeah.

GORDON: Was this common? I mean, was Nixon—

EHRLICHMAN: That was in the nature of excess rhetoric a lot of the time. At least I took it that way . . . [Nixon] knew darned well the Secret Service would not do it. He knew darned well I would not have the Secret Service do it. So he felt comfortable in venting his spleen that way.

Now, as between him and Haldeman, I do not know what came out of that, but he [Nixon] was given to these rhetorical excesses and it is going to be very hard for people, when they listen to the tapes, to be able to separate the real from the hubris.

GORDON: Were there any instances that anybody got beat up as a result of an order from Nixon?

EHRLICHMAN: Not to my knowledge.

GORDON: Can you conceive of it?

EHRLICHMAN: Yeah, I can conceive of Colson going out and blindly carrying out one of these instructions . . .

GORDON: What you just told me sort of ties in with the themes of the Kent State revisionists. One of the theories was that Nixon gave one of these crazy orders in a fit of anger, you know, "knock off some students" or something to that effect, and somebody like Colson took it seriously and put into motion a series of events which culminated in the shootings.

EHRLICHMAN: At Kent State?

GORDON: Yes.

EHRLICHMAN: I do not think that Richard Nixon was focusing on Kent State at that time. His whole focus was on Cambodia and he intended not to have anything to do with demonstrators or domestic problems, or anything else, to my certain knowledge. So I would doubt that.

GORDON: There is one revisionist who thinks there was actually a mock-up of the campus in the basement of the White House—
EHRLICHMAN: Oh, boy.
GORDON: And this is what is going to be the wave of the future. Have you heard of these theories or have any reactions to these allegations?
EHRLICHMAN: I've not heard of them but it does not surprise me because there is a conspiracy theory about everything that has gone on in the Nixon years, apparently.

There is absolutely no substance to it. Kent State occurred as a total surprise to everybody in the White House. I am positive of that.
GORDON: Is there anything you want to say to the revisionists?
EHRLICHMAN: Oh, gosh. Surely they have something better to do with their minds and their time.
GORDON: Do you think Kent State changed the conduct of the Vietnam War at all? What happened at Kent?
EHRLICHMAN: I doubt that you could say that a switch was thrown right at that moment, but it certainly had to have some impact because of the many, many direct interventions by citizens, bearing upon the people who were making the policy at the time.

But it is an intangible. I do not know how you are ever going to measure it.
GORDON: One of the questions I've always had—and this may be more of a Watergate question than Kent State—why did he [Nixon] ever pick [Ohio Senator William] Saxbe as his attorney general?
EHRLICHMAN: God knows . . . [Nixon adviser] Bryce Harlow told me it was because he could be confirmed.
GORDON: I could not understand it because Saxbe was really [critical] of you and [Haldeman] and [his nomination] just made no sense.
EHRLICHMAN: It was not so much that. It was Nixon had no respect for him. And he was quite open about it during the time that Saxbe ran for the Senate and so on.
GORDON: There was a report [in Jack Anderson's syndicated column] that Saxbe was on Nixon's "shit list."
EHRLICHMAN: Yes. I would say that is true. I wrote quite a bit about this [in my book] and then edited it out on the basis that probably nobody ever heard of Saxbe or cared about it.
GORDON: Well, in Ohio, we do.
EHRLICHMAN: Yeah, I know, but how many books do you sell in Ohio? (Laughs)
GORDON: Not too many.

EHRLICHMAN: No, basically it slowed the book down and I could see the reader scratching his head and saying `who the hell is Saxbe?'

No, I had a very long dissertation on the Nixon/Saxbe relationship which is on the cutting room floor right now.

GORDON: Will any surprises come out in the White House tapes? On Kent State?

EHRLICHMAN: No. I do not think so. If Nixon had any—

Well—I'll tell you one thing that might come out would be a tape of that conversation between Nixon and Rhodes, because that telephone was a part of the system.

GORDON: And it would say why Rhodes did not want the federal grand jury?

EHRLICHMAN: Presumably it would. It would be the whole conversation.

GORDON: Did Nixon owe something to Rhodes? That he agreed to do this?

EHRLICHMAN: I don't know. I doubt it.

GORDON: A political favor or whatever?

EHRLICHMAN: I doubt it. Ohio was obviously an important state for [the] 1972 [presidential election], but Nixon and Rhodes had always been sort of political allies.

GORDON: If it was not for Rhodes, would Nixon have crushed the grand jury himself?

EHRLICHMAN: I have no idea. I have no idea.

POSTSCRIPT: Unfortunately, whatever was said between Nixon and Rhodes will not be retrievable. James J. Hastings, Deputy Director of the Nixon Presidential Materials Project at the National Archives, advised me, subsequent to this interview, that the White House taping system did not begin operation until February 16, 1971. That means that White House conversations taking place at the time of the shootings and the early cover-up were not recorded for posterity.

The taping system was dismantled on July 18, 1973, which means that Nixon's private reactions to the news that the Justice Department re-opened the investigation over his objections also will not be available.

Calls to Rhodes' office, to get reactions to Ehrlichman's comments, were not returned. The author frankly feels that even if Rhodes asked Nixon to prevent the federal prosecution, Nixon would have done so anyhow, and that Ehrlichman was simply trying to deflect blame for the cover-up on Rhodes.

APPENDIX II

Excerpts from the Colonel Fassinger Interview

Although it has sometimes been said that millions of words have been written about the shootings at Kent State, some stories remain incompletely told. One story concerns the role played by former Ohio Governor James A. Rhodes, when he visited the campus the day before the killings. We still do not know the full extent of his meddling in the campus disturbances. There has always been the suspicion that Rhodes did more than just talk tough, and that he may have given the National Guard commanders secret orders which may have helped bring about the shooting.

Perhaps the most important untold stories are those of the National Guardsmen who fired. Even though most of the "shooters" were cross-examined at the 1975 trial, we really do not know what prompted them to shoot. (Or perhaps I should say we do not believe them).

During the course of research for this book, I talked informally with many of the Guardsmen, and formally interviewed some of them, including William Perkins, who was understandably quite concerned about what people would think of him.

Perkins implored me to look into the Guardsmen's backgrounds, saying, "We're kind, we're gentlemen, and we're not troublemakers." He wanted to make sure people knew the Guardsmen never wanted "to go out and kill people."

Unfortunately, the officers who were subject to the "order-to-fire" and "conspiracy" accusations, and who were thus subject to the most scrutiny and speculations—Major Harry Jones and Sergeant Myron Pryor—both declined several requests to be interviewed.

On June 7, 1983, however, I was able to interview Lieutenant Colonel Charles Fassinger, the commander of the troops.

We talked for three hours in his home in Northfield, Ohio. Here are the highlights of that interview:

• Asked to clarify who was really in charge of the troops—he or General Canterbury—Fassinger conceded "that has always been a question." Fassinger was not able to provide a definitive answer, but he did note that while he was the highest officer in the chain of command on Blanket Hill on May 4, he still had to follow Canterbury's orders by virtue of the fact that Canterbury outranked him. And Fassinger confirmed that Canterbury did indeed give some "orders" or "suggestions" during the confrontation.

• Fassinger denied that one of the reasons everything went haywire on May 4 was because the Guard rushed to break up the rally without adequately preparing for it. Contradicting General Canterbury's testimony before the Scranton Commission (Canterbury claimed he only learned of the rally at the last moment), Fassinger said that both he and General Canterbury knew that the May 4 rally would be held as early as the previous night. (During the civil trial Fassinger similarly testified that an "intelligence officer briefed me on the general layout of the campus. We went over the maps." Fassinger also testified "I was informed particularly about the fence" that the Guardsmen had almost marched into. That was one of the most controversial logistical moves, and resulted in bitter criticism by the men Fassinger and Canterbury were leading.)

• Asked "If you were writing this book instead of me, what would you want people to learn from Kent State?" Fassinger said: "There ought to be a better way of handling that sort of situation on a college campus." But Fassinger insisted that no one in authority did anything wrong and that the shootings were unavoidable. He said that while he had regrets, he did not feel he had anything to apologize for.

• Talking about how the tragedy affected other Guardsmen, Fassinger denied reports that some Guardsmen were proud of the killings. He said the incident had "a very marked effect" on Sergeant Pryor and claimed that it contributed to the break up of his marriage. (Pryor's ex-wife, however, subsequently told me she left him because of other problems.)

Regarding General Canterbury, Fassinger said: "Canterbury was almost paranoid over it [the shootings and the trials]. It was almost a total obsession . . . He was a basket case." He said some people blamed a heart attack Canterbury suffered on the strain of the investigations and litigation.

• When told that a private, Jeffrey Jones, told me that Major Jones was upset with the men for the firing, and asked if he was also upset with the enlisted men, Fassinger sidestepped the question by saying: "I don't think anybody thought about being mad or not mad" at the troops. He claimed he was too preoccupied at the time.

• Fassinger verified published reports that the situation after the shootings was extremely volatile. He agreed with Ohio National Guard Captain Ronald Snyder's assessment that, before the students were finally persuaded by KSU professors to leave the scene, the potential was there for the country's biggest massacre since Custer's Last Stand.

• He said that to this day he still does not know why the Guardsmen turned and fired. "I know that all of a sudden, for some reason, I turned. I turned in the same direction [as the other soldiers]. I looked to the right where they were looking. And it was instantaneous. It was simultaneous. . . I can't tell you why I did that. I suppose I asked that question 800 million times . . . It bugs me a lot."

• Fassinger claimed that the notion that the Guardsmen might have conspired to shoot the students never entered his mind, either before or after Peter Davies publicly made that charge. He insisted that "you could not get trained [troops] to be that quick and that precise [to] all turn in the commotion that was going on at the same time."

• Fassinger insisted that given the noise level, no Guardsmen could have heard a verbal order and that no Guardsmen could have seen a hand signal because their gas masks blocked their peripheral vision.

• Asked if that many soldiers would do an about-face and fire that many shots (67) for 13 straight seconds without anyone telling them to, Fassinger insisted "they did." He did concede, however, that it was possible for someone at the tail end of line to give an unauthorized order to only a few soldiers, thus triggering a chain reaction.

• Reminded that at the civil trial the plaintiffs' lawyers tried to prove that Pryor was the one who gave the order to fire, Fassinger insisted that Pryor, a first sergeant, would not have had the command authority to give such an order and the troops would never have listened to him "if they recognized his voice."

• When I mentioned that the plaintiffs' lawyers could not make up their minds about what they wanted to prove at the trial, Fassinger cut in, saying: "Amen. Talk about scattered—them and the Justice Department. Every time they'd make one point, then [they would] disprove it with their next expert."

• Fassinger said that sometime within the late 1970s some of the Guardsmen who were sued talked about having a picnic and inviting all of those who were involved. However, "most of us decided that probably did not make a lot of sense. The majority of [defendants] did not want to hear [about it] anymore."

• Fassinger said that in 1970 the Ohio Attorney General, Paul Brown [who later became the Chief Justice of the Ohio Supreme Court], "met all the Guardsmen that were involved at my armory" [at the Akron-Canton airport and assured them they would never be prosecuted by the state of Ohio."

• He denied that Governor Rhodes pressured the troops to crack down against the students or that Rhodes' fiery speech of May 3 affected the troops. He said charges that appeared in Peter Davies' book that Rhodes' speech was broadcast into the Guards' bivouacs were not true.

• Finally, Fassinger said that he did not favor the 1979 out-of-court settlement of the civil damage suits and that he and the other Guardsmen were convinced they would win the second trial. However, Fassinger said that he and the others agreed to the settlement largely because of the pressure exerted by Judge William Thomas and their attorneys, all of whom felt that the settlement would end the litigation and allow everyone to finally put Kent State to rest.

"I think all of us were very hesitant to sign [that statement of regret]. I don't know that anybody volunteered to be the first signature. In fact, that was a whole bone of contention. No one wanted to be the first signature."

CHRONOLOGY

1970

April 30   President Nixon announces the invasion of Cambodia, triggering massive protests on several of the nation's campuses.

May 2   Ohio National Guardsmen are sent to Kent State after the University's ROTC building is burned down.

May 3   Ohio Governor James Rhodes personally appears on campus and promises to use "every force possible" to maintain order. Rhodes denounces the protestors as worse than brownshirts and vows to keep the Guard in Kent "until we get rid of them."

May 4   Four students are killed and nine others are wounded when a contingent of Guardsmen suddenly opens fire during a noontime demonstration.

July 23   Key portions of a secret Justice Department memo are disclosed by the *Akron Beacon Journal.* The memorandum describes the shootings as unnecessary and urges the Portage County Prosecutor file criminal charges against six Guardsmen.

July 31   Attorney General John Mitchell says that both students and Guardsmen apparently violated federal laws and hints that a federal grand jury may be convened "if Ohio authorities do not act."

August 3	After consulting with top Guard officials, Governor Rhodes orders that a "special" state grand jury be empaneled.
October 4	The President's Commission on Campus Unrest concludes the shootings were "unnecessary, unwarranted, and inexcusable."
October 16	The "special" state grand jury exonerates the Guardsmen, but indicts 25 individuals, mostly students, for a variety of offenses that occurred on campus before the shootings.
Later October–November 1	Demands for a federal grand jury mount after it is revealed that the "special" state grand jury ignored key evidence and that one of the "special" prosecutors told a newsman he felt the Guardsmen should have shot more students.
November 30	Assistant Attorney General Jerris Leonard confirms that the Justice Department is reviewing the evidence to determine if a federal grand jury should be convened. Leonard promises a decision before the year is over.

1971

January 28	A federal judge upholds the state's indictments of students, but orders the state grand jury's report to be expunged from the record and physically destroyed due to its bias.
April 30	The first major book on the shootings, *Kent State: What Happened and Why,* by James Michener, is released. Michener says he was unable to uncover proof that there was a conspiracy to fire. However, Michener writes: "It seems likely that some kind of a rough verbal agreement had been reached among the troops" to fire.
June 22	A conspiracy report written by Peter Davies is submitted to the Justice Department. Davies alleges that there definitely was a conspiracy and that a sergeant, Myron Pryor, started it all by firing a pistol as a signal.
August 13	Attorney General John Mitchell closes the case, dismissing the conspiracy allegations and claiming "there is no likelihood of successful prosecutions of individual Guardsmen."
October 20	A 10,000-signature petition urging President Nixon to overrule the decision is submitted to presidential aide Leonard Garment at the White House.

| December 8 | The "special" state grand jury is even further discredited when Ohio officials dismiss charges against 20 of the 25 individuals indicted by the grand jury. Ohio prosecutors claimed they had insufficient evidence to obtain convictions. |

1972

May 4	The second anniversary of the shootings passes without any response to the petition.
July 6	In a letter to the parents of the slain students, Garment says that the new attorney general, Richard Kleindienst, will not reverse Mitchell's previous decision.
October 12	The parents of the slain students file suit in U.S. District Court in Washington. They ask for a court order compelling the Justice Department to conduct the grand jury investigation.

1973

April 30	The spreading Watergate scandal shakes up the Nixon administration. Elliot Richardson becomes the new attorney general; Garment is elevated to the position of Nixon's counsel.
May 1	The parents of the slain students renew their grand jury demands. The students at Kent announce they will resubmit the petition.
May 10	In a meeting with the student petitioners K. William O'Connor, a high-level Justice Department official, admits that the Justice Department already has sufficient evidence to prosecute six Guardsmen.
May 25	In an apparent attempt to preempt a reversal of the no-investigation policy by incoming attorney general Elliot Richardson, the White House closes the case a third time.
June 13	Richardson reopens the case anyway, by announcing the Department is reviewing the file.
June 15	The *Akron Beacon Journal* confirms reports that a House Judiciary subcommittee is quietly investigating the Justice Department's handling of the Kent State investigation.

August 3   Assistant Attorney General J. Stanley Pottinger announces that the Justice Department will officially conduct a new inquiry. Senator Birch Bayh follows Pottinger's announcement by releasing a letter he received from one of the Guard's company commanders. On the basis of that letter Bayh charges that armed FBI informant Terry Norman may have been "the fatal catalyst" for the tragedy.

October 20-   Richardson resigns during the Saturday Night Massacre.
November 1   Nixon nominates Ohio Senator William B. Saxbe to be his fourth attorney general. Saxbe promises to terminate the new investigation if his nomination is approved by the Senate.

November 1-7 The parents of the slain students, the student petitioners, and others demand that Saxbe disqualify himself because of several conflicts of interest.

December 11   In an unusual 8:30 announcement on the eve of Saxbe's confirmation hearings, Pottinger announces that a federal grand jury will be empaneled.

December 12   Saxbe promises to keep his hands off the investigation "if they have, as a result of this grand jury, further proceedings."

1974

February 8   Word leaks out from the grand jury that at least seven Guardsmen invoked their Fifth Amendment rights against self-incrimination and refused to testify.

March 28   The federal grand jury indicts eight Guardsmen on charges they deprived the students of their rights to due process. No conspiracy is alleged, and no indictment is returned against Terry Norman or any Guard officers.

April 17   The U.S. Supreme Court overturns a series of lower court decisions dismissing civil damage suits filed by the parents of the dead students and the nine surviving victims. The ruling paves the way for a civil trial after the criminal proceedings.

October 7-17 Attorneys for James Rhodes unsuccessfully try to block the release of Rhodes' deposition in the civil case until after the Ohio gubernatorial election. The deposition reveals that Rhodes' attorney, in a move reminiscent of the Watergate coverup, offered into evidence an incomplete transcript of Rhodes' May 3, 1970, press conference. Among the remarks deleted was a comment by an official that the Guard would resort to shooting if necessary.

October 29   Opening statements are delivered in the prosecution of the eight Guardsmen.

November 5   Rhodes is elected governor of Ohio again.

November 8   Federal Judge Frank Battisti dismisses the criminal charges against the Guardsmen, ruling that the prosecutors failed to prove their case beyond a reasonable doubt. Battisti suggests the Guardsmen should have been tried instead by state officials.

1975

May 28   A three-month-long wrongful death and injury trial begins. It provides the first opportunity to consider the evidence, five years after the killings.

August 27   After hearing highly conflicting testimony—and after considerable controversy over rulings excluding and including certain evidence—the jury decides not to award damages to the parents of those killed and the nine surviving students.

1977

July 29   Ignoring pleas from the victims and students who set up a makeshift Tent City on the practice football field, Kent State proceeds with the construction of a gymnasium annex over a large part of the site of the May 4 confrontation. 192 protestors are removed from the site and arrested. Subsequent protests are similarly unsuccessful.

September 12   The Sixth Circuit Court of Appeals in Cincinnati overturns the decision of the 1975 civil jury on the ground that Judge Donald Young mishandled an incident involving jury tampering.

1978

December 9   The second civil trial begins amid rumors that there might be a compromise out-of-court settlement.

1979

January 4   The victims settle out of court. The state of Ohio awards them a total of $675,000, to be split 13 ways, and the defendants sign a "statement of regret." Some victims claim the statement is an apology, but the defendants and their attorneys dispute that.

1982

October 4   The major litigation officially ends with a Supreme Court decision paving the way for the release of court documents sealed seven years earlier at the request of KSU and Ohio officials.

1990

May 4   KSU dedicates a memorial to the events of May 4 (not the victims). At the dedication ceremonies, Ohio Governor Richard Celeste apologizes to the families of the slain students and the nine surviving victims.

Notes

Preface

ON THE HISTORICAL SIGNIFICANCE OF MAY 4: It has often been reported—inaccurately—that Kent State marked the first time that protesting college students were killed by authorities. That dubious distinction belongs to South Carolina State in Orangeburg, where, in 1968, three black students trying to exercise their rights to go bowling were killed by South Carolina Highway Patrolmen.

Kent State was not even the first time in Ohio history that the militia had resorted to lethal force to crush a protest. According to an article in the Winter 1974 issue of *Ohio History,* the official journal of the Ohio Historical Society (Charles Peckham, "The Ohio National Guard and its Police Duties, 1894"), in 1894, 76 years before Kent State, Guardsmen stationed in a little town called Washington Court House, Ohio, fired into a mob that was bent on lynching a black man who had just plead guilty to the rape of a white woman. In that incident five men were killed and more than a dozen others wounded.

According to Peckham's account, Colonel A. B. Coit, the commanding officer, was charged with manslaughter and later acquitted after a lengthy trial. Peckham reported: "This trial appears to have been one of the first in Ohio, if not the United States, concerning the legal responsibility for guardsmen for causing the deaths of citizens in carrying out their duty."

DID THE KILLINGS INFLUENCE THE COURSE OF THE VIETNAM WAR?: The best, and to date, only thorough study to assess the antiwar movement's impact on the Johnson and Nixon administration's prosecution of the Vietnam War is *The War Within: America's Battle over Vietnam* by Tom Wells (Berkeley: University of California Press, 1994). Wells argued the protests "played a major role in constraining, deescalating and ending the war" and that the Kent State killings and resultant national furor probably forced President Nixon to prematurely withdraw troops from Cambodia. Beyond that, there is no evidence the killings accomplished anything else.

PAGE
15   "Had a decision" Norman Cousins, "Kent State and Watergate," *World,* June 6, 1973, p. 12.
17   "Sensitized America" Report of the Kent State University's May 4th Memorial Committee, submitted to Kent State Michael Schwartz, December 21, 1984, p. 9.
18   "The first military" Ottavio M. Casale and Louis Paskoff, editors, *The Kent Affair,* Boston: Houghton Mifflin and Company, 1971, p. ix.
18   "the single most" Statement issued by May 4 Task Force, "Faculty Senate Gives Nod to May 4 Memorial Study," *Daily Kent Stater,* November 8, 1973
19   "The Nation has" Address at the Dedication of the Karl E. Mundt Library Speech delivered at General Beadle State College, Madison, South Dakota, June 3, 1969.

Chapter One, "Four Days in May"

THE UNIVERSITY'S INTERNAL REPORT: Kent State's internal report, which presented such damaging evidence against the Kent State police department and its failure to protect the ROTC building from would-be arsonists, is officially called "The Events of May 1-4, 1970 at Kent State University: Minority Report of the Commission on KSU Violence," and is available in the university library.

The report presented the conclusions of an internal University fact-finding commission. Incidentally, there was no majority report. The report is called the Minority Report because only four of the nine members of the commission investigated the events of May 1-4, 1970.

THE COVER-UP OF GOVERNOR RHODES' THREATS: There are actually two versions of the transcript of Governor Rhodes' May 3 press conference in Kent: a complete transcription of the tape, which was entered into evidence as an exhibit at the civil trial, and a shorter version offered by Rhodes' attorneys when he was deposed for the civil suit. The abridged version omits the threat attributed to General Sylvester Del Corso: "We will use any force that is necessary, *even to the point of shooting.*"

WHO THREATENED TO SHOOT STUDENTS?: There was also some confusion as to who actually uttered that threat. Since the speaker apparently said, "I'll be right behind with the National Guard," it was assumed the source must have been Adjutant General Sylvester Del Corso. And Del Corso confirmed making the threat when he was deposed for the 1975 wrongful death and injury trial.

However, at the trial itself, Del Corso testified that he was mistaken at the time he gave his deposition. Roy Thompson, the chief of the Kent city police, testified he made the statement.

Some of the victims' attorneys suspected that since Thompson was not a defendant in the suit, he did Del Corso a favor and took responsibility for the threat.

Regardless of who said it, though, the point is that shooting was very much on the mind of those present at the press conference. No public official or military officer did anything to discourage this loose talk about killing students.

WHO ORDERED THE MARCH AGAINST THE STUDENTS?: The question of who ordered the May 4 rally to be dispersed was never resolved at the trials. General Canterbury testified that he dispersed the crowd at the request of KSU President Robert I. White. White, however, insisted that he made no such request and that had he known he had any say in the matter, he would have allowed the rally to proceed.

There was also testimony at the civil trial by the Guard's public information officer, Sergeant Michael Delaney, that Governor Rhodes gave standing orders on May 3 that all rallies be dispersed. Rhodes denied the allegation under oath.

WAS THE MAY 4TH RALLY LEGAL?: This question—and the related question of whether the First Amendment protected the students' rights to assemble and demand a redress of their grievances (i.e., the end of the war in Vietnam)—was debated at length at the 1975 civil trial. Virtually every witness at the trial agreed that the rally was peaceful until the Guardsmen ordered the students to disperse. However, the defendants' lawyers argued that since the previous days' demonstrations had turned violent, the Guard had every right to expect that this one might too.

In 1977, the Sixth Circuit Court of Appeals, deciding on the appeal of the suits, ruled in favor of the defendants. The appeals court did not pass judgment on the wisdom of the decision, which had been criticized by the Scranton Commission. The Commission concluded: "Even if the Guard had authority to prohibit a peaceful gathering . . . the decision to disperse the noon rally was a serious error. The timing and manner of the dispersal were disastrous. Many students were legitimately in the area as they went to and from class. The rally was held during the crowded noontime luncheon period. The rally was peaceful, and there was no impending violence. Only when the Guard attempted to disperse the rally did some students react violently."

WAS THERE A 14TH VICTIM?: In the text I used the commonly accepted figure of 13 victims, but we cannot be absolutely sure that a 14th person was not shot.

The possibility of a "secret" victim was first raised by James Michener, who, in his book *Kent State: What Happened and Why* claimed there was "fairly strong evidence that a fourteenth student was hit in the left arm, but not seriously; he fled the area with his wound concealed, apprehensive lest he become involved with police investigations." Michener never cited his source, making his claim impossible to verify, and no other evidence ever turned up to indicate that a 14th victim was wounded in the general vicinity where Michener placed him—approximately 600 feet from the firing line.

However, the FBI released to the victims' lawyers (but not to journalists) a statement by a former student named Robert Freeman, who told the Bureau he was hit by pieces of shrapnel while he was standing on the porch of Taylor Hall. I was not able to determine how seriously Freeman was wounded (or even if we would consider him "wounded" at all). Freeman's mother told me, in an October 26, 1981 interview, that Robert died in 1976 and that "her boys didn't tell their mother very much." She suggested I talk with his brother Michael, who would know more about the incident. Michael refused to return numerous calls.

THE GIRL IN JOHN FILO'S PULITZER PRIZE-WINNING PHOTOGRAPH: Mary Vecchio was not a Kent State student. She was a 14-year-old runaway who happened to be in Kent that weekend and accompanied some of her new friends to the noontime rally.

PAGE

24   "We are not sure" "The Justice Department's Summary of FBI Reprints." Reprinted in I. F. Stone, *The Killings at Kent State: How Murder Went Unpunished* (New York: Vintage Books, p. 62). (Hereinafter referred to as the Justice Department Summary.)

24   "Armageddon . . ." "Here's What Happened at Kent, Part I," *Cleveland Press,* May 14, 1970.

24   "unless they wanted" The Report of the President's Commission on Campus Unrest (Washington, D.C.: Government Printing Office, 1970), p. 244. (Hereinafter referred to as the Scranton Commission.)

25   "dipped a cloth" Ibid., p. 248

25   "Members of the" Ibid., p. 249.

26   "The persons involved" "The Events of May 1-4, 1970 at Kent State University: Minority Report of the Commission on KSU Violence." Kent, Ohio, 1970, p. 55. (Hereinafter referred to as the Minority Report.)

27   Other local officials. Among those present at the meeting with Rhodes were U.S. Attorney Robert Krupansky, Ohio Highway Patrol Chief Robert Chiarmonte, Portage County Prosecutor Ronald Kane, Kent Mayor LeRoy Satrom, and Kent city Police chief Roy Thompson.

27   "We are up" Transcript of Governor Rhodes' press conference, May 3, 1970, Box 63, May 4 Collection, Kent State University Archives.

28   "The next phase" Ibid.

28   "I'll be" Trial transcript, Krause v. Rhodes, 390 F. Supp 1072 (N.D., Ohio, 1975), Vol. 41, pp. 10,359-60. (Hereinafter referred to as Trial transcript.)

28   "Flowers are" Peter Davies, *The Truth About Kent State* (New York: Farrar, Straus and Giroux, 1973), p. 23. (Hereinafter referred to as Davies.)

29   "Where they were" Justice Department Summary, p. 71.

29   "The students" Scranton Commission Report, p. 258.

29   "Three Guardsmen" Ibid.

30   "Had had an average" Scranton Commission Report, p. 25.

31   "Had a great time" Trial transcript, vol. 31, p. 7711.

31   "These students are" James Michener, *Kent State: What Happened and Why* (New York: Random House, 1971), p. 331. (Hereinafter referred to as Michener.)

33   "A blind fool" "'Misled at Kent,' says Guardsman," *Cleveland Press,* April 3, 1974.

33   "The shootings could" "Guardsman Ends 10-Year Silence on KSU," *Akron Beacon Journal,* May 4, 1980.

34   "Some among" Scranton Commission Report, p. 267.

Chapter Two, "The Search for the Smoking Guns"

"SNIPER" SILLINESS: The notion that there might have been a sniper at Kent State was brilliantly ridiculed by newspaper columnist Clayton Fritchey, who, in a column syndicated in May 1970, pointed out that every time law enforcement officials had fired into a crowd of unarmed civilians, an invisible sniper was always cited as an excuse. Fritchey wrote that "the unknown sniper is becoming almost as famous as the Unknown Soldier" and suggested that the same sniper must have been present at every civilian disturbance because "in each instance he has shown the same peculiar characteristics. He can, for instance, be spotted and heard (bang, bang) by police, state highway patrolmen, and the militia, but at the same time remain totally invisible and inaudible to all other witnesses on the scene. Secondly, no two snipers could be such incredibly bad marksmen. The unknown sniper has yet to hit an officer of the law, although the police and guardsmen have been packed together in such large masses that it's hard to see how a blind man could have missed them. Also, in the shootings of John F. Kennedy and Martin Luther King, the snipers had to leave behind guns and other evidence in order to make a getaway, but the unknown sniper is a true phantom, for he is able to escape each time without a trace, although surrounded by hordes of law enforcement agents."

THE EXTENT OF THE ROCK THROWING BY THE STUDENTS: The full FBI report, which is now available and which includes more than 500 eyewitness accounts, is not overly helpful in resolving the question of how many rocks were thrown at the Guardsmen at the time of the shootings. If you review the statements, you will find plenty of witnesses who will say the rock throwing was minimal, and others who support the Guards' version.

One can only wonder, however, how the Guards' widely publicized claims of being under a life-threatening assault influenced the eyewitness accounts. The attention given the Guards' claims undoubtedly helped some witnesses see more rocks than were probably actually thrown.

OTHER OBJECTS THROWN AT GUARDSMEN: The Guardsmen's claim of self-defense included a claim by Lieutenant Dwight Cline that he had to dodge a parking meter thrown off the roof of Taylor Hall. Cline, however, was the only one of the 500 witnesses who saw this parking meter flying through the air.

Another Guardsman told the FBI he had to dodge what he described as "a three-inch log." I can at least vouch for the "log." That is because I found the person who threw it: a former student named Pat Vittone. However, Vittone insisted the "log" was just a little stick and that he threw it off to the side of the soldiers so that it would miss them. Moreover, Vittone swears that he threw it after the Guardsmen started shooting first.

INJURY CLAIMS BY GUARDSMEN: Other than the two Guard injuries documented by photographs (Sergeant Shafer's arm and a bruise sustained by James McGee on his right bicep), the only other noteworthy injuries that I am aware of occurred well before the shooting occurred. Philip Raber, a sergeant who refrained from firing his weapon, was struck in the mouth and had a tooth knocked loose during the Guard's initial march across the Commons. That happened about 15 minutes before the shootings. Private James Pierce, who did fire at students, testified that a rock struck him in the testicles while he was standing with his fellow soldiers on the practice football field, about five minutes before the shootings.

Colonel Charles Fassinger and Major Harry Jones both claimed to have been struck by heavy objects and knocked off balance as they walked back up the hill.

After the firing, another Guardsman who did not fire, Sergeant Dennis Breckenridge, hyperventilated and fainted. He had to be carried away on a stretcher.

An FBI report dated May 8, 1970, indicates that photographs were taken of bruises sustained by William James, who received a bruise to his right leg just above the knee, Lloyd Thomas, who received a bruise on his right thigh, and James Pierce, who received a bruise to right thigh. These photographs, however, were never entered into evidence by the defense attorneys.

WAS THERE A "SURGE" OF STUDENTS TOWARD THE GUARDSMEN?: The Scranton Commission reported: "As the Guardsmen reached the top of the hill, some students surged from the east face of Taylor Hall and the southern end of the parking lot up toward the guardsmen on Blanket Hill." Yet the Commission also concluded: "The leading edge of this crowd appears to have advanced to a point no closer than 20 yards from the guardsmen, with the main body 60 to 75 yards away, before the gunfire began and they reversed their direction. It is possible that some of them had no aggressive intent but instead began running up the hill in the direction of the Guard to get a good vantage point on Blanket Hill, after, as they expected, the guardsmen retreated down the far side of the slope."

The Commission ultimately concluded the shootings were "unnecessary, unwarranted, and inexcusable."

THE 8 MILLIMETER MOVIE OF THE SHOOTING: In addition to the still photographs, there was also an 8 millimeter home movie of the shootings taken by a student named Chris Abell from the fifth floor of Wright Hall, a dorm approximately 1,600 feet from Taylor Hall. An analysis of the movie conducted by a photo-interpreting firm, Electromagnetic Systems Laboratories in Sunnyvale, California, was very damaging to the National Guard. As Joseph Kelner reported in his book, *The Kent State Coverup:* "The evidence of the film is that at no time before Troop G opened fire were they being approached by more than 17 students, that none of the approaching students was closer than 85 feet, and that 10 of them were more than 175 feet away."

Kelner devoted an entire chapter to the movie and a tape recording made by another student, calling it "Absolute Proof in Sight and Sound." As damning as these statistics are, I chose not to include the conclusions in the main text because the authors of the report ("Anaylsis of Photographic and Acoustic Data Pertaining to the Kent State Incident," February 25, 1974) allowed themselves a 30% margin of error on those figures.

WHAT THE VICTIMS WERE DOING ON MAY 4: Of the 13 students known to have been shot, seven played varying roles in the protest, while the other six were bystanders.

The closest student to the Guardsmen, Joseph Lewis, Jr., testified that he was shot while standing still and giving the Guardsmen the finger.

Dean Kahler, who was shot in the spine and permanently paralyzed after he dropped to the ground in an unsuccessful attempt to dodge bullets, admitted throwing two or three rocks at the Guardsmen earlier.

Alan Canfora and Tom Grace, the two hard-core radicals among the wounded students, subsequently tried to soft-pedal their involvement. The Justice Department Summary of the FBI report concluded both "probably had flags" which were waved to aggravate the troops and that both "were encouraging the students to throw rocks at the Guardsmen." (Canfora was proud of his behavior but Grace denied waving a flag and insisted all he had done was join in the chanting).

Robby Stamps, a less radical political activist, denied throwing any rocks at the Guard, but the summary states he was "active in taunting the Guard" (all quotes from page 100).

The summary also placed fatalities Jeffrey Miller and Allison Krause "at the front of the crowd taunting the Guardsmen" (p. 99) and reports that Miller made obscene gestures and threw a tear gas cannister at them at one point, while Krause shouted obscenities at them. The summary states that: "Debris, similar in composition to rocks found on the Kent State campus, was found in the pockets of the jacket that Allison Krause was wearing" (p. 80).

The other victims—John Cleary, Scott Mackenzie, Doug Wrent-more, James Russell, and fatalities William Schroeder and Sandra Scheuer—were apparently just in the wrong place at the wrong time. Schroeder, who attended Kent State on a ROTC scholarship, had just finished a test in war tactics and had apparently stopped to watch the action. Sandra Scheuer was killed while walking to her 1:00 P.M. class.

THE UNIFORMITY OF MOVEMENTS BY THE GUARD: The 24 witnesses who told the FBI that the Guardsmen, before firing, turned "together," "in unison," or used similar phraseology, were Bemas Clifford Black, Stephen C. Buck, Stephen Cohen, Robert Foley, Pennie Fordham, William Gregg, Philip Haas, John Henie, Linda Hetz, Barbara Knapp, Barry Marc Leven, Juopko Linna, Bennett Ray Parsons, Charles M. Rascoll, Donald Schwartzmiller, Debbie Shryock, Jeffrey Tusing, Donald Tuson, William Waldman, Janet Wiley, James Woodring, Julio Arturo Sanjiel, and Thomas Sweet. Other students who reported this uniformity of the Guardsmen's movements to the KSU Commission on Campus Violence were Joseph L. Carter, John Goodall, James D. Howell, James Minard, James D. Rodkey, Christian Gillepsie, Richard Cupp, (first name unknown) Pimienta, Phil Zelsnick, Gayle M. Gamble, Michael Lynch, (first name unknown) Thatcher, Lafe Tolliver, Paul Onshot, Jr., and Professor Jerry M. Lewis.

Although they did not give statements to the FBI, witnesses John Weisner, James Abrams, John T. Oplinger, David Seffens, Rick Levinger, Gene Williams, Paul Schlemmer, *New York Times* reporter John Kifner, John Dienert, and Peter Winnen were all quoted in news accounts that the Guardsmen turned in unison.

Additionally, witnesses Harry William Montgomery, Alan Canfora, Robert Pickett, Sergeant Myron Pyror, and Private James McGee corroborated this uniformity at the 1975 civil trial.

That makes 55 witnesses in all who paid attention to the synchronization of the Guardsmen's movements (just a few more than all the witnesses to the Kennedy assassination who thought the first shot originated from the grassy knoll).

REMOVAL OF THE NAME TAGS: The removal of the Guardsmen's name tags was not discovered until the discovery process for the civil trial; and unfortunately, the victims' attorneys never pursued the question of why the tags were removed.

The closest to an official explanation was given by Major Harry Jones, in his deposition of September 19, 1974. Jones testified that the tags were removed because "we had problems with that before," meaning that bright and resourceful rioters were able to identify individual soldiers and called their houses to harass their families.

The problems with Jones' explanation were that it meant that a protestor upon seeing, say, Major Jones' name tag, would have to be able to (a) correctly guess his first name, (b) determine which Guard unit he served in; and (c) figure out what geographical area the men from that unit came from. Assuming that a clever and resourceful demonstrator could figure all that out, the demonstrator would then, in Jones' case, have to go through the Akron phone book and pick out the right Jones family out of 783 possibilities!

Jones' explanation was an insult to our intelligence. It seems much more likely that the tags were removed to prevent the Guardsmen from being identified by investigators after the shootings.

TESTIMONY REGARDING A VERBAL ORDER TO FIRE: Only three of the 52 Guardsmen in A Company, 145th Infantry (James Farriss, Robert James, and Robert Shade), and only one of the 18 men of G Troop, 107th Armored Cavalry (Rudy Morris), told their superiors they heard a verbal order to fire. Most of the principal "shooters" in G Troop testified they acted on their own without hearing an order.

There were a few instances during the 1975 civil trial when the issue of whether or not there was a verbal command to fire came up, and each time the Guard's defense attorneys suggested that the Guardsmen who thought they heard the word 'Fire!' really only heard part of the order, 'Cease fire,' or the one order that was confirmed: 'Fire over their heads,' issued by Sergeant Matthew McManus after the shooting already begun.

One Guardsman who told the FBI he heard a command to fire, Rudy Morris, even tried to shift the blame for the order onto the students when he was deposed for the civil trial. In testimony obviously inspired by his attorney, Morris told the victims' attorneys: "I only stated that I heard the word 'fire,' which well could have been from students; it could have been from Guardsmen who may have said 'Don't fire,' 'Cease fire,' 'Watch your fire,' 'Place your fire.' It could have come from anyone in any given sentence.'"

DID SERGEANT PRYOR GIVE A HAND AND ARM SIGNAL TO FIRE?: Although it was never publicly reported (this information is buried in the trial transcripts), Major Jones was asked by the Justice Department during its federal grand jury investigation about the possibility that Sergeant Pryor gave a signal to fire. The prosecutors showed Jones John Darnell's photograph showing Pryor in front of the firing line, and asked Jones if that photograph seemed to depict Pryor giving "a hand and arm signal to fire." Jones answered: "It would, yes."

However, when Jones was subsequently asked the same question at the 1975 civil trial, he changed his answer, which prompted the victims' attorneys to ask if they could introduce Jones' federal grand jury testimony into the record. Judge Donald Young ruled that the attorneys could not do so under existing rules of evidence (which, ironically, changed the day after Jones testified: July 1, 1975).

Young ruled that all the attorneys could do was to allude to Jones' earlier testimony in an attempt to refresh his memory.

Plaintiffs' attorney Nelson Karl then asked Jones if he ever testified anywhere that the photograph depicted Pryor giving a signal to fire. Jones then said he could not recall his earlier testimony.

"As you are looking at it now," Karl pressed, "do you not see that as a signal to commence firing?" Jones backed down and testified: "It could be interpreted as a hand signal to fire. There is a possibility, according to the interpretation of the individual."

THE OTHER WITNESSES AGAINST SERGEANT PRYOR: Stewart Pennell, Jr. told the FBI he "was about 30 feet from the Guardsmen" when

all of a sudden I saw one of the Guardsmen turn around with a sweeping motion of his hand which held a handgun, and this Guardsmen pointed it at the approaching students. Almost immediately 6 or 8 Guardsmen with rifles turned around and started firing at the demonstrators . . . I know the man with a handgun fired at least three shots.

Rick Levinger, a protestor, told the FBI:

Suddenly, one of the Guards dropped to one knee in front of the Guard, with a pistol in his hand. He fired three shots toward the parking lot. I then heard a shout, which I couldn't understand, come from someone in the Guard unit area. One row of the Guard then turned toward us and dropped to their knees, raising their rifles to their students.

Lewis Joel Goldberg told the FBI:

He saw a National Guard leader in front of the Guardsmen firing a pistol in the air. He stated approximately ten National Guardsmen knelt down and then fired their rifles upward in the air. He stated the same Guardsmen next aimed at the crowd and fired.

According to photographer John P. Filo:

They turned around and faced the students. They all dropped to one knee, at least the ones I could see, except for the man crouched with a pistol. The distance at that point from the students was 30 to 40 feet. The troops suddenly began firing. The Guardsmen with the pistol began firing into the crowd. I heard no gunshots prior to that and had seen no stones thrown at the troops.

Student Dale Alan Morckel told the FBI that:

Shortly before the shots were fired, the officer apparently leading the Guardsmen was talking to his men; at this time, he had his hand on his pistol. He then turned around with his gun in his hand, moving it up and down in a warning fashion.

Student William Penoyer told the FBI:

The Guardsmen turned and fired as a group as though they were following a command. One Guardsmen, in front of the group, using a pistol, appeared to fire a second or two before the others.

A seventh student, Karl Kessler, reported the Guardsmen got hit by a rock on the shoulder, then turned halfway around and fired his .45 caliber pistol.

WHY WAS THERE AN AMBULANCE ON THE COMMONS BEFORE ANYONE WAS SHOT: Someday some future chronicler of the Kent Affair is going to discover that an ambulance was summoned to the Commons even before the students began to gather at noon. And that chronicler is probably going to ask, as I did: "What is an ambulance doing there? No one has been shot yet."

The thought will probably occur to him—as it occurred to me—that perhaps someone knew something was about to happen and had already made preparations.

I asked several people if they knew why an ambulance was on Commons before the shootings, and got nowhere until I stumbled across a reference to it in a statement Kent State patrolman Bob Stewart provided to his superiors in the KSU police department. I called Stewart and he told me: "It was no big deal. The Guard asked for a public address system so it could address the crowd. We couldn't find a bullhorn. The only one we could find was connected to the ambulance."

GUARDSMEN WHO TALKED ABOUT SHOOTING BEFORE IT HAPPENED: For the record, there were several unverified and/or secondhand reports that the Guardsmen in G Troop talked about shooting students before actually doing so. One source of these reports was a student named Thomas Sweet, who told the KSU Commission on Campus Violence that he overheard Guardsmen calling their wives on May 3, 1970, and that the tenor of the calls was that the "Guard was not going to take any more crap from the students beginning Monday, May 4."

Another source was Mark Nehilla, a Kent State sophomore who told the FBI in 1973 that he hitchhiked from Kent to his hometown in Pittsburgh in April 1971, and was picked up by a man who identified himself as a Guardsmen who was "a member of the unit involved in the shootings." Nehilla said the Guardsmen told him "how afraid he was as well as how afraid everyone in his unit was . . . He indicated that their nerves were shot, they were tired, and angry from being yelled at and pelted with rocks. While they were nursing their bruises they began to think about what they would have to do [unclear] and how they were going to go about it. According to him [on Sunday, May 3] about 8 [to] 10 of the men were talking about how they were fed up with the harassment and rock throwing and it was about time to end it. These individuals began to make plans for the next day if the students continued to throw rocks. Some individuals in this group wanted to use their rifles and scare the kids and others said it was too risky and someone could get hurt. He said that some of the Guards were against violence and thought that small group was crazy. According to him, some of the Guards were really serious about using their guns, and he wanted no part of such action."

According to Nehilla, the driver said, "The men who shot into the crowd were the same ones who had been talking about it the night before [and] that after the shootings, all of the men decided to keep their mouths shut as to who shot where so as not to expose those men who hit people . . . He told me they were not thinking very clearly because of the pressure and fear and I took this to mean he meant himself as well as the other Guards."

Nehilla was able to provide the FBI with a general description of the driver and his car, but no other FBI reports have surfaced indicating that any Guardsman was asked about Nehilla's report. The attorneys for the victims were also apparently unaware of Nehilla's story when they deposed the Guardsmen for the civil trial. They made no attempt to ask the soldiers about this very plausible-sounding scenario.

THE "WHITE HOUSE-DID-IT" THEORY: The records of President Nixon's 1970 telephone calls have now been made available by the National Archives, and there is no indication that Nixon talked directly with

Rhodes, or with anyone else who was even remotely connected with the Kent State killings, during the period of April 30-May 4, 1970. Nixon's first logged telephone conversation with anyone involved in the Kent State incidents came two days later, on May 6, 1970. The logs indicate that Nixon talked for eight minutes to Governor Rhodes, as well as to many other politicians (no doubt to assess the political impact of the killings and the Cambodian invasion).

THE SOURCE OF THE ACCOUNT THAT NIXON TOLD RHODES TO MAKE AN EXAMPLE OF SOMEONE AT KENT STATE: The original source of the *Gallery* magazine account that Nixon phoned Rhodes after the R.O.T.C. building burned and demanded that Rhodes 'make a goddamn good example of someone' at Kent State was Robert Stamps. In 1978 Stamps had filed a lawsuit against Cuyahoga Community College, claiming the college reneged on an offer of employment after it discovered he was one of the nine students wounded at Kent State. The news of the lawsuit made all the local papers, and as Stamps tells it, he was awakened that night at 3:00 A.M. by a caller who claimed to have worked for Army Intelligence and who knew intimate details about his personal life that no one should have known.

According to Stamps, the caller claimed that the federal government was responsible for the shooting and that a plot had been firmed by several undercover agents at the Perkins Pancake House on Main Street, a block from campus, on the day before the shootings.

The caller also left his name and telephone number with Stamps, who turned it over to his attorney, Sanford Rosen, for further investigation.

Stamps also repeated the story to researcher Charles Thomas, who in the April 1979 issue of *Gallery,* treated the story as fact and cited this alleged meeting as proof of a federal conspiracy.

However, when I subsequently asked Rosen about it, he told me the lead was investigated and "nothing productive came up."

Rosen referred me to one of his co-counsels, Andrea Biren, who told me she interviewed the caller and "it was obvious the man had personal problems."

Biren conceded the call was weird, but said the caller was unable to provide her with any concrete information about federal involvement in the shootings.

THE .22 CALIBER BULLETS FOUND AT THE SCENE: Major Harry Jones denied firing the .22 Beretta he carried, but .22 caliber bullets were recovered from the scene, raising questions as to whether Jones perjured himself.

The first .22 caliber bullet was discovered by Pfc. Lee Scalf, who initially told the FBI the bullet was spent, and then changed his story when he was deposed for the civil trial.

The second bullet was found by Colonel Charles Fassinger, who testified he found it in the first parking stall in Prentice Hall.

The third .22 bullet was found by Major Jones himself when he and Captain John Martin were in the Prentice Hall dormitory.

Incredibly, the FBI never ran any laboratory tests to determine if any of these bullets could be traced to the .22 Beretta Major Jones was armed with.

THE UNACCOUNTED FOR .32 CALIBER BULLET: Another unsolved mystery is why the FBI lab was sent on May 11, 1970, a .32 caliber bullet that was also found at the scene. None of the students were known to have been hit with a .32, and the Guardsmen were not supposed to have carried .32s; although we do know some soldiers, such as Captain Ron Snyder, carried their private weapons to campus.

PAGE

49   "A crowd estimated" "General: The Guard Were Not Ordered to Fire," *Akron Beacon Journal,* May 5, 1970

49   "A sniper opened" "Rhodes Asks FBI Probe in Kent Deaths," *Plain Dealer,* May 5, 1970

50   "Some of the students" "Single Shot May Be KSU Clue," *Akron Beacon Journal,* May 5, 1970.

50   "All (77) Guardsmen were hit" "Rhodes Asks FBI Probe in Kent Deaths," *Plain Dealer,* May 5, 1970.

52   "Regardless of the" Justice Department Summary, p. 87

53   "Was in a position" Ibid.

56   "What would a hot" Michener, p. 371.

56   "One of the most shocking" "Guard's Prosecutor Admits He Never Expected to Win," *Akron Beacon Journal,* May 4, 1975.

56   "Had to be" Justice Department Summary, p. 95.

56   "The totally unnecessary" Peter Davies, *An Appeal to the United States Department of Justice for an Immediate and Thorough Investigation of the Circumstances Surrounding the Shootings at Kent State,* p. E8148. Entered into the Congressional Record by Congressman William S. Moorhead, July 22, 1971, p. E- 8143. (Hereinafter referred to as the Davies Report.)

57   "If there was" "The Campus Upheaval: An End to Patience," *Time,* May 9, 1969, p. 22.

57   "A depressing number" Michener, p. 453.

57   "What he called" "Special KSU Prosecutor: Should've Shot All Troublemakers," *Akron Beacon Journal,* October 24, 1970.
58   "That the students" Memorandum from J. Edgar to FBI officials Clyde Tolson, Cartha DeLoach, Alex Rosen, William Sullivan and Thomas Bishop, May 11, 1970.
58   "How do I feel?" See, e.g., Michener pp. 446-455, passim; "My God! They're Killing Us," *Newsweek,* May 18, 1970, p. 31; CBC Sunday Magazine, May 10, 1970, reprinted in Ottavio Casale and Louis Paskoff, *The Kent Affair* (Boston: Houghton Mifflin & Company, 1970), p. 29; and "Ohio Guard Says Mail Favors its Actions," *New York Times,* June 1, 1970, p. 24.
58   "Didn't feel they" Report of the Inspector General: Kent State University, 4 May 1970, p. I-8.
59   "They have been" Michener, pp. 365-5.
59   "A strong feeling" Ibid., p. 361.
59   "I saw them" Ibid., p. 367.
59   "That on the football" Ibid., p. 361.
59   "Was an accident" Ibid., p. 410.
60   "A few" Davies Report
60   Davies' letter to author, September 17, 1971.
61   "The approximate" Minority Report, p. 241.
62   "Maybe ten" Trial transcript, vol. 23, p. 5,621.
62   "If they rush us" Report of the Inspector General: Kent State University Riot, 4 May 1970, p. I-8.
63   Federal grand jury testimony of James McGee, February 1974, p. 4,982.
63   "Part of our" Deposition of Rudy Morris, February 1975, pp. 30-31.
64   Acoustical analysis. "Analysis of Recorded Sounds From the 1970 Shooting Episode at KSU," Cambridge, Mass.: Bolt, Beranek and Newman, Inc., February 28, 197.
64   "You tap a" Trial transcript, vol. 21, p. 5,079.
65   "An explosion" Deposition of Major Harry Jones, September 19, 1974, pp. 114-115.
65   "I don't see" Trial transcript, vol. 21, p. 5,077.
65   Trial transcript, vol. 21, p. 5079.
66   "Mighty mad" Interview with Jeffrey Jones, November 8, 1973.
66   "Who gave you?" Inspector General's Report, p. G-16.
67   "Amen" Interview with Charles Fassinger, June 7, 1983.
67   "I carried a" Trial transcript, vol. 50, p. 969.
68   Deegan essentially. Trial transcript, vol. 16, pps. 3,940-43.
70   "To make a" Charles Thomas, "The Kent State Massacre: Blood on Whose Hands?", *Gallery,* April 1979, p. 101.

70   Lack of planning, Justice Department Summary, p. 75.
72   "The bidding of" Trial transcript, vol. 21, p. 5,269.
72   "The troops were under" "Kent State: The Search for Understand-
     ing," *Akron Beacon Journal,* May 24, 1970.
72   "That's a mild" Trial transcript, vol. 29, p. 7,263.
73   "I had a conversation" Ibid., vol. 21, p. 5,069.
73   "Come on" Ibid., vol. 19, p. 4,523.
73   "Come on, come on" Joe Eszterhas, "Troops 'Lost All Their Cool,'
     Cleveland *Plain Dealer,* May 5, 1970, and Michener, pp. 365-6.
73   "I definitely had" Trial transcript, vol. 21, p. 5,110.

The Strange Case of Terry Norman

THE WITNESSES AGAINST NORMAN: Amazingly, at the time Senator Bayh accused Norman of being "the fatal catalyst" for the shootings,
there was not a single witness who had been publicly identified who had
actually seen Norman fire his gun. All of the witnesses against Norman
had been standing behind police and National Guard lines by the ruins of
the ROTC building, and watched Norman run toward them after the
shootings and surrender his pistol to the campus police.

The claims of these witnesses, though, seem to be significant. Two
of these witnesses, Michael Delaney, the Guard's public information officer, and Fred DeBrine, a newsman for NBC, thought they heard Norman say: "I had to shoot! They were going to kill me."

Delaney, DeBrine, and Joe Butano, the soundman of the NBC crew,
say they heard KSU detective Tom Kelley, upon taking possession of the
gun, blurt out: "My God! He fired four times! What the hell do we do
now?"

In addition to these three witnesses, Sergeant Richard L. Day, Jr., in
a statement provided to his superiors, claimed: "I heard the young man
say: a student grabbed my camera and started to beat me up—I shot
him."

Norman's response to these claims (when he was deposed for the
civil trial) was: "There are a lot of mistaken people."

Detective Kelley has variously claimed he was kidding, that he was
just testing Norman's reaction, and that he was misunderstood. He told
one reporter what he probably said was: "I hope to hell he didn't fire the
gun."

COULD NORMAN HAVE SHOT A STUDENT?: Although Sergeant
Day's statement indicated Norman admitted shooting someone, no .38
caliber bullets were recovered from the scene, and none of the medical

reports indicate that any of the 13 victims sustained wounds consistent with a bullet fired by a .38 caliber pistol.

Of course, not all the bullets were recovered. Some students took bullets home with them as souvenirs.

Day is the only witness who thought he heard Norman admit shooting someone. Had Norman actually shot a student, there would have been a cover-up at Kent State far greater than anyone has possibly imagined.

WHAT THE GUARDSMEN HAD TO SAY ABOUT NORMAN: At the time of the shootings, Norman was behind the Guardsmen, in a dip in the hillside I call "Terry Norman Gulch." Most of the Guardsmen did not see him at the time of the shootings.

In fact, of the 77 Guardsmen who were on Blanket Hill, the only one who has ever said he even noticed him during the shootings was Sergeant Dennis Breckenridge, who told the FBI he noticed Norman after hearing an initial shot of unknown origin from his rear. Breckenridge, however, did not say he saw Norman with a gun. Instead, he indicated Norman "was in the process of throwing a 'baseball-type' gas grenade . . . into the crowd of demonstrators."

THE BALLISTICS TEST: While the ballistics test conducted by the FBI revealed that Norman's gun was fired since it was last cleaned, it could not tell us whether Norman fired his gun at Kent State; if he fired it on May 4; and if he did fire it on May 4, if he fired it before, during or after the Guard's volley.

All the tests really revealed was that the FBI lied about the results of the test (no doubt to discourage any public prying into its use of Norman as an informant.)

THE ATTEMPTS TO INFLUENCE WITNESSES: In an April 16, 1973 interview, former graduate student Harold Reid told me that he first saw Norman after the shootings hovering over a student laying on the ground with the pistol pointed in the student's direction. Reid was under the impression that Norman had just shot the man. That is why he, KSU Alumni Director William Barrett, and several others began chasing Norman across the length of the Commons into the arms of the National Guard and Kent State police.

Reid was subsequently escorted to KSU police headquarters, where he was asked to write a statement of what he was witnessed. According to Reid, while he was still writing his statement Tom Kelley, the plainclothes detective who took the pistol from patrolman Harold Rice, entered the room and announced that Norman's gun had not been fired.

Before that, Reid thought the gun had been fired. Reid said Kelley's announcement was "probably done to influence my thinking. To this day, if I saw a person in the position he [Norman] was in, I'd say it had been fired. However, in the state of confusion, I could not come out and say I heard it."

HOW THE KSU POLICE TRIED TO DISTANCE THEMSELVES FROM NORMAN: Although KSU detective Tom Kelley ultimately admitted he used Norman as an informant, supplied him with three rolls on film on May 4, and helped him get press credentials, the KSU police initially tried to disown him (in a manner reminiscent of the "Mission Impossible" tape: "If you or any member of your crew are caught, the secretary will disallow any knowledge of your actions.")

For at least three years after the shootings the KSU police steadfastly denied having any relationship with Norman. In a March 1973 interview with the author, former KSU Police Chief Donald Schwartzmiller even went to great lengths to discredit Norman. Schwartzmiller portrayed Norman as a "frustrated, hoped-to-be policeman" who volunteered to take identification photographs of students at antiwar rallies for free because "that was his only way of getting into police work."

Schwartzmiller claimed the police department's relationship with Norman was severed, though, by him a year before the shooting because of an unrelated incident.

Telling a tale reminiscent of the one Hobart College officials told about the infamous *provocateur* Tommy the Traveler, Schwartzmiller claimed that he ordered Norman off campus because he heard Norman brought "a trunkload of rifles" onto campus during a tense period of protests in 1969.

"Upon hearing this and knowing the atmosphere of the campus community at the time," Schwartzmiller said, "I ordered him off campus and ordered that if he were ever seen again, that he be arrested for trespassing.

"I considered him an undesirable. I'm not saying he was a . . . nut, but I mean, under pressure, this guy might break and start pulling the trigger."

The trouble with Schwartzmiller's story is that Schwartzmiller did not have the authority to summarily kick a student out of school without a due process hearing.

Moreover, a check of university records revealed that during the one-year period Schwartzmiller claimed Norman was persona non grata at Kent, Norman was at that time enrolled as a student.

While Schwartzmiller tried to portray him as an unreliable informant, Detective Kelley thought highly enough of Norman to write a letter of recommendation for Norman when Norman applied for a job with the Washington, D.C. police.

The Washington, D.C. police also trusted Norman to handle sensitive assignments. In his May 5, 1975, deposition for the civil trial, Norman testified: "I worked with the civil disturbance unit and also our SWAT team."

THE FBI'S LYING ABOUT NORMAN: FBI Director J. Edgar Hoover also lied about the Bureau's relationship with Norman. In 1970 Hoover responded to an inquiry from Congressman John Ashbrook, claiming that: "Mr. Norman was not working for the FBI on May 4th, nor has he ever been in any way connected with the Bureau."

As Norman himself later told investigators: "That statement is false."

In 1973 the FBI finally admitted that one month before the shootings Norman provided "information of value" about a neo-Nazi organization, for which he was paid $125.00.

And although the FBI continued to tell the House Judiciary subcommittee that Norman was not taking pictures for them, a statement Norman provided to the Kent State police on May 4, 1970, has recently surfaced.

In that statement Norman wrote: "I was requested to take pictures for the purpose of identification and prosecution of violators by Detective Tom Kelley of the Campus Police Department and Bill Chapin of the FBI office."

THE FBI'S REFUSAL TO INVESTIGATE NORMAN'S ROLE: One of the more disturbing aspects of the FBI's investigation is its refusal to interrogate a number of witnesses to the Terry Norman incident.

The FBI had to have known there were suspicions that Norman started the shooting because DeBrine reported what he had heard on the local NBC News. Most of the initial news accounts also reported the Guard's claim there was a sniper on campus; so there really was no excuse for not interviewing witnesses who tried to volunteer information.

Guard Sergeant Michael Delaney and NBC cameraman Jorge Gomez both told me they tried to volunteer their statements to FBI agents, but the agents were not interested in listening.

Guard Captain John Martin made the same claim when he wrote Senator Bayh about Norman. Martin wrote: "The FBI seemed to show no interest whatsoever in [his soldiers'] statements whenever I reported them."

DID NORMAN HAVE TWO GUNS ON MAY 4?: Captain Martin sometimes wondered if the FBI tested the same weapon Norman turned over to the KSU police. The question of whether Norman had a second gun was raised because of a claim made by NBC soundman Joe Butano, a member of the NBC camera crew which saw Norman surrender the pistol.

Butano and other members of the crew had met Norman on the afternoon of May 3, and Butano, who shared Norman's enthusiasm for guns, told me that in the NBC company car, Norman showed him a .357 magnum, not the .38 caliber pistol turned over to the police. (Butano and a freelance reporter, Bob Hoiles, even took the shells out and played with them.)

When he was deposed for the civil suit, Norman denied that he was armed with two guns on May 4.

HOW MANY GUNS WERE TAKEN FROM NORMAN? If Norman had only one gun, why then did Guard Sergeant Michael Delaney initially claim that Norman handed over the gun to him, and that he gave the gun to Harold Rice of the KSU police?

Former KSU public information officer Paul Schlemmer confirmed seeing this.

That is not the story told by the Kent State police. Each KSU police officer at the scene gave a statement indicating that Norman surrendered the gun directly to KSU Patrolman Harold Rice, who in turn handed it to plainclothes detective Tom Kelley.

TERRY NORMAN HUDDLING WITH THE GUARDSMEN: At the civil trial, a photograph surfaced showing that Norman had penetrated the ranks of the National Guardsmen while they were on the football field minutes before the shooting. When shown the picture, Norman admitted to being in the middle of a circle of Guardsmen, but said he could not recall the substance of his conversations with the Guard. He said: "I did not secretly conspire . . . to do anything."

(One witness, whose name was blacked out when the FBI reports were released, told the FBI: "As stones were being thrown at the National Guard he was picking some of them up and at one point I saw him throw a stone back at the students. I felt his presence with the guard during their action and also his taking part in some action as being unwarranted.")

NORMAN'S ROCK THROWING AT THE STUDENTS: Norman's rock throwing, seen by this witness and Sgt. Breckenridge (above), was also witnessed by two other individuals. Captain John Martin, in a statement to the Guard Inspector General's office, said he saw Norman place himself "somewhere between the National Guardsmen and the students and he seemed to run out, throw this object, and come back . . . I remember thinking to myself at the time, 'My gosh, where did that idiot come from, and what's he doing?"

Norman himself admitted throwing "two or three" rocks at students (although demonstrator Tom Masterson, who later wrestled with him, placed the number more like "half a dozen, a dozen.")

MY CONCLUSION ABOUT THE COVER-UP OF NORMAN'S ROLE: Based on the evidence to date, my feeling is that the reason the FBI and the campus police covered up the fact they used Norman as an informant, and never fully investigated the possibility he may have started the shootings, was not because these agencies *knew* he fired his weapon, but because they did not know what to think and were *afraid* he may have somehow been involved in the tragedy.

Did Norman ever fire his gun? As far as I know, there is only one witness who was on Blanket Hill who thought he saw Norman fire at the same time the Guardsmen fired. There are, however, four witnesses (Delaney, DeBrine, Butano and Day) who thought they heard Norman and/or detective Tom Kelley admit the gun had been fired after he ran back to the practice field. So what Norman did on Blanket Hill still remains a mystery.

One thing can be said: Contrary to persistent rumors that he disappeared after the shootings, Norman returned to Kent State during the summer of 1970 and enrolled in a geography class. Would he have done that if he had really shot someone or discharged his weapon on the campus?

PAGE

76   "but not at us" Mickey Porter column, *Akron Beacon Journal,* May 5, 1970.

Chapter Three, "Who Burned ROTC?"

KSU FOREKNOWLEDGE OF THE ROTC FIRE: Although I think he was just covering his tracks, the historical record should reflect the fact that after Detective Tom Kelley told the *Beacon Journal* (in a taped interview) that he knew about ROTC fire in advance, he changed his story when deposed for the civil trial. In a deposition dated April 4, 1975, Kelley testified: "I never knew they were going to burn anything."

DEBBIE SHRYOCK'S STORY: One of the more interesting stories about the ROTC fire was told by Debbie Shryock, a former reporter for the *Daily Kent Stater,* who claims she was friends of three of the men who were responsible for initially starting the fire—men, she said, who were never subsequently indicted by the state grand jury and who could never understand why the wrong people were prosecuted.

According to Shryock, the reason her friends had such a difficult time starting the fire was because the decision to burn the building was not made until the last minute and because "they had never burned a building and they did not know how to do it."

Shryock said she witnessed their amateurish attempts to start a fire, first with matches, and then their subsequent short-lived success at starting a fire when someone threw an ignited cloth in the building..

Shryock, like numerous other witnesses, insisted that the fire appeared to be out at the time the police finally arrived at the building and chased the students away.

Shryock also told me that she and her friends were the same ones who subsequently publicly raised questions as to how the fire rekindled after the students left the scene, and why, when her friends started the initial blaze on the south side of the building, the south end subsequently was left standing, while the north end was destroyed.

The latter claim, however, was disputed by faculty observer Glenn Frank, who told me that "the photographic evidence does not bear it out."

AGENTS PROVOCATEUR: For background information on how government informants behaved during the era of anti-Vietnam War protests, see: "Against Provocation," *Saturday Review,* March 29, 1971; "FBI Mayhem," *New York Review of Books,* March 18, 1976; Frank Donner, "The Confession of an FBI Informer," *Harper's,* December 1972; "Ron Rosenbaum, "Run, Tommy, Run," *Esquire,* July 1971; "Political Trials," *The Nation,* June 4, 1973; "Dirty Tricks on Trial," *Ramparts,* August-September 1973; "Agents Provocateur," *The Nation,* April 5, 1975; "'Horror Stories, Et Cetera'—But What's the Et Cetera?," *Miami Herald,* July 12, 1973, and "Watergate Acts Seen as More Widespread," *Washington Post,* May 17, 1973.

For undercover activities specifically at Kent State, see Ted Joy, "Espionage at Kent State," *The Nation,* January 29, 1973, which detailed allegations that a KSU patrolman infiltrated a radical group, the Vietnam Veterans Against the War, in 1972, and tried to get the veterans to commit acts of violence against policemen and property.

These and other accounts of provocateurs particularly fascinated several reporters for the *Akron Beacon Journal,* who spent a considerable amount of energy investigating this angle. In an article published in the March 31, 1974, edition of the newspaper ("Undercover Agents' Role Left Unanswered by Jury"), reporters John Dunphy and Pat Engle-

120

FAIN Ohio

hart reported that they had identified two undercover agents who were on campus that weekend. According to the article, one man, John Bernard, claimed he was "working for Army Intelligence and other federal agencies."

The *Beacon Journal* reported shortly after the man was interviewed for the article that "he quit his job as an insurance man in Akron and moved to a Columbus suburb, saying his life had been endangered by the interview."

The second undercover agent—a man Dunphy told me had the same name as the former president, Richard Nixon—"said he was part of a federal narcotics strike force sent to the campus to make a drug arrest. He said several undercover agents comprised the strike force and were quickly ushered out of town after the shootings."

Galen Keller, a paralegal for the victims who had access to all the investigative files, alleges that a police informant may have been involved in the disturbance in downtown Kent on Friday night, May 1, 1970. Keller informed the victims' attorneys that a still unreleased Ohio Highway patrol report indicates that a demonstrator "mentioned by many witnesses as being the one who got things going downtown Friday night" turned around and gave the Kent city police the names "of individuals he saw performing illegal acts."

PAGE
82   "Don't pack your cameras" "KSU Policeman Denies Saying Norman Fired Gun," *Akron Beacon Journal,* August 8, 1973.
83   "Took the unusual" Memorandum and Supporting Documents of Plaintiffs in Opposition to All Defendants' Summary Judgment Motions. Legal brief filed in the U.S. District Court, March 31, 1975.
83   "We had two squads" Chester Williams' statement to the FBI, May 1970.
83   "Policy of nonintervention" Minority Report, pp. 59- 60.
83   "The persons involved" Ibid., p. 67.
84   "That fire went" Ibid., p. 55.
84   "Had thought themselves" Ibid., p. 77.
85   "ROTC going" Interview with Donald Schwartzmiller, May 20, 1974.
85   "Can you take" Quoted in the Minority Report, p. 60.
85   "Thought he was loony" Interview with Walter E. Moore, April 12, 1982.
86   "Hell, no" Joe Eszterhas, "Ohio Honors Its Dead," *Rolling Stone,* July 10, 1971.

86   "Once again" Memorandum from President Robert I. White to Chester Williams, July 3, 1970.

86   "He [Schwartzmiller] had" Memorandum from Chester A. Williams to President Robert I. White, "Answer to allegations concerning Mr. Schwarztmiller on July 31, 1970," dated August 15, 1970.

88   "The FBI feels it has identified" Pg. 69, original Justice Department Summary, Stone.

Chapter Four, "The Early Coverup"

J. EDGAR HOOVER'S ROLE IN THE COVER-UP: In carrying out Nixon's order to "knock down" the news report that the Guardsmen could be prosecuted, FBI Director J. Edgar Hoover even wrote to *Akron Beacon Journal* publisher John S. Knight accusing his paper of printing falsehoods and insisting that the FBI "did not draw any conclusions" from its investigations. In a rebuttal, published prominently on the front page of the *Beacon Journal* on August 7, 1970, along with Hoover's accusations, Knight noted that Hoover evaded the fact that the newspaper's information was accurate, and that the only mistake the newspaper made was in attributing the information to the FBI instead of to the Justice Department attorneys who evaluated the information provided by FBI agents.

"An exercise in semantics," Knight wrote, "must not be permitted to obscure the fact that our article was essentially correct and not 'distorted,' as you allege."

DID THE OHIO ATTORNEY GENERAL'S OFFICE PLAY A ROLE IN THE COVER-UP?: In my interview with Scranton Commissioner Joseph Rhodes, Jr., Rhodes told me that a representative from the Ohio attorney general's office tried to persuade the Commission not to subpoena any Guardsmen because "it would ruin their case against them." This had to have been a cover story since the state prosecutors never intended to indict any Guardsmen.

THE STATE GRAND JURY'S ZEAL TO INDICT HUNDREDS OF STUDENTS: In a memorandum from Robert Murphy to Assistant Attorney General Jerris Leonard dated November 24, 1970, Murphy recapped a conversation he had with state prosecutor Robert Balyeat after the state grand jury exonerated the Guardsmen and the Justice Department began its review of the case. Murphy quoted Balyeat as saying: "It appeared at the outset of the proceeding that [the] Ohio Grand Jury was inclined to indict literally hundreds of students on charges, including failure to obey

252   FOUR DEAD IN OHIO

a lawful order to disperse. He [Balyeat] told the Grand Jury that this was neither practical nor desirable."

Murphy wrote: "Balyeat told me that in considering what charges could be brought against the Guardsmen, he ruled out murder because no intent could be shown, and he ruled out manslaughter because of the lack of ballistics evidence. He also ruled out consideration of assault and/or battery charges as being inappropriate for a situation in which four people had died. This, of course, limited considerably the possible charges that could be brought against the Guardsmen. Balyeat felt that the only case that was worth bringing to the Grand Jury's special attention was the [Lawrence] Shafer case. He did not reach the question on whether the Ohio statute, which purports to clothe Guardsmen with immunity in suppressing riots, was applicable in this situation. He does feel, however, that self-defense, which is a subjective matter in Ohio, is most probably a sufficient defense to any charge that could be brought against the Guardsmen."

THE MISSING NIXON MEMO: The Justice Department claims it cannot locate a copy of Nixon's original memorandum ordering Attorney General John Mitchell to close the case. Apparently it has disappeared.

SHIFTING THE PROSECUTION BURDEN ON THE VICTIMS: One of the reasons the Justice Department's closure of the case seemed so suspicious was because the Department in effect kept telling the victims of the shootings—and later the student petitioners—"We'll investigate the killings if you get the evidence to us." As Reverend John Adams pointed out, it was absurd for the Department to tell grieving parents and college students to do their own investigating when the Justice Department had all the financial resources and the judicial machinery at its disposal.

Moreover, by this time, the Justice Department's summary of the FBI had already been made public, and the summary seemed to contain sufficient evidence to proceed with a grand jury investigation and prosecution of the Guards.

PAGE
93   "a cover-up surpassed" Richard G. Zimmerman, "Watergate Bonus: New KSU Probe," Cleveland *Plain Dealer,* December 16, 1973.
93   "time is right" "US Probe of KSU Killings is Pushed," *Akron Beacon Journal,* May 14, 1971
93   "something hidden in" Conversations with Paul Keane and Robert Gage, July 1972. Confirmed in my interview with Dr. Olds, April 25, 1974.

95 "a complete preliminary" Memorandum from Cartha DeLoach to Alex Rosen, May 8, 1970.

96 "the students got" Memorandum from J. Edgar Hoover to FBI officials Cartha DeLoach, Alex Rosen, Williamv Sullivan and Thomas Bishop, May 11, 1970.

96 "Their conduct showed. . ." Memorandum, "Kent State: Preliminary Conclusions and Recommendations," from Robert Murphy to Jerris Leonard, undated (circa June 1970).

98 Interview with Glenn Olds, April 25, 1974.

98 "going after" Interview with Arthur Krause, July 6, 1974.

98 "assist Mr. Kane" Memorandum from Jerris Leonard to Will Wilson, assistant attorney general, Internal Security Division, July 7, 1970.

99 "setting forth" Letter from Jerris Leonard to Ronald Kane, July 9, 1970.

99 "Taking all the" Memorandum, "Potential National Defendants in the Kent State Shootings," from Jerris Leonard to Ronald Kane, undated but sent between July 9 and 24, 1970.

100 "The President said" Memorandum from J. Edgar Hoover to Clyde Tolson, William Sullivan, Thomas Bishop, C. D. Brennan, James H. Gale, and Alex Rosen, July 24, 1970.

100 "The President was" Memorandum from J. Edgar Hoover to Clyde Tolson, William Sullivan, Thomas Bishop, and Alex Rosen, July 24, 1970.

101 "As instructed" Memo from Thomas Bishop to William Sullivan, July 24, 1970.

101 "furnished this" Ibid.

102 "apparent violations" "Mitchell Eyes Prosecution by U.S. in Kent State Case: Apparent Violations of Federal Law," *Akron Beacon Journal,* July 29, 1970.

102 "The pretrial publicity" "Prosecution of Guard in Kent Deaths Hinted," *Washington Post,* July 24, 1970.

103 "turned the tables" Memorandum from Alex Rosen to William Sullivan, July 24, 1970.

103 "grasped control" Interview with Ronald Kane, November 6, 1981.

103 "for the purpose" Ibid.

104 "the ultimate investigation" "KSU Probe Plans Laid by Brown," *Akron Beacon Journal,* August 12, 1970.

104 "state officials seem" "Doubts Sure to Follow State's KSU Investigation," *Akron Beacon Journal,* August 9, 1970.

104 "He [Ford] served" "Key Figures in Grand Jury Probe," *Kent Record-Courier,* September 4, 1970.

"To identify the" As cited in "White Tells Panel at KSU: '3 Groups Wanted to Shut Us Down,'" *Akron Beacon Journal,* August 19, 1970.

105 "subpoena any" Ibid.

105 "assess the guilt" "Authorities Thought Revolution Had Come to Kent," *Akron Beacon Journal,* August 21, 1970.

106 "The Commission ordered" Letter from William Ziegler to Dana Stewart, late 1970.

107 "fired in the honest" "KSU Jury Indicts 25; Defends Guard," *Akron Beacon Journal,* October 16, 1970.

107 "neither necessary nor" Memorandum, "Potential National Guard Defendants in the Kent State Shootings," from Jerris Leonard to Ronald Kane, undated but sent between July 9 and 24, 1970.

107 "unnecessary, unwarranted, and inexcusable" Scranton Commission Report, p. 289.

108 "conceived in fraud" Remarks of Stephen Young, Congressional Record, December 17, 1970, vol. 116, no. 203.

108 "a shooting situation" Justice Department Summary, p. 84.

108 "should have shot" "Should've Shot All Troublemakers," *Akron Beacon Journal,* October 24, 1970.

109 "The President has decided" "Ehrlichman Memo Reveals Nixon Bid to Bar Kent Probe," *Washington Post,* May 5, 1978.

109 "Please ask" Ibid.

110 "Quite disturbed" Memorandum from J. Edgar Hoover to Clyde Tolson, William Sullivan, Thomas Bishop and Alex Rosen, July 24, 1970.

110 "Summary of the" "Highly confidential" memorandum from Jerris Leonard to John D. Ehrlichman, May 1970.

110 "These reports" Ibid.

111 "hidden" Conversations with Paul Keane and Robert Gage, July 1972, confirmed in my April 25, 1974 interview with Olds.

111 "doesn't always work" "Mitchell Backs Hoover's Right To Talk Like Everybody Else," *New York Times,* December 19, 1970.

111 "because of serious" Memorandum, "Kent State University," from K. William O'Connor to Jerris Leonard, March 9, 1971.

112 "The government has" "No U.S. Action Likely on Kent," *Washington Post,* March 21, 1971.

113 "There is no" Michener, p. 409.

113 "Long enough" John P. Adams, "Kent State—Justice and Morality," *Cleveland State Law Review,* Winter 1973, p. 44.

114 "This theory is" Peter Davies, "An Appeal for Justice," *Congressional Record,* July 22, 1971, p. E- 8145.

114 "The parents and" Ibid., p. E-8144.

115 "Safely after" Christian Science Monitor August 14, 1991

114 "The appropriate time" "U.S. Probe of KSU Killings is Pushed,"
     Akron Beacon Journal, May 14, 1971.

115 "No likelihood" "U.S. Shuts Door on KSU Probe," *Cleveland
     Plain Dealer,* August 14, 1971.

115 "Successful investigation" John P. Adams, "Kent State— Justice
     and Morality," p. 44.

Chapter Five, "The Struggle for Justice"

THE RADICALS WHO OPPOSED A FEDERAL GRAND JURY IN-
VESTIGATION: The radicals at Kent who opposed a federal grand jury
on the grounds it would only indict more protestors, and not the National
Guardsmen, were not as paranoid as they seemed at the time. FBI
memos subsequently released under the Freedom of Information Act reveal that even after Mitchell announced the "no-grand-jury" decision on
August 13, 1971, high level FBI officials tried to pressure Mitchell into
indicting more students if the state of Ohio decided not to proceed with
its prosecutions, as was widely expected at the time. One teletype sent to
the Special Agent in Charge of the Cleveland field office from "Director,
FBI" on August 25, 1971, two weeks after Mitchell's announcement, requested that the Cleveland office of the FBI continue to quietly monitor
developments in the Kent 25 cases on those very grounds.

THE AUTHOR'S OWN INVOLVEMENT IN THE KENT STATE
CASE: The reason I never advertised the fact that I helped get the National Guardsmen prosecuted was because I did not want the publicity to
jeopardize my chances of getting interviews with either the Guardsmen
or their attorneys. I ultimately succeeded in that regard.

My work with Keane and Rambo (primarily as their publicist) gave
me a unique perspective. Unlike some chroniclers of the Kent case, who
seemed to view the case only through the filter on their own narrow academic specialties, I had a window to what many of the most important
players were thinking and doing behind the scenes as events unfolded in
the case.

I was also Peter Davies' closest contact on the Kent State campus
between late 1971 and 1975. I only met Peter in person a few times, but
over a three-year period we spoke by phone several times a week and
often at considerable length. Peter would often bounce ideas off me and
we'd swap information.

We both felt very strongly that the Guardsmen should be prosecuted.
However, that close contact also led to my disillusionment over his
methodology and theorizing. We had fundamentally different approaches

to the case. I believed one should examine the evidence, and then see which theories best fit the facts. Peter thought it should work the other way around.

PAGE

117 "The Justice Department's" Bill Gordon, "Kent: One Year Later," *UCLA Daily Bruin,* May 3, 1971.

118 "Dormitory counselors" "Olds Won't Sign Petition on Shooting," *Akron Beacon Journal,* October 5, 1971.

118 "Begging from the" Interview with Paul Keane, March 6, 1972.

119 "The creative or" Interview with Glenn A. Olds, April 25, 1974.

119 "Kent State doesn't" Interview with Greg Rambo, November 11, 1971.

119 "I assure you" Letter from Attorney General John Mitchell to Ohio Congressman William Stanton, December 20, 1971.

120 "The petition is" Conversations with Paul Keane and Greg Rambo, November 1971. Confirmed in Olds interview.

120 "The matter of a" "Nixon to Answer KSU Petition Soon?" *Akron Beacon Journal,* November 14, 1971.

120 "The dropping" "Another KSU Chapter Ends—Cases Dropped," *Akron Beacon Journal,* December 8, 1971.

123 "Second-guess" "Kleindienst Says He Won't Reopen File on KSU Case," *Akron Beacon Journal,* February 23, 1972.

123 "A review and" "White House: Decision to Come," *Daily Kent Stater,* February 24, 172.

124 "We're getting" Conversation with Paul Keane, March 10, 1972.

124 "Sufficient new" Letter from Leonard Garment to parents of the four slain students, July 6, 1972. Quoted in "White House Restates Position on Kent State," *Washington Post,* July 12, 1972.

125 "Telling the petitioners" Conversation with Arthur Krause, July 1972.

126 "Something hidden in" Conversations with Keane and Gage, July 1972, confirmed in Olds interview.

126 "All we can do" "The A.M.," *Kent State University Daily Summer News,* August 15, 1982.

Chapter Six, "The Struggle for Justice (Continued)"

THE PROFESSOR WHO TURNED ON THE VICTIMS: Although one professor tried to take credit for helping get the federal grand jury investigation, the truth is that no one on the Kent State faculty did anything more than sign his name to the petition calling for the investigation.

The aforementioned professor, Jerry M. Lewis, wrote several articles about May 4 for sociological journals and was initially believed to have been a supporter of the victims. The families of the victims even invited him to attend some of their private meetings with their attorneys in which confidential litigation strategy was discussed.

At one meeting, held on September 17, 1973, just after the Justice Department reopened the case, Lewis stunned those in attendance. During the middle of a discussion on ways to keep the pressure on the Justice Department so it would empanel the federal grand jury, Lewis took a position against the victims, saying: "The radicals on campus will not like it (an investigation)."

Arthur Krause, the father of slain student Allison Krause, exploded. He had just spent the last three and a half years working for the investigation, and virtually screamed at Lewis: "Jerry, that's the stupidest thing I've ever heard of."

The humiliated professor kept quiet for the rest of the meeting, but a memo discovered in the University archives reveals that just a few days after acting as a mouthpiece for the few radicals left on campus, Lewis did a 180 degree shift and became a volunteer informant for the Kent State administration. Lewis sent a memo to KSU President Glenn Olds volunteering to brief Olds on what transpired at the meeting.

(Had he known about it, Krause would have had another fit. The former president of the university, Robert I. White, was one of the defendants in the victims' lawsuit.)

Years later, when Lewis was assigned to a committee charged with considering whether to build a memorial to the dead, this ethical breach was brought to the attention to another Kent State president, Michael Schwartz, who was warned Lewis' presence on the committee would alienate the victims. Schwartz seemed to show the same contempt for the victims by saying: "I alienate people all the time."

PAGE
129 "stay quiet" "Kent Case Just Won't Stay Quiet in the Grave," Cleveland's *Plain Dealer,* September 13, 1981.
130 "We're never" Tape recording of colloquium, "Kent State: Outside the Law," May 3, 1973.
131 "Convocation of" Statement prepared for NSA Magazine, published by College Press Service, January 23, 1974.
131 "Struggle for" "Kent State: Struggle for Justice," Transcript of *Bill Moyer's Journal,* Educational Broadcasting Corporation, aired on WNET-TV, January 16, 1974.
132 "Forced the press" Interview with Paul Keane, January 12, 1973.
133 "Does Kent State" Interview with Paul Keane, January 12, 1973.

133 "plunged almost" "A Man Who Says He 'Lost' 2 Daughters at Kent State," *Life,* August 27, 1971.
134 "a quixotic" Ibid.
135 "Nothing" Interview with Max Keller, January 26, 1981.

Chapter Seven, "Reopening the Investigation"

WHY THE WHITE HOUSE ALLOWED THE PETITIONS TO BE RE-SUBMITTED: The White House probably would not have agreed to meet with the students and accept the resubmitted petitions if it had not been for Kahler's threats to bang on the White House gates with his wheelchair. The threat obviously had an impact on the White House, because a year later (May 22, 1974), when I interviewed Leonard Garment's deputy, Bradley Patterson, he brought up the subject himself, saying: "We cannot have people outside the White House banging on the gates."

PROSECUTING GUARDSMEN ON MISDEMEANORS: Even though K. William O'Connor insisted that the Guardsmen could only be indicted for misdemeanors, the Justice Department subsequently indicted the Guardsmen under the felony provisions of the statute. That made it look as if O'Connor was not leveling with the petitioners—or, as Dean Kahler cracked: "Maybe O'Connor was not up on his law that day."

With the benefit of hindsight, though, it appears that O'Connor was correct. Had the Guardsmen been convicted, it is quite possible that the judge might have sentenced them under the misdemeanor provisions of the statute. The Justice Department lacked (and was unable to develop during the subsequent federal grand jury) any proof linking any specific Guardsman to any specific victim. Thus, there was no way of proving that "death resulted" from any discharge of weapons.

DID THE NATIONAL GUARD TRY TO MAKE TERRY NORMAN A SCAPEGOAT?: At the time Captain Martin sent his letter to Senator Bayh raising questions about Norman's role on May 4 there was a great deal of speculation to the effect that the National Guard was trying to set up Terry Norman as a scapegoat for the shootings.

As one of the attorneys who represented the Kent 25 observed: "The Justice Department announces its probe and then the Guardsmen suddenly remember that Terry Norman said he fired his gun. It was an obvious frame-up to get themselves off the hook."

One cannot discount the possibility, but after talking with Martin and reviewing the statements he provided to the Guard's Inspector General's office, I am inclined to take a more innocuous view of these turn of events.

My feeling is that the questions about Norman nagged Martin—just as they nagged many newsmen and professors on the campus. My suspicion is that when Martin sent the bits and pieces of information he had about Norman to Bayh, he did not foresee the impact and repercussions his letter would have.

His letter became a key link in the chain of events that led to the indictment of the Guardsmen, including two of Martin's sergeants. Had Martin foreseen this, I suspect he might not have sent the letter.

THE JUSTICE DEPARTMENT'S REASONS FOR REOPENING THE CASE: One of the documents in the Nixon collection released by the National Archives suggests that the Justice Department never had any intention of empaneling the federal grand jury and only reopened the case to head off the threat of a Congressional investigation. This August 8, 1973 memo from White House aide Leonard Garment to Nixon's chief of staff Alexander Haig, written after Garment had consulted with Assistant Attorney General J. Stanley Pottinger, advised Haig that: "the Richardson/Pottinger argument is that this further investigation will not lead to a federal grand jury proceeding, but will put the Justice Department in a better posture vis-a-vis a Congressional investigation."
Garment, who opposed the federal grand jury, did not buy that argument. Garment warned Haig "we will gradually find ourselves embroiled in a full-fledged grand jury proceeding."

The memo was passed on to Nixon, who apparently agreed. Nixon underlined Garment's warning with the word "Al!!", indicating that he wanted some action taken against the investigation.

WHY THE CASE WAS NOT REOPENED: When the case was reopened, Pottinger claimed his review was prompted by a letter from an "investigative reporter" offering new information. That reporter was actually Peter Davies, who on March 29, 1973, wrote to Pottinger offering to provide new information that Terry Norman fired his gun on May 4 if the Department demonstrated "a genuine interest in taking formal depositions from the witnesses."

The Department, however, gave Davies the brush-off. The response to this offer came on May 23, when a letter bearing Pottinger's name and Robert Murphy's signature was sent to Davies stating: "The information you have furnished does not warrant a change in the early decisions concerning the empaneling of a grand jury."

Davies, however, had never submitted the new information he dangled. The Department acted as if it was not interested in what Davies had to offer.

According to Davies, several months later, after the case was reopened, Murphy apologized to him for the brush-off, claiming that the letter was sent by someone else in the Department while he was out of the office.

THE CREWDSON CONNECTION: It is possible that in claiming he saw information in FBI files that would greatly "pain the parents," Crewdson was shown a document containing an accusation against one of the slain students that was not necessarily true.

For example, Crewdson could have been shown an FBI report suggesting that fatality Jeffrey Miller was armed with a gun. The gun, of course, turned out to be a "throwdown" planted by Captain Ron Snyder (see Chapter Nine), but the FBI or Crewdson might not have known that from just reviewing the file.

Unfortunately, Crewdson will not go beyond what he told Davies. So far he has only spoken about his conversation with Davies on background.

WAS A WOUNDED STUDENT A GOVERNMENT INFORMANT?: Davies really let his imagination run wild on the issue of potentially embarrassing information about the victims. Privately he began asking not "Was one of the victims a government informant?" but "Which one of the victims was a secret agent?"

Memos in his papers in the Yale archives indicate his suspicions centered around a wounded student whose father, Davies believed, worked for the CIA.

There is not a shred of evidence that this student was anything other than a protestor.

THE ALLEGED BRIBE ATTEMPT: The Crewdson Connection was not the only bizarre incident in the Kent Affair that Davies has cited in espousing his more recent "the-White-House-did-it/there-was-a-big-conspiracy" thesis. In his public speeches, and in private conversations, he has frequently alluded to an alleged attempt to offer Arthur Krause a half-million-dollar bribe in exchange for the dropping of Krause's civil suit against Governor Rhodes and the Guardsmen.

Davies outlined the story of the allegation in a March 30, 1975, memorandum to Mike Epstein, an investigator for the Senate Intelligence Committee. According to Davies, in early 1971 a motion picture producer contacted Krause with the idea of doing a film about his daughter and the killings. When the producer learned that Krause would be in

New York to attend a screening for a PBS documentary, the producer suggested that Krause meet a friend of his—a top official in the American Civil Liberties Union. Krause did so on April 10, 1971, accompanied by Davies.

Davies told Epstein the bribe attempt "came when he [the ACLU official] brought up the subject of money, and was asking Art if that's what he was after through the lawsuits against Rhodes, Del Corso and Canterbury. 'If it's a question of money,' he said, 'that can be arranged.' Then he said something like, 'How much do you want? Half a million, a million?' This could, of course, have been simply flippancy on [the ACLU official's] part, except it was all said very seriously. And when Art asked where [the official] was going to get that kind of money, the lawyer truly stunned us by saying that there were ways to make such a payment through the Ford Foundation!!!"

The ACLU official, as Davies correctly pointed out, had an highly unusual relationship with J. Edgar Hoover—one that baffled his associates in the Civil Liberties Union.

Davies' version, of course, would only make sense if the federal government were somehow involved in the tragedy, therefore having very strong motives to head off a public trial.

When I spoke with Krause about the allegation in 1977, he confirmed that money was discussed, but said the discussion was "subject to interpretation" and it was also possible that the ACLU official was just exploring the possibility of an out-of-court monetary settlement.

That seems to be the most logical explanation for this incident, which cannot be independently confirmed since the ACLU official died in the early 1970s.

The very fact that Davies was present at the meeting also casts doubt on the validity of his allegation. If someone wanted to offer Arthur Krause a bribe, it seems unlikely he would do so in the presence of a witness.

SERGEANT PRYOR'S LAWSUIT AND THE PUBLICATION OF DAVIES' BOOK: The reason Davies' book was so watered down was because at the time of publication a malicious libel suit filed by Sergeant Myron Pryor was still pending. Davies had accused Pryor of instigating the shooting in his 1971 report.

The suit may have been filed to discourage Davies from writing his book. It was dismissed on March 27, 1975, by U.S. District Judge Constance Motley, who chided Pryor's lawyers for doing "nothing to seriously prosecute this claim." Motley said, in her opinion: "If ever there was a case that deserved to be dismissed for lack of prosecution, this is it."

PAGE

139 "without prosecutive action" Memorandum, "Kent State University," from K. William O'Connor to Jerris Leonard, March 9, 1971.

139 "Leonard wanted" Conversation with Paul Keane, May 10, 1973.

140 "pretty thin stuff" "Kent Riot Evidence is 'Thin," *Washington Post,* May 13, 1973.

140 "The most any" "O'Connor Against May '70 Probe," *Daily Kent Stater,* May 11, 1973.

140 "I pointed out" Letter from Bill Gordon to Paul Keane, May 17, 1973.

141 "The answer on" Letter from Leonard Garment to Paul Keane, Greg Rambo, and Dean Kahler, May 25, 1973.

141 "Mr. Garment" "The Letter," (editorial), *Daily Kent Stater,* May 30, 1973.

142 "Believe it or not" Interview with Peter Davies, June 24, 1974.

142 "If Nixon is" Note from Paul Keane to Bill Gordon, mid- June 1973.

142 "Taking a fresh" "U. S. Aide Reconsiders KSU Probe: Olds Working Behind Scenes," *Akron Beacon Journal,* June 13, 1973.

143 "The Justice Department" Conversation with Pat Englehart, June 16, 1973.

143 "I asked the" Transcript of J. Stanley Pottinger's press conference, June 15, 1973.

143 "if we had any" Ibid.

144 "Suspicious minds" Nathan Lewin, "Kent State Revisited: Another Skelton in the Closet?," *The New Republic,* August 18 and 25, 1973.

144 "Why, in light" Ibid.

145 "Stop that man!" "Kent State: The Search for Understanding," *Akron Beacon Journal,* May 24, 1970.

145 "at students just prior" Justice Department Summary. pp. 89-90.

146 "I had to shoot" Interview with Michael Delaney, March 21, 1973.

146 "My God!" Interviews with Michael Delaney, March 21, 1973, and Fred DeBrine, March 20, 1973.

147 "for Detective Tom" Norman's statement to the Kent State police, May 4, 1970.

147 "for which he" U.S. Congress, Committee on the Judiciary, "Nomination of Clarence Kelley to be Director of the Federal Bureau of Investigation," June 19, 20 and 25, 1973, p. 142.

147 "On May 4" Letter from John Martin to Birch Bayh, July 24, 1970.

148 "The FBI seemed" Ibid.

149 "state of shock" Author's telephone conversation with Peter Davies, August 2, 1973

149 "I had a" Peter Davies, "Another White House Horror Story?" *The Village Voice,* November 3, 1973.

151 "A personal memorandum" "Schorr Case: Memo Points to Haldeman," *New York Times,* December 30, 1973.

151 "Golden" Philip Nobile, "Extra! An Exclusive Report on How the New York Times Became Second Banana," *Esquire,* May 1975, p. 97.

151 "In normal times" Harrison Salisbury, *Without Fear or Favor: The Times and Its Times* (New York: Times Books, 1980), p. 439.

152 "Pain to the nation" Peter Davies, "Another White House Horror Story?" *The Village Voice,* November 3, 1973.

152 "That was just" Interview with Roy Meyers, August 27, 1974.

152 "jumped on it" Interview with David Hess, August 13, 1974.

152 "If that son" Interview with Pat Englehart, June 6, 1974.

152 "Meandering bullshit" Interview with John Dunphy, November 21, 1974.

155 "an emotional response" Congressional Record, November 16, 1970, p. 37,289.

155 "cruel and unjust" "Parents of KSU Victims Rap Saxbe," *Akron Beacon Journal,* November 2, 1973.

155 "an examination of" "Students at Kent State Fight Saxbe Move," *Akron Beacon Journal,* November 5, 1973.

155 "It would be" "KSU Probe Shouldn't Stop," editorial, *Akron Beacon Journal,* November 6, 1973.

156 "The case remains" "Saxbe and Kent State," editorial, *New York Times,* November 15, 1973.

156 "The history of" "Another Whitewash?", editorial, *St. Louis Post-Dispatch,* November 20, 1973.

157 "Murphy made" Interview with Steven Sindell, April 21, 1975.

157 "The day-to-day" Interview with Robert Murphy, May 29, 1975.

157 "If, however" U.S. Congress, Committee on the Judiciary, "Nomination of William B. Saxbe to be Attorney General," December 12 and 13, 1973, p. 3.

Chapter Eight, "The Prosecution of the National Guardsmen"

HOW A CONSPIRACY MIGHT HAVE BEEN PROVEN: The only way prosecutors could have proven that there was a conspiracy (or order to fire) was to get one of the Guardsmen in G Troop, who was on the hill, to come forward and testify against his fellow soldiers.

I spent quite a bit of time tracking down several soldiers whom I suspected might have fit that category. Like others before me, I was not successful, but I was never satisfied that every screw was turned or that every potential "rat" was interrogated.

WHY LEON SMITH AND MATTHEW McMANUS WERE INDICT-ED: The most puzzling aspect of the indictment was the fact that both McManus and Smith were indicted for firing their shotguns, yet only one student, James Russell, was wounded by shotgun pellets, apparently on a ricochet. It seems highly unlikely that Russell could have been wounded by both men. The reason McManus and Smith were indicted were because both foolishly gave statements which could be interpreted as meaning that their shotgun blasts wounded someone.

THE SUSPICION THAT THE SELF-DEFENSE CLAIM WAS FABRI-CATED: In 1970, after writing (in the Justice Department's summary of the FBI report): "We have some reason to believe that the claim by the National Guard that their lives were endangered by the students was fabricated subsequent to event," Robert Murphy asked the FBI to try and identify the Guardsmen who gave the interview to Knight Newspapers and who talked about the common story. The FBI, however, was unsuccessful in its efforts.

The FBI got as far as Neil Shine, the city editor of the *Detroit Free Press,* who conducted the interview. Shine told the agents he was never told the name of the Guardsmen in question, and that the interview had been arranged by two of his reporters, Bill Schmidt and Julie Morris.

I spoke with both Schmidt and Morris, but neither was able (or willing) to shed any additional light on the Guardsman's identity.

DID BATTISTI HELP THE DEFENSE WIN THE CASE?: In an article that appeared in E*xit,* a Cleveland weekly ("How to Program a Jury," June 2, 1975), former *Plain Dealer* reporter Terence Sheridan raised some suspicions about Battisti's conduct at the trial, and ultimately about the validity of his opinion.

Sheridan charged that Battisti "diligently directed defense strategy in and out of court." Sheridan reported that when the defense attorneys tried to prove in court that the crowd was wild and bombarding the Guardsmen with rocks, Battisti in effect told them to "knock off that line of questioning . . . or you are going to make the government's case: rocks, provocation, bullets . . . summary punishment—specific, that is, goddamn *intent.* Later in his chambers, the judge was less circumspect: 'He said we better knock it off. He got very blunt and looked over at Murphy as he was saying it. He was telling us we were establishing the prosecutors' case and he looked right over at Murphy when he said it. Murphy was really disgusted. When we walked out of the chambers he was really mad. I guess he was hostile because the judge was working against him, telling us how to overcome Murphy, and Murphy didn't like that."

PAGE
160 "Terry Norman has" Interview with J. Stanley Pottinger, January 21, 1975.
161 "acting under color" United States of America v. Lawrence Shafer, James D. McGee, William E. Perkins, James E. Pierce, Ralph W. Zoller, Matthew j. McManus, Barry W. Morris and Leon Smith. Indictment issued March 29, 1974. Reprinted in the *Daily Kent Stater,* April 3, 1974.
161 "There's no question" Interview with C.D. "Gus" Lambros, January 31, 1975.
162 "Anybody who thinks" Conversation with Paul Keane, April 1, 1974.
162 "The system" Interview with Peter Davies, June 24, 1974.
163 "More or less" Pretrial hearings, United States v. Shafer, October 17, 1974.
163 "Are you sure?" Pretrial hearings, United States v. Shafer, September 23, 1974.
163 "The jury was "Terence Sheridan, "How to Program a Jury," *xit,* June 2, 1975, p. 8.
164 "There was no" United States v. Shafer et al., 384 F. Supp 496 (1974), October 29, 1974.
164 "It was a" Ibid.
165 "Leon Smith" Ibid.
165 "I had a rock" Leon Smith's statement to the Ohio Highway Patrol, June 9, 1970.
166 "Highly unusual" "Guard Case Dismissal Possible," *Akron Beacon Journal,* November 8, 1974.
166 "I might have" Ibid.
166 "We really don't" United States v. Lawrence Shafer et al., November 8, 1974.
166 "The government has" Memorandum Opinion and Order of Federal Judge Frank J. Battisti, United States v. Lawrence Shafer et al., November 8, 1974.
167 "The Justice Department" Interview with Greg Rambo, February 19, 1975.
167 "Big and horrible" Conversation with Peter Davies, January 22, 1975.
167 "By avoiding" Ibid.

168 "No slouch" Interview with C. D. "Gus" Lambros, January 31, 1975.

168 "Her father had" "13 Long Seconds," *Akron Beacon Magazine,* May 4, 1980.

169 "A gathering of" Interview with C. D."Gus" Lambros, January 31, 1975.

169 "I suppose" Interview with Robert Murphy, March 25, 1974.

169 "Six Guardsmen" Justice Department Summary, p. 84.

170 "We have some" Ibid.

170 "Just closed my" "Kent State: The Search for Understanding," *Akron Beacon Journal,* May 24, 1970.

170 "An aberration" Interview with J. Stanley Pottinger, January 21, 1975.

170 "While the judge's" David Hess, "Laws on Civil Rights Need to Be Revised," *Akron Beacon Journal,* November 17, 1974.

171 "Whether a certain" Interview with Michael Diamant, November 25, 1974.

171 "Normally, proof" Memorandum Opinion and Order of Federal Judge Frank Battisti, United States v. Lawrence A. Shafer et al., November 8, 1974.

172 "Very different" Ibid.

172 "Left the courtroom" Terence Sheridan, "How to Program a Jury," E*xit,* June 2, 1975, p. 6.

Chapter Nine, "The Civil Trials"

WERE ANY OF THE WOUNDED STUDENTS INVOLVED IN THE PRE-MAY 4 PROTESTS?: One of the key arguments Kelner made on behalf of the plaintiffs in the civil trial was that the 13 victims should not be penalized for the ROTC fire or the other acts of violence perpetrated by other students. Each of the nine surviving students testified they were not involved in the property destruction.

There is still an unresolved question, though, as to whether Alan Canfora told the truth when he testified he was not involved in the protest that led to the burning of the ROTC building. Canfora claimed he was not there at the time, but one member of Kent 25, Rick Felber, told me he definitely was.

Canfora has been caught lying on other issues. In a January 18, 1982, interview for this book, Alan Canfora admitted that he lied to the FBI about where he was located when he was shot. Canfora told the FBI he was 50 to 75 feet further from the troops than he actually was. Canfora said the reason he lied was because he was worried about getting indicted by the state grand jury (which he was).

Years later, Canfora falsely told reporters that he was a spokesman for the other victims (many of whom were embarrassed by his attempts to make a career of May 4).

Canfora's lack of candor was of great concern to Arthur Krause, the father of Allison Krause. During the civil trial Krause confided to friends: "We're going to lose the trial because of Canfora's lying."

BLAKEMORE'S VIEW: Akron attorney Robert Blakemore, who represented KSU President Robert I. White, was quoted in the October 10, 1976 issue of the *Beacon Journal's Beacon Magazine* as saying "I thought the plaintiffs should have collected damages in that one."

In an interview for this book, however, Blakemore amended that statement, saying he felt that only those victims who did not participate in the May 4 confrontation deserved compensation. Blakemore did not feel the protestors "had a right of recovery. They (the protestors) had as much obligation of foreseeing what happened as the other people."

THE THREAT AGAINST JUROR WILLIAMS: Ironically, after the appeals court ordered a new trial on the basis of jury tampering, the U.S. Attorney in Cleveland, William Coleman, according to the September 13, 1977, edition of the *Akron Beacon Journal,* quietly dropped his investigation of the alleged incident because he had doubts that juror Williams was really threatened.

PAGE
177 "to present a clear" "Law Favored the State in Kent Trial: Plaintiff's Lawyer Muddied the Case," *Plain Dealer,* August 31, 1975.
182 "highly destructive" Tape sent to author by Professor David Engdahl, May 12, 1976, in response to author's questions.
182 "Kelner was out" Conversation with Peter Davies, October 15, 1976.
183 "Burning, looting, rioting" Trial transcript, vol. 2, pp. 121 and 138.
184 "An avalanche of detail" Trial transcript, vol. 4, p. 624.
185 "They didn't" Author's notes of conversation reviewing the day's trial developments at Dean Kahler's house, June 3, 1975. In attendance were Kahler, his girlfriend Valerie Manning, wounded survivor Scott MacKenzie, and other friends of Kahler's.
186 "any guff" Trial transcript, vol. 7, p. 1,308.
187 "we went back" Engdahl tape, May 12, 1976.
187 "Lawyers for" "Law Favored the State in Kent Trial: Plaintiffs' Lawyers Muddied the Case," *Plain Dealer,* August 31, 1975.
188 "They tried to" Interview with David Engdahl, October 24, 1975.
188 "Please disperse" Justice Department Summary, p. 76.

188 "They weren't" Letter to *Daily Kent Stater,* October 2, 1975.
188 "Your claim" Trial transcript, vol. 14, pp. 3,754-6.
188 "Picked up as a" Ibid., vol. 18, p. 4,301.
188 "Did you give" Ibid., vol. 17, p. 4,035.
189 "Anything that could" Ibid., p. 4,064.
189 "Well, hell" Ibid., vol. 20, pp. 5,002-5.
189 "Things that happened" Ibid., p. 4,817.
190 "The big break" Joseph Kelner and James Munves, *The Kent State Coverup* (New York: Harper and Row, 1980), p. 123.
190 "Hurry up" Trial transcript, vol. 21, pp. 5,077, 5,146.
190 "It's my honest" Ibid., vol. 20, p. 5,028.
190 "I'm not going to" Ibid.
191 "They [the plaintiffs]" Interview with Burt Fulton, November 14, 1981.
191 "That defense attorneys" "Tone is Serious as KSU Trial Concludes," *Akron Beacon Journal,* July 27, 1975.
191 "When the lawyers" "Kent State Trial: Feuding Between Lawyers Opens Up in Courtroom," *Plain Dealer,* July 11, 1975.
192 "A strategy decision" Engdahl tape, May 12, 1976.
194 "Straight Army type" Ibid.
194 "Good standards" Trial transcript, vol. 39, p. 9,727.
194 "As far as the" Interview with Jack Schulman, November 19, 1974.
194 "State of war" Trial transcript, vol. 35, p. 8,824.
195 "Were out for" "Strategy Bared at KSU," *Akron Beacon Journal,* August 12, 1975.
195 "Two to five" Trial transcript, vol. 43, p. 10,880.
196 "I don't think" "KSU Civilian Shot Story Disputed," *Akron Beacon Journal,* August 20, 1975.
196 "I thought Joy Bishop" Interview with David Engdahl, October 24, 1975.
197 "Misguided leftists" Trial transcript, vol. 44, p. 10,976.
197 "I've had blood" Ibid., vol. 49, pp. 12,307-8.
198 "We the jury" "Jury Clears Guardsman, Rhodes in Kent Killings," *Plain Dealer,* August 28, 1975.
198 "They're still" "KSU Verdict Jolts Victims," *Akron Beacon Journal,* August 28, 1975.
198 "Lay down your" "Kent Jurors Recount Deliberations," *Plain Dealer,* August 30, 1975.
198 "A small oak" "Kent Trial Made History Here," *Cleveland Press,* August 25, 1975.
198 "There wasn't any" Engdahl tape, May 12, 1976.
198 "It somehow offends" "Defendants Ask KSU Court Cost," *Akron Beacon Journal,* October 24, 1975.

199 "The thirteen plaintiffs" Kelner and Munves, *The Kent State Coverup,* p. 260.

199 "An attempt to pervert" Krause v. Rhodes, 570 F. 2nd 563 (6th Circuit, 1977).

199 "Every litigant is" Ibid.

200 "It is time" Letter from David Engdahl, undated, but sent in late November 1977 "to the Kent State Families."

200 "Extremely serious" Ibid.

200 "At the first trial" Letter from Sanford J. Rosen to Rev. John P. Adams, November 21, 1977, for distribution to the Kent State clients.

200 "Desperation measure" Engdahl letter, November 1977.

201 "In the eyes of" Letter from Joseph Kelner to Rev. John P. Adams, November 17, 1977, for distribution to the Kent State families.

201 "There was a" Interview with Sanford J. Rosen, March 29, 1981.

201 "Honestly pessimistic" Ibid.

202 "Totally out" Interview with Burt Fulton, November 14, 1981.

202 "The snag was" Interview with Sanford J. Rosen, March 29, 1981.

203 "The Governor is not" "Kent State Epitaph: $675,000, Regret," *Los Angeles Herald-Examiner,* January 5, 1979.

203 "In retrospect" Statement issued in Cleveland, Ohio, January 4, 1979, by the defendants. Reprinted in the January 4, 1979 *Akron Beacon Journal.*

204 "A fundamental stimulus" Thomas Hensley, *The Kent State Incident: Impact of Judicial Process on Public Attitudes* (Westport, Ct.: Greenwood Press, 1981), pp. 123-4.

204 "eminently reasonable" Ibid., p. 124.

204 "Absolutely possible" Interview with Sanford J. Rosen, March 29, 1981.

205 "Any experienced" Kelner and Munves, p. 268.

205 "There is no" Interview with Sanford J. Rosen, March 29, 1981.

205 "It is true" "The Kent State Verdict," editorial, *New York Post,* August 29, 1975.

206 "Kent State" Ibid.

Annotated Bibliography

Books For the General Reader

The Middle of the Country, Bill Warren, editor. New York: Avon Books, 1970. The foreword of this paperback, which reached the newsstands within two weeks of the shootings, admits: "This book was hastily conceived and hastily executed." It consists of angry reactions to the tragedy by Kent State students and faculty members—only a few of whom were actual eyewitnesses.

The book was subsequently cited once in a footnote in James Michener's *Kent State.* I cannot recall it being used as a source of information anywhere else.

Thirteen Seconds: Confrontation at Kent State, Joe Eszterhas and Michael Roberts. New York: Dodd Mead & Company, 1970. One KSU professor dismissed this book as another "journalistic quickie," but it did include interesting profiles of Adjutant General Sylvester Del Corso and the four slain students. The book was written by two *Plain Dealer* reporters while the immediate aftermath was still unfolding and offers no conclusions (although Eszterhas and Roberts wrote elsewhere they felt the Guardsmen committed murder.)

The Killings at Kent State: How Murder Went Unpunished. I. F. Stone. New York: New York Review Book, 1970. This paperback reprinted three essays that Stone wrote for *The New York Review of Books* in which he denounced the early cover-up.

The Kent Affair: Documents and Interpretations. Ottavio M. Casale and

Louis Paskoff, editors. Boston: Houghton Mifflin, 1971. The editors, both professors of English at Kent State, apparently tried to duplicate what historian Bernard Fall did in *The Vietnam Reader.* Assuming the reader could form his own judgments, they reprinted conflicting official reports (including excerpts of the Scranton Commission report and the report of the special Ohio grand jury), original news and broadcast stories, newspaper editorials, faculty resolutions and letters to the editor.

Kent State: What Happened and Why, James Michener. New York: Random House, 1971. Michener's study, published on the first anniversary of the shootings, was the first major examination of the tragedy by an independent author. Michener and a team of Reader's Digest investigators spent several months in Kent interviewing as many witnesses to the events of May 1-4 as were willing to cooperate at the time. The result was a massive 559-page book that was considered by many (at least outside of Kent) to be the definitive book on May 4.

The book had many admirable qualities. As KSU Professor James Best wrote in an essay: "Michener has the uncanny ability to recreate the ambiance of a situation . . . you can almost hear the demonstrators and see the gas masked guardsmen."

Unfortunately, reliability was not one of the book's strong points. The accuracy of eyewitness accounts were repeatedly attacked at the trials, as were Michener's interpretations. (See in particular "James Michener's K*ent State:* A Study in Distortion," by *Thirteen Seconds* co-authors Joe Eszterhas and Michael Roberts, *The Progressive,* September 1971, and "Not a Great Deal of Error . . . ?," a survey conducted by KSU speech professors Carl Moore and D. Ray Heisey, mimeographed, 1971).

The Truth About Kent State: A Challenge to the American Conscience, Peter Davies and the Board of Church and Society of the United Methodist Church. New York: Farrar, Straus & Giroux, 1973. This book has sometimes inaccurately been referred to as an elaboration of Davies' privately published 1971 study alleging the Guardsmen conspired to shoot the students. Actually, the book was a much more cautious reiteration of his thesis that the killings "may well have been a premeditated barrage by about ten experienced, riot-trained guardsmen."

The book served its purpose of helping force the Justice Department to reopen its investigation to look into Davies' conspiracy charge.

I Was There: What Really Went on at Kent State, Ed Hill and Mike Grant. Lima, Ohio: C.S.S. Publishing, 1974. This was the Guardsmen's answer to Davies' book. It was dedicated to Guardsmen everywhere. Actually, since two (not one) Guardsmen wrote the book, the title should have read *We Were There*. And since the co-authors were not there, as one of the indicted Guardsmen complained, perhaps the title should have read: *We Was There, But We Was on the Other Side of the Hill and Couldn't See Nuthin', But Who's Going to Know the Difference?*

The Kent State Massacre, R. W. Whitney. Charlottesville, N.Y.: SamHar Press, 1975. A 32-page book written for high school history classes. It was part of the publisher's "Events of Our Time" series.

The Kent State Coverup, Joseph Kelner and James Munves. New York: Harper and Row, 1980. This book, co-authored by the chief counsel for the victims during the first wrongful death and injury trial, details Kelner's attempts to hold the Guardsmen and Ohio Governor James A. Rhodes accountable for their actions.

This is the only book devoted to the civil litigation. The book did not follow up on or re-evaluate Davies' charge of a conspiracy, even though that issue dominated public debate. Kelner argued that he lost the case because the judge and the jury were biased against the victims.

Not in Vain, Gerald Green. New York: Donald I. Fine, 1984. A *roman a clef* that takes place at fictional Joshua College. Green, a coauthor of the 1981 NBC docudrama, "Kent State," disguised the identities of real people and scrambled details, but remained remarkably faithful to the facts and captured many of the larger hidden truths about the event.

Green also offered an intriguing new twist: a conscience-plagued colonel in a position to blow the whistle on the coverup of the Joshua Massacre. In effect the character Green created was the "Deep Throat" Guardsmen investigators searched for in vain for years. Green's novel imagines what might have happened had such a man existed.

The Fourth of May: Killings and Coverups at Kent State, William A. Gordon. Buffalo: Prometheus Books, 1990. The hardback edition of this book.

Scholarly Studies (Or At Least What Passes For Scholarship)

Communication Crisis at Kent State, Philip K. Tompkins and Elaine Vanden Bout Anderson. New York: Gordon and Breach, 1971. A case study of how communications breakdowns contributed to the shootings.

Violence at Kent State: The Students' Perspective, Stuart Taylor, Richard Shuntich, Patrick McGovern and Robert Gethner. New York: College Notes, 1971. Reports the results of a student survey conducted by four KSU psychology professors.

No Heroes, No Villains. Robert M. O'Neil and Associates, San Francisco: Jossey-Bass, 1972. Discusses the implications that the Kent State and Jackson State killings had on academic freedom.

Kent State and May 4th: A Social Science Perspective, Thomas R. Hensley and Jerry M. Lewis. Dubuque, Iowa: Kendall/Hunt Publishing, 1978. A textbook which includes summaries of the litigation up to 1978, and sociological analyses.

Kent State: Ten Years Later, Scott Bills, editor. Kent: Kent Popular Press, 1980. A mishmash of essays, mostly from a leftist perspective. Its introduction states that the aim of this retrospective "is to provide a structural means by which different, even provocative views might penetrate the 'truth' of May 4th"—whatever that is supposed to mean.

Mayday: Kent State, Gregory Payne. Dubuque, Iowa: Kendall/Hunt, 1978. Would you believe a book on the making of the 1981 NBC docudrama? Payne, a professor of rhetoric and consultant for the docudrama, used the text in his classes.

Kent State: Impact of Judicial Process on Public Attitudes, Thomas R. Hensley. Westport, Ct.: Greenwood Press, 1981. The title pretty much says it all. Of all the professors at Kent to write about May 4, though, Hensley deserves credit for venturing the furthest out of the Ivory Tower. His analysis of the 1979 out-of-court settlement of the civil suits was excellent.

Kent State/May 4: Echoes Through a Decade, Scott Bills editor. Kent, Ohio: Kent State University Press, 1982. A collection of essays and interviews obtained by a historian who, according to a university press release, concerned himself not with the surviving victims, the families of the dead students, or the Guardsmen, but with a "different order of victims, those whose personal and professional lives and perceptions were disrupted" by the killings. Many of the interviews were with friends of the University or with footnote figures who were accessible to the author but whom no other historian would waste his time with. My review of the book was titled: "KSU Historian Flubs Cast of Characters."

Other Selected Sources

"A Man Who Says He 'Lost' 2 Daughters at Kent State," *Life,* August 27, 1971, p. 65. This is one of a number of profiles and articles about Peter Davies. See also "A Selfless Quest for Justice," *People,*

April 15, 1974, p. 60; "KSU 'Investigator' Tastes Bitterness," *Akron Beacon Journal,* October 3, 1971; "Mission: Kent State," by Mary McGrory, *New York Post,* October 2, 1971; "One Man's Kent State," by Tim Coder, *The Herald,* New York, March 31, 1972; "The Questions on Kent State," by Philip Nobile, *Lorain Journal,* July 18, 1974; and "Author Denies Judge's KSU Shooting Exploitation Charge," *Akron Beacon Journal,* June 7, 1977.

"A Newsweek Poll: Mr. Nixon Holds Up," *Newsweek,* May 18, 1970, p. 30. A Gallup Poll conducted one week after the shootings found that 58 percent of the public blamed the students themselves, while only 11 percent blamed the National Guardsmen.

Adams, John P. *At the Heart of the Whirlwind.* New York: Harper and Row. This memoir describes Adams' role in helping to get the federal grand jury, as well as the role he played in other civil rights causes.

_____. "Kent State: "Why the Church?" *American Report,* November 12, 1971, p. 22-S.

_____. "Kent State: Justice and Morality." *Cleveland State Law Review* 22 (Winter 1973), p. 167.

Adjutant General of Ohio. Annual Report FY (Fiscal Year) 1970. Mimeographed. Delivered to Ohio Governor James A. Rhodes, November 1, 1970.

Ambrose, Stephen E. "The Armed Forces and Civil Disorders." Essay in *The Military and American Society: Essays and Readings,* edited by Stephen E. Ambrose and James A. Barber, Jr. New York: The Free Press, 1972. Ambrose criticized the Guard's lack of professionalism and argued that "the Guard lacks the discipline, training, or leadership to meet its responsibilities." See also Hill, Jim Dan. "The National Guard in Civil Disorders: Historical Precedents." Essay in *Bayonets in the Streets: The Use of Troops in Civil Disorders,* edited by Robin Higham. Lawrence, Kansas: The University Press of Kansas, 1969.

Anderson, Maggie and Alex Gildzen, editors. *A Gathering of Poets.* Kent, Ohio: Kent State University Press, 1992. A collection of poems solicited by the University for the 20th anniversary.

Armao, Rosemary, and Farkas, Karen. "One Day in May." Cleveland's *The Plain Dealer Magazine,* April 26, 1985. A retrospective, fifteen years later.

"Canfora Cleared in Vice Case." *Akron Beacon Journal,* March 27, 1984.

"Civil Rights Protector: John Stanley Pottinger." *New York Times,* March 30, 1974. Profile of the assistant attorney general who reopened the investigation.

"Close-up of the 'Kent State 25,'" *U.S. News and World Report,* November 23, 1970, p. 517. See also "Dismissals at Kent State," *Time,* December 20, 1971, p. 11; and Molyneaux, David. "The Kent State Trials End." *Rolling Stone,* January 20, 1972.

Cohen, Charles E., Briggs-Bunting, Jane, and Gurvis, Sandra, "Twenty Contentious Years Haven't Ended the Pain Inflicted by the Tragic Shootings at Kent State," *People,* April 30, 1990, p. 117. Other 20th anniversary retrospectives include Dowling, Claudia Glenn, "Kent State: 20 Years Ago in Life." *Life Magazine,* May 1990, p. 137; Lesie, Michele, "KSU gains perspective on tragic day," *Plain Dealer,* April 29, 1990, p. 1; Wilson, Robin, "As Kent State prepares to Unveil Memorial, Critics of University Plan a Silent Protest." *Chronicle of Higher Education,* May 2, 1990, p. A-31, Pesman, Curtis; "Minimal Memorial?" Chicago Tribune, May 2, 1990, Section 5; Harrison, Eric and Shryer, Tracy, "New Kent State Memorial Stirs 20-Year-Old Anger." *Los Angeles Times,* May 2, 1990, p. 1; Kahn, Joseph P., "Twenty years later, shadows linger over Kent State;" *Boston Globe,* May 3, 1990, p. 39; and Geewax, Marilyn; "Battle Lines Remain at Kent State as Memorial Draws Crowd, Unrest," *Atlanta Journal,* May 5, 1990, A-3. Wounded student John Cleary summed up the problem with the Kent State memorial: "It doesn't have a sense of focus; it doesn't explain what happened."

Cousins, Norman. "Kent State and Watergate." *World,* June 6, 1973, p. 12. Cousins was the first to ask: "Had a decision been made at a national level that the student demonstrations across the nation had gone far enough and that an example had to be made?"

Cusella, Louis P. "Real-fiction versus historical reality: Rhetorical purification in 'Kent State'—The Docudrama," *Communications Quarterly,* 1982, 30, p. 159-164. Slain student William Schroeder's former roommate, now a professor of communications at the University of Dayton, argues that the NBC docudrama failed to realistically portray the Bill Schroeder he knew: "He was not a superman. The docudrama functioned to correct, refine and cleanse the images of the four students who were killed."

Davies, Peter. *An Appeal to the United States Department of Justice For an Immediate and Thorough Investigation of the Circumstances Surrounding the Shootings at Kent State, May 1970.* Davies' original conspiracy report, entered into the Congressional Record by Congressman William S. Moorhead, July 22, 1970, p. E8143.

_____. "Citizens Battle for Justice." *The Nation,* November 19, 1971, p. 557.

_____. "A Bitter Anniversary." *New York Times,* May 4, 1973.

_____. "Another White House Horror Story?" *The Village Voice,* November 8, 1973, p. 1. Recounts Davies' bizarre conversation with *New York Times* correspondent John Crewdson and Davies' speculations about its significance.

_____. "Four Years After Kent State, Unanswered Questions." *New York Times,* May 4, 1976.

_____. "Kent State Questions." *New York Times,* May 4, 1976.

_____. "Gunsmoke." *New York Times,* May 4, 1977.

DeMott, Benjamin. "Alone in Cover-Up Country." *The Atlantic,* October 1973, p. 115. One of the more perceptive reviews of Davies' book. For a review by a defense attorney, see Harvey A. Silvergate, "Shrouded in Tension and Ambiguity," *Washington Post Book World,* November 17, 1973.

Dickenson, James. "Kent Petitioners Bank on Political Arithmetic." *The National Observer,* December 4, 1971. For other accounts of the student petition for the federal grand jury investigation, see Downing, Robert. "What Two Students Learned at Kent State," *Cleveland* magazine, November 1972, p. 60; and McGrory, Mary. "Kent State Tragedy Haunting Nixon." *Washington Star,* November 16, 1971.

Dunphy, John. "Guard's Prosecutor Admits He Never Expected to Win," *Akron Beacon Journal,* May 4, 1975.

Ehrlichman, John. *Witness to Power.* New York: Simon and Schuster, 1982. Recounts the meetings Ehrlichman and Nixon had with six KSU students a few days after the shootings, but does not discuss Nixon's role in the cover-up.

Electromagnetic Systems Laboratory. "Analysis of Photographic and Acoustic Data Pertaining to the Kent State Incident." February 22, 1974. Report prepared for the Department of Justice, but never entered into evidence at the criminal trial because of its inconclusive findings. The plaintiffs, however, used it during the 1975 civil trial.

Elkins, Stanley. "Lessons and Judgments." *Commentary,* October 1971, p. 99. In reviewing James Michener's book, Elkins, a professor at Smith College, argued that his "driving urge to be 'fair' and conciliatory has tied up all Michener's analytical energies."

Engdahl, David. "Due Process Forbids Soldiers in Civil Disorders." *American Report,* November 12, 1972, p. 6-S.

_____. "Soldiers, Riots, and Revolutions: The Law and History of Military Troops in Civil Disorders." *Iowa Law Review,* 57 (October 1971), p. 1.

Engdahl, David, Renzo, Anthony F., and Laitos, Luize Z. "A Comprehensive Study of the Use of Military Troops in Civil Disorders With Proposals for Legislative Reform." *Colorado Law Review,* Volume 43, No. 4, June 1972, p. 399.

Engdahl, David. "The Legal Background and Aftermath of the Kent State Tragedy." *Cleveland State Law Review,* 22 (Winter 1973), p. 3.

_____. "Kent State Update." *American Report,* February 6, 1973, p. 6.

Englehart, Pat, and Dunphy, John. "Undercover Agents' Role Left Unanswered by Jury." *Akron Beacon Journal,* March 31, 1974. See also "Operation Provocation." *New York Post,* December 8, 1973. Asks how widespread the use of *agents provocateur* was during the antiwar protests of the late 1960s and early 1970s, and whether secret agents were involved in the Kent State disorders. See also Semas, Philip. "How the FBI Tried to Subvert Campus Rebellion." *Chronicle of Higher Education,* September 5, 1975, p. 5.

Eszterhas, Joe. "Ohio Honors its Dead." *Rolling Stone,* June 10, 1971.

Evans, Rowland, Jr. and Novak, Robert D. *Nixon in the White House.* New York: Random House, 1971. Describes "the stark sense of terror, close to panic, pervading the White House after Kent State."

"The Events of May 1-4, 1970 at Kent State University: Minority Report of the Commission on KSU Violence." Kent, Ohio, 1970. The report of the University's internal fact-finding commission, written primarily by KSU English professor Doris Franklin. Available in the KSU library.

Farkas, Karen. "KSU memorial snafu sends planner packing." *Cleveland Plain Dealer,* July 2, 1986. Account of how KSU disqualified Ian Taberner, the winner of the nationwide design competition for the May 4 memorial, supposedly because he was a Canadian citizen (contest rules required the winner be American-born). Critics charged the real reason KSU dumped Taberner was because he was amenable to including the names of the victims on the memorial. May 4 Task Force President Lisa Sanders told me that wounded student Alan Canfora helped get Taberner fired by pretending he was a spokesman for the families and prevailing on Taberner to fight for the inclusion of the names, while negotiations to work around the contest rule were still pending and Taberner's status was shaky. KSU officials proceeded to build the design created by second-place winner Bruno Ast and, only days before the memorial was dedicated, finally acceded to demands that the memorial commemorate those killed.

"FBI Files on the Fire Bomb and Shooting at Kent State." Wilmington, Delaware: Scholarly Resources, Inc., 1985. The 46 volumes of FBI reports on microfilm. The originals are in FBI headquarters in Washington.

Feagler, Dick. "Kent Jury Closes Show Across the Street," *The Cleveland Plain Dealer,* March 30, 1974. Expressed disappointment with the indictment of the eight Guardsmen because "it said that the cause of all this was somebody named Lawrence Shafer and somebody named James Pierce . . . For many, what happened at Kent seemed bigger than what somebody named [Matthew] McManus did. Or what somebody named Pierce did."

"Four Random, Pointless Deaths." *Newsweek,* May 18, 1970, p. 34.

Frankel, Max. "Nixon: He Faces a Divided, Anguished Nation." *New York Times,* May 10, 1970.

Frisby, Michael. "Kent Case Just Won't Stay Quiet in the Grave." Cleveland's *Plain Dealer,* September 13, 1981. Account of the efforts by the state of Ohio and Kent State University to block scholars' and researchers' access to certain investigative files.

Furlong, William. "The Guardsmen's View of the Tragedy at Kent State." *New York Times Magazine,* June 21, 1970, p. 12. Unfortunately, the Guardsmen interviewed here, while in Kent at the time, were not involved in the tragedy. Interviews with Guardsmen who were actually involved were extremely rare. Michael Roberts of Cleveland's *Plain Dealer* managed to interview six unidentified Guardsmen after Davies' conspiracy charges were leveled ("KSU Shootings Still Leave Guard Bewildered," *Plain Dealer,* September 12, 1971). Other than that and brief reaction statements to various developments, the only major newspaper interview conducted by a Guardsmen who fired at students (Sergeant Lawrence Shafer) was "Guardsmen Ends 10-Year Silence on KSU," by John Dunphy, *Akron Beacon Journal,* May 4, 1980.

Gitlin, Todd. *The Sixties: Years of Hope, Days of Rage.* New York: Bantam Books, 1987.

Gordon, Bill. "Kent Students Wait for Nixon Response." *American Report,* January 28, 1972, p. 2.

_____. "Kent State University's Petition to the White House: Ten Months of Deceit." Office of the KSU Student Government, August 9, 1972. Reprinted in the *Congressional Record,* August 18, 1972, p. E-7603.

_____. "Kent State Update: The Case for Action Grows." *American Report,* June 16, 1973, p. 5.

_____. "Kent State Indictments Leave Crucial Questions Unanswered." *American Report,* April 15, 1974, p. 16.

_____. "Will a Memorial Be Built at KSU and What Will it Say?" *Plain Dealer,* April 27, 1983.

_____. "Kent State is Facing Its Past." *Plain Dealer,* December 19, 1983.

_____. "Is KSU Trying to Forget?" *Plain Dealer,* December 6, 1984.

_____. "Memorial Maneuverings at Kent State." *Pittsburgh Post-Gazette,* April 4, 1987.

Greene. Daniel St. Albin. "When a World Collapse: Kent State's Wounded Tell Their Grim Story." *The National Observer,* May 3, 1975, p. B-1. For interviews with all nine surviving wounded students, see "Nine Lives: Looking Up the Survivors in 1970," [Akron] *Beacon Magazine,* May 4, 1980.

Haldeman, H. R. *The Haldeman Diaries: Inside the Nixon White House.* New York: G. P. Putnam's Sons, 1994.

Henderson, Ron. "18 Months Later: Families of the Kent State Dead Speak Out." *American Report,* November 12, 1971, p. 12-S.

Hildebrand, William H., Keller, Dean H., and Herrington, Anita D., editors. *A Book of Memories: Kent State University, 1990-1992.* Kent, Ohio: Kent State University Press, 1993. A memorial book tracing and celebrating the history of Kent State.

Himmerstone, Robert G. "The Fifth Victim at Kent State." *Life,* October 16, 1970, p. 41. Profile of Dean Kahler.

Holstein, Elaine Miller. "And Still No Honest Apology." *New York Times,* April 23, 1990.

Holstein, Elaine Miller. "Anniversary." *The Progressive,* May 1988, p. 34.

_____. "For the Attorney General." *New York Times,* July 6, 1973.

Howard, Bob. "The Manipulation of May 4 For Political Ends." *Left Review 2* (Spring 1978), p. 14.

"Investigations: The Kent State Case." *Newsweek,* May 25, 1970, p. 33.

Jindra, Chris. "New Kent Trial: A Question of Rights—'How Far Does the Constitution Go?,'" *Chicago Tribune,* July 13, 1975.

Jindra, Chris. "Law Favored the State in Kent Trial: Plaintiffs' Lawyers Muddied the Case." *Plain Dealer,* August 31, 1975. See also "Last Act at Kent State." *Time,* September 8, 1975, p. 11.

"Justice Delayed." Transcript of *Bill Moyers' Journal.* Educational Broadcasting Corporation. Aired on WNET-13, December 19, 1972.

"Justice Mocked." *The Nation,* December 18, 1980.

Keane, Paul. "Keeping Kent State Alive for History." Speech prepared for Kent State's twelfth annual May 4 commemoration program.

Kelner, Joseph. "There Must be a Public Trial." *New York Times,* August 23, 1971.

_____. "Kent State: A Footnote to History," *Trial,* November/December 1971, p. 21.

_____. "The Kent State Killings: Among the Victims Was Justice." *Los Angeles Times,* May 4, 1980.

Kelner, Joseph and Kelner, Robert S. "Kent State Revisited: A Footnote to History." *New York Law Journal,* May 19, 1988, p. 1.

"Kent State Continued." *Time,* November 9, 1970, p. 16.

"Kent State: Four Deaths at Noon." *Life,* May 15, 1970, p. 30.

"Kent State in '71." *The Nation,* December 13, 1972, p. 30.

"Kent State Indictments." *The New Republic,* April 13, 1974, p. 8. See also "The Shield is Gone." *The Nation,* April 13, 1974, p. 450.

"Kent State: Making Peace With the Past." Akron *Beacon Magazine,* May 4, 1980. Special issue.

"Kent State: Martyrdom That Shook the Country." *Time,* May 18, 1970, p. 12. See also "Mr. Nixon's Home Front." *Newsweek,* May 18, 1970, p. 26, and "My God! They're Killing Us." *Newsweek,* May 18, 1970, p. 31.

"Kent State Reopened." *Time,* December 24, 1973, p. 17.

"Kent State Revisited." *Time,* December 6, 1971, p. 21.

"Kent State: Struggle For Justice." Transcript of *Bill Moyers' Journal,* Educational Broadcasting Corporation. Aired on WNET-13, January 16, 1974.

Knight Newspapers. "Reporting the Kent State Incident." New York: American Newspaper Foundation, January 1971.

Krause, Arthur. "May 4, 1970." *New York Times,* May 4, 1972.

_____. "My Daughter Was Murdered." *Reform Judaism,* February 1974.

_____. "A Memo to Mr. Nixon." *New York Times,* May 7, 1978.

Krause v. Rhodes, 390 F. Supp., 1072 (N.D., Ohio 1975). Transcript of the 1975 civil trial.

Lewin, Nathan. "Kent State Revisited: Another Skeleton in the Closet?" *The New Republic,* August 18 and 25, 1973, p. 16. Lewin asked "whether there is not a skeleton rattling in this closet, and whether the renewed interest in Kent State was designed to head off some startling disclosure as to how and why the case was initially quashed."

Lewis, Jerry M. "The Kent Story." *New Politics 8* (Fall 1970), p. 44.

_____. "Review Essay: The Telling of Kent State." *Social Problems* 19 (Fall 1971), p. 267.

_____. "Trivial Truths." *Northern Ohio Live,* February 23-March 8, 1981, p. 6. Criticisms of the NBC docudrama.

Lombardi, John. "A Lot of People Were Crying and the Guard Walked Away." *Rolling Stone,* June 11, 1970.

Lough, Thomas S. "The FBI Setup at Kent State University, May 4, 1970." Mimeographed, 1987.

Mahon, John K. *History of the Militia and the National Guard.* New York: Macmillan Publishing Company, 1983.

"Man in the Middle," *Time,* November 23, 9170, p. 81. Story about former KSU President Robert I. White.

McGrory, Mary. "Kent State Case Goes On and On." *New York Post,* April 11, 1977.

"Michener Changes Kent State Theory." *New York Times,* April 30, 1972.

"Mockery of Justice." *Commonweal,* November 27, 1970, p. 211.

Morrison, Joan, and Morrison, Robert K. *From Camelot to Kent State: The Sixties Experience in the Words of Those Who Lived It.* New York: Times Books, 1987. This oral history includes a graphic interview with wounded student Tom Grace.

Munves, James. "More Than People Died at Kent State." *The Nation,* April 26, 1980, p. 492.

Nixon, Richard. *RN: The Memoirs of Richard Nixon,* Volume 1. New York: Warner Books, 1975. Nixon tried to justify the shootings by citing approval in public opinion polls.

_____. *No More Vietnams.* New York: Arbor House, 1985. Seeing "the pictures in the newspapers of the two girls and two boys who had been killed at Kent State," Nixon wrote, was "the most profoundly depressing moment for me during the war years of my presidency."

"Ohio Regrets." *The Nation,* January 20, 1979, p. 37.

Oplinger, Doug. "Turmoil . . . KSU Protestor-Minister No Stranger to Controversy." *Akron Beacon Journal,* September 11, 1977. Profile of Reverend John P. Adams. See also "Memories of Gentle Man Committed to Peace, Justice," by Dave Boerner, *Akron Beacon Journal,* December 13, 1983, and "Adams Will Be Missed," *Kent Record-Courier* (editorial), December 14, 1983.

Page, Tim. "At Kent State, They Still Hear the Drumming." *Newsday,* March 15, 1989.

Peckham, Charles A. "The Ohio National Guard and its Police Duties, 1894." *Ohio History,* LXXXIII (Winter 1974). Notes the only other known instance in which Ohio Guardsmen fired into a crowd of civilians.

Pekkanen, John. "A Boy Who Was Just There Watching It and Making Up His Mind." *Life,* May 15, 1970, p. 36. Story about fatality William Schroeder.

Peterson, Richard E., and Bilorusky, John A. "May 1970: Campus Aftermath of Cambodia and Kent State." Berkeley: The Carnegie Commission on Higher Education, 1971. A study of the extent of the disruptions on higher education across the country in the aftermath of the Cambodian invasion and Kent State.

Pruden, Wesley. "A Bereaved Father Wouldn't 'Shut Up.'" *The National Observer,* August 1973. Profile of Arthur Krause. See also "Tormented Crusader," by James Ricci, Akron *Beacon Magazine,* June 25, 1972, and "Parents of Kent State Victim Keep Case Opened," by Bryce Nelson, *Los Angeles Times,* December 26, 1973.

Rasanen, George P. "Congress at Fault at Kent State." Cleveland *Plain Dealer,* September 22, 1973.

"Report of the Inspector General: Kent State University Riot, 4 May 1970." The official Ohio National Guard report.

"Report of the Kent State Grand Jury." Kent, Ohio: Committee for Truth and Justice. Mimeographed, 1972. When the federal government refused to conduct a "real" federal grand jury, some students held their own "mock" grand jury. This is their report.

"Report of the President's Commission on Campus Unrest." Washington, D.C.: Government Printing Office, 1970.

"Rhodes' Records End in Landfill Archives," *Plain Dealer,* November 10, 1982. Before leaving office, Governor James A. Rhodes' papers were "accidentally" buried 40 feet underground in a Columbus, Ohio dumpsite.

Rowan, Carl T. "Why the Young May Be Cynical About 'Justice.'" *Washington Evening Star,* July 18, 1971.

_____. "Kent State Tests Commitment to Law." *Washington Star News,* September 9, 1973.

Rubin, Trudy. "A Re-examination of Kent State: Did Mystery Man Fire First Shots?" *Christian Science Monitor,* July 12, 1973, p. 3.

_____. "Kent State: New Light on Man with Pistol." *Christian Science Monitor,* August 11, 1973, p. 1.

Sanford, David. "Kent State Gag: A Very Special Grand Jury." *The New Republic,* November 7, 1970, p. 14.

Schollenberger, Charles. "Justice Denied at Kent State." *The New Republic,* May 12, 1973, p. 13.

_____. "Heroes as Well as Victims at Kent State." *The Voice* (Wooster College), May 31, 1974.

_____. "Gaining Access to Federal Records on the Kent State Tragedy." The Freedom of Information Center, University of Missouri School of Journalism, April 1979.

Semas, Philip W. "Indictment of 8 in Shootings at Kent State U. Reopens Question: Why the Delay?" *Chronicle of Higher Educa-tion,* April 8, 1974, p. 1.

_____. "Counsel for the Kent State Victims Makes His Case Against the Judge." *Chronicle of Higher Education,* September 15, 1975, p. 5.

Sheridan, Terence. "How to Program a Jury." *Exit,* June 2, 1975, p. 6.

Sindell, Steven. "Kent State: Opening the Doors." *Trial* 10 (July 1974), p. 43.

Smith, Curt. *Long Time Gone: The Years of Turmoil Remembered.* South Bend, Ind.: Icarus Press, 1982. In the only interview Nixon gave since leaving office in which the subject of May 4 came up, Nixon told Smith: "I can't think back upon that without a haunting sense of

sadness, tragic, even though I don't blame the National Guard."
Nixon also denounced antiwar protestors as hypocrites, trash, and
sanctimonious frauds.

Sorvig, Kim. *To Heal Kent State: A Memorial Meditation.* Philadelphia:
Worldview Press, 1990. This privately published account discusses
Sorvig's proposal for a memorial, which did not win the nationwide
memorial competition. The book does not deal directly with May 4
issues.

Stevens, Mark, and McGuigan, Cathleen. "Kent State Memorial."
Newsweek, September 11, 1978. Chided the KSU administration for
rejecting the offer of a George Segal commemorative sculpture by
saying: "Educational institutions should not fear the free flow of images and ideas." The statue, which was commissioned by a private
Cleveland foundation, was subsequently donated to Princeton. For
other articles on the early attempts to memorialize the tragedy, see
also Dyal, Robert, "Too Little and Too Late: The Kent State Faculty
and Administrative Response in the Decade After May 4, 1970," *The
Left Review,* Spring 1980, p. 33; Canterbury, William, "Parents tell
KSU to Keep its Memorial," *Akron Beacon Journal,* September 24,
1977; and "Remembering Kent State" (editorial), *New York Times,*
October 22, 1977. The *Times* felt KSU's 1977 proposal to "honor a*ll*
the parties involved in the tragic confrontation, including the National Guard, was remarkably insensitive. To honor the killers would be
an insult to the victims."

Stone, I. F. "Strange Lessons for the Young." *New York Review of Books,*
November 2, 1970. Puncturing the myth that Kent State was a
hotbed of radicalism, Stone wrote: "This is a campus where you
meet activists who have never heard of the *Nation* or read the *New
Republic* and students who think themselves avant-garde because
they read *Time* and *Newsweek.*"

"The Truth About Hoover," *Time,* December 22, 1975, p. 20. Notes how
the late FBI director, at the end of a meeting with Justice Department officials to discuss an investigation, "talked only about one
topic: his belief that one of the coeds had been sexually promiscu-
ous."

"The Truth About Kent State: Story Behind the Book." *Publishers Weekly,* September 3, 1973, p. 204.

Thomas, Charles. "The Kent State Massacre: Blood on Whose Hands?"
September 3, 1973, p. 204.

_____. "Unhappy Anniversary." *The Nation,* May 24, 1980, p. 632.

U. S. Congress, House. Representative John Sieberling's insertion of the
Justice Department's summary of the FBI report into the Congressional Record, January 14, 1973, p. E-207.

U. S. Congress. Committee on the Judiciary. "Nomination of Clarence
Kelley to be Director of the Federal Bureau of Investigation." June
19, 20, and 25, 1973. Includes the FBI's response to Congressional
questions about Terry Norman.

_____. Committee on the Judiciary. "Nomination of William B. Saxbe to
be Attorney General." December 12 and 13, 1973.

U. S. Department of the Interior. National Park Service. "National Regis-
ter of Historic Places: Inventory Report on Kent State, May 4,
1970," by James Sheire, 1978.

Verkuil, Paul. "Immunity or Responsibility for Unconstitutional Conduct: The Aftermath of Jackson State and Kent State." *North Carolina Law Review,* April 1972, Vol. 50, no. 3, p. 548.

Viorst, Milton. *Fire in the Streets: America in the 1960s.* New York:
Simon and Schuster, 1979. The final chapter profiles wounded student Alan Canfora.

Von Hoffman, Nicholas. "KSU: 'See, the System Works.'" *Plain Dealer,*
April 8, 1974.

Wechsler, James A. "Unsolved Murders." *New York Post Magazine,* December 24, 1972, p. 5.

_____. "Justice Obstructed?" *New York Post Magazine,* October 7, 1975,
p. 35.

"When the National Guard is Called . . ." *U. S. News and World Report,*
May 18, 1970, p. 32. See also Vasquez, Juan M., "The Guard is
Poorly Trained for Riot Duty," *New York Times,* May 10, 1970.

"Who Guards Against the Guard?" *Newsweek,* May 18, 1970, p. 33.

Wallace, Weldon. "After Four Years, Kent State Wants the Tragedy
Purged." *Baltimore Sun,* April 29, 1974.

Wells, Tom. *The War Within: America's Battle over Vietnam.* Berkeley:
University of California Press, 1994.

"When The War Came Home." *Inquiry,* May 5, 1980, p. 3. Argues that
"the Kent State shootings were more than just an attack on the four
students who were killed and the nine who were wounded . . . They
were an officially sanctioned assault on the entire antiwar movement, a warning to everyone in this country who raised a voice
against the holocaust in Southeast Asia."

Wilkinson, Francis. "Trigger Happy: The Cult of Kent State." *The New
Republic,* May 13, 1991, p. 16.

Wills, Garry. "Mitchell Quibbling Over Kent State Investigation." *Santa
Monica Evening-Outlook,* August 1971.

Wischmann, Lesley. "Four Dead in Ohio." *American History Illustrated,*
May/June 1990, p. 24.

Zaroulis, Nancy, and Sullivan , Gerald. *Who Spoke Up: American*

Protest Against the War in Vietnam, 1963-1975. New York: Double-
day & Company, 1984.
Zimmerman, Richard G. Condon, George E., Jr., and Jindra, Chris.
"Guard Wrong at Kent: Del Corso—Students No Threat to Soldiers," *Plain Dealer,* September 29, 1975.

Interviews

This book was also based on more than 200 interviews that were
conducted between 1971 and 1988. In all, I interviewed 170 individuals,
some two or three times.

I also had many other informal or off-the-record conversations with
other key figures in the Kent Affair, including all eight of the indicted
Guardsmen, and the two key officers, Sergeant Myron Pryor and Major
Harry Jones. Oftentimes these informal discussions were just as valuable
as the formal interviews in terms of helping to piece together the parts to
the puzzle or weighing the conflicting facts.

The following is a list of those interviews.

WHITE HOUSE OFFICIALS: John Ehrlichman (February 18, 1982);
John Dean (March 1, 1983); Leonard Garment (November 4, 1974);
Bradley Patterson (May 22 and 24, 1974).

JUSTICE DEPARTMENT OFFICIALS: J. Stanley Pottinger (January
21, 1975); Robert Murphy (December 10, 1974; March 25, April 4 and
May 29, 1975); and Paul Lawrence (December 18, 1974). Former Attorney General Elliot Richardson also answered questions in letters dated
July 12, 1974 and February 24, 1976.

OHIO OFFICIALS: John J. Gilligan (January 8, 1975); Eric Gilbertson
(November 2, 1982).

ATTORNEYS FOR THE VICTIMS: David Engdahl (July 24, September 10 and November 14, 1974; May 12, 1975); Steven Sindell (July 24,
1974; January 23 and April 21, 1975); Sanford J. Rosen (March 29,
1981); paralegal Steven Keller (November 30, 1974); law clerk Andrea
Biren (March 27, 1981).

DEFENSE ATTORNEYS: C. D. "Gus" Lambros (April 11, 1973; February 27, 1974 and January 31, 1975); Bernard Stuplinski (November 25,
1974 and March 25, 1975); Michael Diamant (November 25, 1974 and
March 25, 1975); Edd Wright (November 13 and 21, 1974); Jack Schul-

man (November 19, 1974); Burt Fulton (November 14, 1981); Robert Blakemore (November 9, 1981).

PARENTS OF THE SLAIN STUDENTS: Arthur Krause (July 6, 1974); Florence Schroeder (May 22, 1974).

SURVIVING WOUNDED STUDENTS: Dean Kahler (May 15, August 6 and October 25, 1973; June 3 and November 7, 1974; April 28, 1975; June 9, 1976); Robby Stamps (February 15, 1981); Alan Canfora (January 18, 1982 and March 1, 1988); Joseph Lewis, Jr. (November 9, 1973); Mrs. Joseph Lewis, Sr. (Joe's mother, October 25, 1973).

FRIENDS OF THE VICTIMS: Rev. John P. Adams (June 1, 1974); Peter Davies (August 6, 1973 and June 24, 1974); Paul Keane (December 19, 1971; January 23 and March 6, 1972; January 12 and April 17, 1973; May 15, 1973 and January 19, 1974); Gregory Rambo (November 11, 1971; March 6, 1972; August 6, 1973, January 17, October 1 and November 14, 1974; and February 19, 1975).

OHIO NATIONAL GUARDSMEN: Colonel Charles Fassinger (June 7, 1983), William Perkins (November 17, 1974); Michael McCoy (March 12, 1975); Jeffrey Jones (November 8, 1974); Ralph Tucker (August 7, 1973 and March 25, 1975); Ed Deericks (October 3, 1973); Ron Snyder (March 18, 1975); Richard Lutey (July 22, 1973); Larry Vanhorn (September 18, 1974); Ed Conti (July 22, 1973). Russell Kitchen (October 17, 1973); Joseph Lambe (October 17, 1973); James Lutey (October 10, 1974); Michael Stephenson (September 20, 1974); Jerry Taylor (September 20, 1974); Bruce Mendelson (April 7, 1973); Gary Wilcox (September 18, 1974); Ray Silvey (January 15, 1972).

REGARDING TERRY NORMAN AND THE NORMAN AFFAIR: Fred DeBrine (March 20, 1973); Jorge Gomez (April 25, 1973); Joe Butano (July 26, 1973); Guard Sgt. Michael Delaney (March 21, April 18 and July 19, 1973); Harold Reid (April 16, 1973); William Barrett (April 3 and 16, 1973); Donald Schwartzmiller (March 29, 1973; July 12 and August 6, 1973; May 20, 1974 and April 24, 1975); Marty Williams (August 1, 1973); Robert Tilton (July 17, 1973); Dominic Scalise (October 5, 1973); Prof. John Flower (April 24, 1973); Prof. Earl Roberts (July 12, 1973); Prof. Richard Worthing (April 23, 1972); Prof. Marvin Koller (January 19, 1982); Robert Hoiles (March 29, 1973); Paul Tople (March 25, 1973); Paul Schlemmer (April 3, 1973); David Kline (March 27, 1973); Greg Zalar (March 31, 1973); Steve Titchenal (October 12, 1973); Don Roese (October 16, 1973); Pat Vittone (July 16, 1973);

David Scribner (July 13, 1973); Fred Patterson (March 31, 1973); Jack Wright (July 14, 1973); Ken Deck (July 15, 1973); Helen Cullison (July 9, 1973); Jim King (July 9, 1973); Ruth Stefanek (July 16, 1973); Thaddeus Garrett (July 17, 1973); Chet Williams (July 12, 1973); Juanita Morris (July 21, 1973); Arthur Thompson (September 5, 1973); Connie Walsh (March 28, 1973); Larry Cochran (September 4, 1973); Bill Heckman (July 17, 1973); Debbie Shryock (August 15, 1973; February 21, 1974 and January 26, 1988); Ralph Oates (January 9, 1987).

OTHER KSU AND LAW ENFORCEMENT PERSONNEL: Chuck Seimer (April 23, 1975); Jack Crawford (May 5, 1982); Chuck Stine (February 24, 1981); Ross Jamerson (April 12, 1982); Walter E. Moore (April 12, 1982); Fred Miller (May 30, 1974); David Helmling (May 14, 1982 and February 1, 1988); Art Schake (September 8, 1986).

STATE GRAND JURORS: Robert Hastings (June 21, 1974); Elizabeth Heisa (July 28, 1974)

SCRANTON COMMISSIONERS: James Ahern (May 21, 1974); Joseph Rhodes, Jr. (June 10 and July 1, 1974); staff attorney Kenneth "Red" McIntyre (May 21, 1974).

NEWSMEN: John Dunphy (November 21, 1974); Pat Englehart (June 6, 1974); David Hess (August 13, 1974); Roy Meyers (August 27, 1974); Neil Shine (April 1, 1982); Sandra Bullock (October 22, 1982).

OTHER KENT STATE ADMINISTRATORS, PROFESSORS AND MEMBERS OF THE BOARD OF TRUSTEES: KSU President Glenn A. Olds (April 25, 1974); James Bruss (April 24, 1973); Ted Curtis (October 29, 1981); Prof. Steven Paulsen (March 12, 1975); Prof. Benjamin McGinniss (April 10, 1973); Prof. Rosemary Lavicka (June 11, 1973); Prof. Jerry M. Lewis (September 4, 1984); Prof. Glenn Frank (February 3, 1988); Prof. Stan Christensen (February 6, 1988); Prof. Dennis Cook (March 1, 1988); Prof. Tom Lough (March 1, 1988); Prof. Walter Adams (March 2, 1988); Richard Cunningham (August 6, 1984); Robert Beck (January 9, 20 and October 1, 1987 and February 8, 1988); Prof. Jim Dalton (January 5, 1987); Dr. Ottavio Mark Casale (October 12, 1987); Harry Ausprich (September 12, 1984).

OTHER ATTORNEYS: Ronald Kane, Portage County Prosecutor (November 6, 1981); Perry Dickinson, special Ohio prosecutor (October 30, 1981); James Hogle, Kent 25 attorney (May 13, 1974 and October 27, 1981); William Whitaker, Kent 25 attorney (July 25, 1974); Alan Parker,

House Judiciary Subcommittee (February 14, 1974); Charles Kirkwood (May 28, 1983).

FORMER STUDENTS: Rick Felber (December 6, 1981); Ruth Gibson (February 2, 1988); Jerome Stoklas (March 16, 1978 and November 4, 1981); Bill Ling (March 23, 1973); Bob Radigan (June 17, 1974); Jody Zahler (June 3, 1975); Tom Brunbach (June 12, 1974); Timothy Frerkis (November 1, 1981); James Woodring (January 17, 1972); Peter Winnen (July 27, 1976); Robert Peabody (November 14, 1971); John Bell (September 21, 1984); Jeff McVann (September 4, 1984); Lisa Sanders (October 1 and 31, 1986); Bob Edgar (January 16, 1987); Joe Gregor (October 12, 1987); Ken Krizner (January 27, 1987); Gere McClellan (December 17, 1986); Ron Yung (January 27, 1987).

OTHERS: James Michener (August 8, 1973); Max Keller, docudrama producer, (January 26, 1981); James J. Hastings, Deputy Director, Nixon Presidential Materials Project, National Archives (May 28, 1997); James Doyle, spokesman, Watergate special prosecutor (February 24, 1981); Eric Both, ambulance driver, June 14, 1974); Mary Jane Pryor, Myron's ex-wife (August 8, 1983); George Walter Harrington (November 2, 1981); L. Samuel Copeland (April 2, 1982); Ian Taberner (January 24, 1987); Bruno Ast (January 19, 1987 and October 12, 1987); Arthur Rubiner (October 20, 1986); Harry Tripp (January 15, 1987); Fred Bricker (December 29, 1986); Foster Armstrong (December 29, 1986); Pete McCall (December 30, 1986); Bill Zorn (January 14, 1987); Charles Madonio (May 1, 1974).

Index

Brown, James, 180-1
Brown, Paul, 101-2, 104, 220
Brown, William, 120
Bruss, James, 132
Buck, C. Stephen, 235
Bullock, Sandra, 183
Bureau of Criminal Investigation
 (BCI), 55, 89, 120
Butano, Joe, 82, 243, 247-8

Callum, Joseph B., 122
Cambodia, invasion of, 18, 23, 29,
 118, 202, 210, 214, 228, 240
Canfora, Alan: 234, 235, 187, 278;
 charges dismissed against,
 122; lies to FBI, 266-7;
 location when shot, 32, 53-5;
 provokes Guardsmen, 34;
 pimping indictment, 275
Canfora, Rosemary, 122
Canterbury, General Robert H.,
 30-1, 33-4, 49, 56, 62, 64, 73,
 106, 155, 178, 218-9, 261;
 criticized by enlisted men, 33;
 explanation for shooting, 49;
 testimony against Robert I.
 White, 181, 229; why not
 prosecuted, 96
Caris, Judge Albert, 103
Carter, Joseph L., 235
*Case of the Murdered President,
 The,* 49
Case, William, 180-1
Chapin, Bill, 147, 246
Chaucer, 207
Chiarmonte, Robert, 231; threatens
 shooting, 28
Chosen Few, 24
Christensen, Delmar, 106

Christian Science Monitor, 115,
 145
CIA, 152
Cicero, 190
Civil trials, 175-205; appeal, 197-
 199; defendants, 177-181;
 new trial ordered, 199;
 opening statements, 182-3;
 settlement, 201-205; statement
 of regret, 202-4
Clark, Ramsey, 177
Clawson, Ken, 112
Cleary, John, 187-8 235; criminal
 trial testimony, 165; location
 when shot, 32, 53-5
Cleveland Press, 24, 152
Cline, Lt. Dwight, 179; parking
 meter tale, 232
Cohen, Stephen, 235
COINTELPRO, 87, 151
Coleman, Frederick, 267
Colson, Charles, 214
Columbia University, 28, 200
Congressional Record, 114
Conspiracy, charges of, 15, 17, 59-
 63, 113-5, 130, 134-5, 154,
 161, 168-70, 239, 240, 259,
 264; contingency order
 testimony, 62, 74; first shot as
 signal, 60, 63-4; Guardsmen's
 huddle, 59-60, 62-3, 113, 154;
 investigated by the federal
 grand jury, 160-1, 168-9;
 national plot theory, 15, 18,
 61, 69-71, 214-5, 239-240,
 260-1; and Mark Nehilla, 239,
 and James Nichols, 153;
 precision of turn, 61-2, 219,
 235; removal of name tags, 63,

About The Author

William A. Gordon was born in Akron, Ohio during the blizzard of 1950. Since city streets were closed to traffic, Ohio National Guardsmen had to be summoned to take his mother to the hospital.

Mr. Gordon is a graduate of Kent State and the author of three other books, including *The Ultimate Hollywood Tour Book* and *Shot on This Site: A Traveler's Guide to Places and Locations Used to Film Famous Movies and TV Shows.* He currently lives in a suburb of Los Angeles, California.